Salsa Crossings

A BOOK IN THE SERIES

Latin America Otherwise: Languages, Empires, Nations

Series editors

Walter D. Mignolo, Duke University

Irene Silverblatt, Duke University

Sonia Saldívar-Hull, University of Texas, San Antonio

Salsa Crossings

DANCING LATINIDAD IN LOS ANGELES

Cindy García

Duke University Press ::: *Durham and London* ::: 2013

Printed in the United States of America
on acid-free paper ∞
Interior designed by Bea Jackson
Cover designed by Amy Ruth Buchanan
Typeset in Minion Pro with Lobster display

Library of Congress Cataloging-in-Publication Data
García, Cindy, 1968–
Salsa crossings : dancing latinidad in Los Angeles / Cindy García.
pages cm — (Latin america otherwise : languages, empires, nations)
Includes bibliographical references and index.
ISBN 978-0-8223-5481-9 (cloth : alk. paper)
ISBN 978-0-8223-5497-0 (pbk. : alk. paper)
1. Salsa (Dance)—Social aspects—California—Los Angeles.
2. Salsa (Dance)—California—Los Angeles.
I. Title. II. Series: Latin America otherwise.
GV1796.S245G37 2013
793.3'30979494—dc23 2013004646

For Vivi

who loves cha cha chá

Contents

About the Series

Latin America Otherwise: Languages, Empires, Nations is a critical series. It aims to explore the emergence and consequences of concepts used to define "Latin America" while at the same time exploring the broad interplay of political, economic, and cultural practices that have shaped Latin American worlds. Latin America, at the crossroads of competing imperial designs and local responses, has been construed as a geocultural and geopolitical entity since the nineteenth century. This series provides a starting point to redefine Latin America as a configuration of political, linguistic, cultural, and economic intersections that demands a continuous reappraisal of the role of the Americas in history, and of the ongoing process of globalization and the relocation of people and cultures that have characterized Latin America's experience. *Latin America Otherwise: Languages, Empires, Nations* is a forum that confronts established geocultural constructions, rethinks area studies and disciplinary boundaries, assesses convictions of the academy and of public policy, and correspondingly demands that the practices through which we produce knowledge and understanding about and from Latin America be subject to rigorous and critical scrutiny.

"Globalism" (the neoliberal project for homogenizing the world) failed, but the consequences are with us in several spheres of our lives. Popular dance, very much like highbrow art and museums, responds directly or indirectly to the consequences of globalism as it impinges on the world beyond the United States and the former western states of the European Union. In former Eastern Europe we find today responses very similar to what salsa means and does in the United States.

Cindy Garcia's meticulous and insightful explorations in *Salsa Crossings* provide a case study that is, at the same time, a sign of the times. During the Cold War popular music was basically unidirectional: from the United States to the rest of the world. Since the end of the Cold War and the rise of globalism, music and popular culture travel in several directions at the same time, engendering conflicts among the population that are the actors and consumers of popular culture. Garcia's investigations reveal that, on the one hand, the popularity of salsa in the United States could play as community building among Latino/as. On the other hand, it makes Spanish Caribbean music visible in the national culture of the United States. However, it is also a source of conflict among Latino/as, as they dispute salsa's authenticity outside of the Caribbean. Salsa's authenticity is not, of course, an issue in the Spanish Caribbean, but it is when it is exported to the United States and enters larger national configurations in which Latino/as struggle for their status. As a consequence, salsa is exploited for a purpose that goes beyond community building and internal political conflicts within the community. It becomes a source of income and market competition. Salsa, in other words, is also a commodity in the global cultural market.

Garcia's book is an outstanding contribution to the growing and already impressive field of Latino/as scholarship. It dissects internal intra-cultural conflicts (within the communities of Latino/as) as well as inter-cultural conflicts (between Latino/as "minor culture," the Anglo national and hegemonic culture). The argument is compelling and grounded in solid and sophisticated field research. It is also a single contribution to the goals of *Latin America Otherwise*: to show that we are all beyond the epoch in which Latin America was over there and Latino/as over here. Such division is vanishing daily. The "fact" of salsa and this analysis of its manifestations and functions clearly show that Latin America is here and Latino/as are over there.

Preface

HOW TO MAKE IT TO THE DANCE FLOOR IN LOS ANGELES

This salsa story began in October 1999, when some graduate students from UCLA, Collette and Stephanie, were grumbling to me about the previous Saturday night; they had spent it at El Reino de la Salsa in Hollywood.[1] No one had asked them to dance, so they danced with each other, feeling like complete outsiders.

When I asked them to recommend a place to go dancing (I was new in town), they warned me not to go to El Reino de la Salsa if I hoped to dance. The people there, they said, were unfriendly and stuck up and had not even acknowledged their presence. But I had also heard from a male acquaintance that El Reino de la Salsa was one of the best salsa clubs in Los Angeles, known for its live music and Cuban salsa. He felt as though he belonged to the "salsa family" that had emerged within this club's intimate setting. I decided to try my luck at this place, given my interest in finding a Latino-based dance club in which to root my L.A. social life as well as my ethnographic inquiry.

I had illusions of inviting Collette and Stephanie back to the club once I had performed some of the groundwork to establish myself as a member of the "family." These plans were dashed, however, when, on my first night at El Reino de la Salsa, like Colette and Stephanie, I could not make it to the dance floor. My ability to belong amid the crowd of dancers was dependent on a man asking me to dance. More specifically, it was dependent on a man appraising me as a desirable dance partner. That first night at El Reino de la Salsa, I spent a lot of time sitting around, taking note of how men and women went about forming these temporary partnerships—enactments of the usual heteronormative routine in which women generally wait to be asked by men before they step onto the dance floor. Why, I asked myself, did this heteronormative formation seem so much more heightened than I'd ever noticed before?

The doorman reluctantly seated my friend Jan and me at an empty table tucked into the corner by the door. From my chair I had an unobstructed view of people coming and going, in to dance and out to smoke. When the doorman brought over two other women—we soon learned that their names were Yolanda and Dora—to join us, he told us that we are lucky to have been seated at a table, since none of us had made reservations.

Despite the inauspicious welcome, we four were determined to enjoy the evening. Yolanda and Dora, who told me they were from El Salvador, were thrilled to be there on a rare night out; they had rounded up their boyfriends to do babysitting duty. Jan doesn't speak Spanish, so couldn't converse with Yolanda and Dora unless I translated. After our introductions, however, Yolanda and Dora didn't make any further attempts to use my translation services. Neither did Jan. Yolanda and Dora spoke mostly with each other, and sometimes with me, in Spanish.

Yolanda, Dora, Jan, and I were passed over as dance partners when the musicians opened with a salsa, so I surveyed the scene. A man and a woman in their sixties (I later found out their names, Javier and Ernestina, and that they came to the club every weekend) beat the other couples to the floor. She held the hem of her blue-sequined dress so lightly that the skirt appeared to smoothly sway on its own; then she startled us as she abruptly stepped out to the side, her sequins swishing in response. She and Javier embraced. He paused. Poised on the ball of her foot, she was ready for him to begin at any moment, in any direction. He dramatically waited several counts and then pushed forward across the floor, navigating in between the other couples without taking his eyes off Ernestina.

A white woman in a tight, sleeveless, sequined, pastel-colored leopard-print dress and purple high heels entered the club. She tossed her shoulder-length, permed and dyed red hair, kissed the doorman on the cheek as if she had been here before, and was swept up almost immediately by a male partner; she was on the floor, dancing salsa, within sixty seconds of her arrival. It was stunning. Most of the other people had eased into dancing at a slower pace, as if getting warmed up to the music and to each other.

"How did she make it to the floor so fast?" I wondered. Maybe she was a regular visitor to the club. Perhaps people knew her and liked how she danced. Or maybe it was her outfit. At this thought, I realized that most of the women who were dancing were wearing sequins or leopard prints, high heels, hoop earrings, and miniskirts. Their black-suited partners might not have found my Target pants and minimal heels very appealing. I wasn't yet sure how the sequins fit in, but many of the women dancing had assembled outfits that signified "Latinaness," albeit the kind belonging to the forbidden, exotic dancing Latina bodies represented in Hollywood movies, such as *Shall We Dance?* (2004) and *Dirty Dancing: Havana Nights* (2004).

As the band drew out the last note of the set, the red-haired woman's purple heel caught the hem of Ernestina's dress, and the sequins unraveled and scattered. Javier stooped to help Ernestina collect them. Recorded music came over the loudspeakers as the band and its following took a break, making space on the floor for The Unsequined: those adorned in less flashy attire who seem to be more concerned with dance as a form of socializing. Then a Latino came to the table to invite Dora to dance. Once on the floor, they intertwined their fingers and approximated the rhythm, slowing down or skipping steps to resynchronize as they chatted in place.

While I scanned the room, I took note of the activities and outfits of one other class of club-goers: Women Not Dancing. About eight Latinas in their twenties, all in black dresses, got up from a table and left, without having danced. Maybe they had just come to the club for the dining experience and hadn't wanted to dance, or maybe no one had wanted to dance with them. Maybe they had wanted to dance, refused to subject themselves to the gendered rules of this club, and decided to go to lesbian night at the salsa club in Silver Lake instead.

Then I noticed another group: White Women Dancing with White Women. Two white women—they reminded me of Collette and Stephanie—faced each other, dancing to differing beats. One of them tossed her hair, while the other waved her arms in the air and spun around. Two other white women were dancing together, embracing on the opposite side of the floor, exaggeratedly pushing their hips from side to side with painstaking effort. None of these four white women had danced when the band was playing. While inwardly I cheered their determination to dance without waiting for men to ask them in this decidedly queer-unfriendly space, I also cringed at their mimicry of the "Latina-like" moves they had seen throughout the evening.

When I used to go to clubs in San Jose with my cousins or friends, we'd take a similar approach, dancing with each other. Usually we didn't make it through the first song, however, before men would come and spin us off in different directions. At times we women would prefer to dance together and refuse offers that would, in effect, split us apart. At El Reino de la Salsa, however, I hadn't yet manufactured this kind of arrangement with the women at my table, and I was not exactly eager to align myself with the Latina-mimicking white women. Stuck at the table in the corner, desiring to dance but without any offers, I was sure this would change once people saw that I know how to salsa. I figured that if I could just electrify everyone with my dancing, maybe the ordinariness of my unsequined outfit wouldn't matter.

I had never had any trouble fitting in to the dance scene at clubs in Colorado, Costa Rica, Cuba, or California's Bay Area, where I grew up. I had been dancing for years, beginning as a child, with my family in Milpitas, California. We danced to salsa, *cumbia,* merengue, soul, and disco music, although no one ever differentiated the genres by name. In Boulder, Colorado, beginning in 1993, I took my first formal lessons in social partner dances with Carmen Nelson. A native of Guatemala who had studied dance with Liliana Valle in Costa Rica, Nelson structured her classes around Valle's concept of *baile popular,* dances from Latin America popularized in Costa Rica, dances of everyday nightlife, including salsa, merengue, *cha cha chá, bolero, bolero son,* and *swing criollo* performed in social contexts.

In 1997 I studied dance for a year with Valle, the artistic and pedagogical director of the Merecumbé Centro de Enseñanza e Investigaciones de Baile Popular in San José, Costa Rica. In 1998 I spent five weeks studying *baile popular* with instructors in Havana and at the Escuela Nacional de Arte in Cuba. My interpretations of the social scenes in Los Angeles salsa clubs were greatly influenced by both the informal dance practices of my Mexican American family and the *baile popular* pedagogies of my formal instructors. In neither of these situations did one dance genre seem to overshadow the others.

When I began my ethnographic research, I quickly learned that this was not always—or even often—the case. Salsa eclipsed all other genres in the Los Angeles clubs I first attended: El Reino de la Salsa, The Legend, Copa Cabana West, Valentino's on Mondays. Latino dance clubs advertised on the web and those endorsed by club patrons turned out to be salsa clubs. That is, Latina/o and non-Latina/o patrons went to these places almost exclusively to dance, and salsa was the dance that mattered most. Had the centralization of salsa affected how patrons across club cultures interpreted their nighttime corporealities? Conversely, had these desired corporealities effectively centralized salsa, making it the only dance that mattered?

When I asked about Las Feliz Edades, a club near my home on the East Side, patrons cautioned me not to go there. Las Feliz Edades, I was told, did not really "count" as a salsa club because the people there were mostly "low-class immigrants" who danced "their old, traditional styles," like *cumbia*, merengue, and *punta*.[2] I was told, "They don't know how to dance salsa there" and "They care more about socializing and drinking than dancing." The disparaging tones of these descriptions came from dancers whose fixations on the latest L.A. salsa moves marked them as *salseras/os* and distanced themselves from the "socializers" at Las Feliz Edades.

Meaning more than simply "one who dances or plays salsa," the term *salsera/o* is often associated in many locales with someone who not only demonstrates a high degree of knowledge of salsa but also has the ability to generate social prestige through her or his performances of it. In Los Angeles, however, the term *salsera/o* refers not simply to a person with knowledge of and a skilled performance of salsa dancing but to a person with apparent mastery of L.A. salsa in particular. It is by demonstrating mastery of this dominant, local style of salsa that salseras/os gain prestige, locally and globally. What does this style entail? Practitioners of L.A. salsa create moves in part by mining the legacy of an exoticized *latinidad* produced in Hollywood for American film and television.[3]

In Los Angeles patrons of salsa clubs divide dance practices into categories of salsa/not-salsa. Salsa has become the referent by which even non-salseras/os (such as socializers) locate themselves. Non-salseras/os commonly claim, "We don't dance that flashy American salsa style" or "No bailo salsa, bailo cumbia!"[4] Non-salseras/os learn to recognize that alternatives to L.A. salsa practices are predominantly measured against and on the terms of L.A. salsa. Without a reference to salsa, their dance practices would not register outside of their social circles. Non-salseras/os thus learn to identify themselves in relation to the dominant practice of salsa, inadvertently yet inevitably reinscribing the binary opposition of salsa and its others: cumbia, merengue, and cha cha chá, for example.

I had intended to research and write about *baile popular*, but salsa has consumed my work. Local understandings of dance reframe *baile popular* as either not-salsa or only-salsa. I have thus taken on, challenged, stretched, relished in, struggled with, cursed, and submitted to salsa as a dominant analytical framework. My Los Angeles dance club investigations entail the qualitative, ethnographic study of salsa (and not-salsa) as an everyday or everynight social practice.

When the band at El Reino started up again, the red-haired woman with the hem-ripping purple heels followed a new partner to the floor to dance L.A. salsa. As they faced each other, they flung their arms above their heads, punctuating the air with their fingertips. Then they performed a series of rapid turns; with his hand on the back of her neck, he pulled her body toward his, and then abruptly pushed her away, only to pull her back in by the wrist. As the turns ended, he hoisted her over his head, upside-down, her legs opening into a split. Allowing her body to almost drop headfirst to the floor, he caught her by the hips, while she stabilized herself by pushing away from the floor with her hands and wrapping her legs around his waist. He then flipped up her skirt and slapped out a rhythm on her sequined buns-turned-congas. She lifted her torso upward and whipped her hair around as she landed on her feet once again.

I was simultaneously fascinated by their incredible virtuosity and disturbed by how precisely they performed the exaggerated combination of violence and sexuality often represented as *latinidad* in U.S. popular culture.[5] It's not that I could not see the possibility that women might gain pleasure and empowerment from performing eroticism in a social space.[6] What nagged at me was that the Latina eroticism performed was mediated predominantly by a history of cultural representations of Latinas as one-dimensionally exotic.[7]

The couple had danced an exoticism that was fed by and simultaneously reinforced the web of associations of Latinas as hypererotic, a legacy of colonialism. In this dance, exotic Latinaness was apparently made even more desirable with the addition of sequins and ballroomesque arm moves. After a long time sitting, I noticed that women (Latina and otherwise) who did not embody this Latina stereotype and who did not execute L.A. salsa's swift turns, endless flourishes, dramatic lifts, and sparkly outfits, did not succeed in putting their bodies into circulation as dancers.

Without the stability of the sociofamilial groups I had been a part of in other places, I realized that navigating the Los Angeles club scene alone, especially as a woman who did not perform dominant, local conceptualizations of Latinaness, did not feel like a leisurely activity. Was it possible for newcomers to belong to the scene without performing exoticizations of *latinidad*?

With the abundance of clubs in the Los Angeles area, I thought that I might be able to escape the pressures to perform the sequined Latinaness required by L.A. salsa by going to a different club. Perhaps I could fit in among the "socializers" at a club like Las Feliz Edades, where the dancing sounded more familiar and less exotic, where women were included in the social dance scene even if they did not measure up to the exotic dance and outfit standards for L.A. salseras.

As I was to find out, even though many of the practices at Las Feliz Edades overlapped with my own, my status as a fair-skinned American academic ethnographically soaking in details marked me as an outsider. To an extent, I felt like an intruder, venturing into a social haven for mostly immigrant patrons who wished to escape the anti-immigrant American gaze. At the not-salsa club of Las Feliz Edades, patrons deliberately distanced themselves from the L.A. salseras/os. As I was to conclude later, an analysis of the distinctions between salsa and not-salsa interlaces with the politics of migration, citizenship, and belonging that underlie local dance cultures.

In salsa contexts at clubs like El Reino, I started my research as a wallflower, a (non)participant observer. This unsolicited, sedentary position afforded me the opportunity to survey the choreography of belonging, to assess how patrons bestow social membership within the parameters of nightclub culture and salsa ideologies. To these observations I brought an analytic framework of choreography in order to understand the social and political relationships of bodies in motion. Susan Foster (1998: 4) posits choreography as a set of culturally situated codes and values regarding gestures, movements, and speech through which identities, and thus social memberships, are configured. What are the choreographic codes of membership at work in salsa and not-salsa clubs? I asked.

Through a close analysis of bodily practices, both on and off the dance floor, at several clubs, I have assessed how choreographies of belonging overlap with discourses of *latinidad*.

In the context of staged concert dance performances, choreographers are listed, and their choreographic intentions often summarized, in a program. One then interprets choreography based on the performance, considering what the dancers were "supposed to do" within an overall plan that organizes elements such as space, time, and effort. In the social settings of nightclubs, however, there are no program notes, no explicit choreographer, and no summary of what an observer is about to witness. The social codes and dance values in play often become apparent through the tensions that arise when someone breaks with the choreography.

In the ethnography that follows, I analyze dominant club choreographies and their disruptions—the stumbles, mediocre motions, and miscues—in order to understand how women make it to the dance floor. In the course of my research, it became apparent that gendered choreographies in L.A. salsa clubs are tangled up with the politics of globalization, transnationalism, migration, and citizenship, politics not immediately associated with spaces of leisure in a city known for its movie productions, movie stars, and abundance of rich people working in the movie industry. I thus examine how the Hollywood movie industry relates to my concerns about the social, political, and economic implications of the hierarchies of gender, ethnicity, class, and nation within clubs. I address these macropolitics of belonging throughout the book as I present how classed, racialized, and gendered social bodies—bodies of Latin American migrants, Chicanas/os, Latinas/os, and non-Latinas/os—participate in salsa settings.

The salsa stories I recount point to choreographies of power. They show that to move up the salsa social hierarchy, local salseras/os must perform an exoticized L.A.-style salsa that distances them from club practices associated with undocumented Mexican laborers. They indicate that in Los Angeles, dancing "like a Mexican" is equated with dancing salsa "wrong." They reveal that belonging as a Latina/o citizen in the United States is in dialogue with the parameters for social membership in salsa clubs. And these stories show that many L.A. Latinas/os attempt to eliminate from their own performances any dance techniques that can locate them as migrants, as poor or working class, as Mexican, or as undocumented, whether or not these categories accurately characterize them.

During my ethnographic research in Los Angeles, I found that social membership and mobility in the nightclubs depends on one's repertoire of select bodily techniques and movement practices. From the timing of exiting the dance floor to the sequined shimmer of a spin and the intricate lift of a properly tweezed eyebrow, dancers tie themselves not simply to a salsa style but also to a particular conceptualization of *latinidad*. This book is concerned with enactments of *latinidad* in salsa spaces.

Grounding Critical Ethnography

Feminist ethnographic methodologies have profoundly influenced this project. The fieldwork took place between 1999 and 2005 in Los Angeles, the city to which I moved in order to study practices of *baile popular*. By studying the gendered salsa relationships amid the hierarchies of class, race, and nation, I have heeded Kamala Visweswaran's (1995: 113) argument that the decolonization of feminist ethnography necessitates the integration of gender with other axes of difference.

Visweswaran (1995: 113) also calls for homework: the critical analysis of one's own position in conjunction with fieldwork. Understanding the ways I became implicated in Los Angeles salsa clubs requires that I consider the degree to which I can claim the status of native ethnographer. And this requires that I call into question the extent to which I can frame Los Angeles, or even salsa clubs within Los Angeles, as home. Native ethnographers such as José Limón went back home to study the practice of polka dancing in south Texas, but my own home is neither singular nor obvious. The Bay Area city of Milpitas is the place in which I grew up and the one that feels most like home. Many place-bound notions of home, however, do not take into account the mobility of populations and that social relationships might occur outside the place, even across distances (Rouse 1991: 14). In my case, many of the people I knew there have moved away, including my parents and me. This place is my home only in memory.

Los Angeles, the place I chose to call home during my research, became the site in which I studied the way salsa practices contribute to the configuration of U.S. *latinidad*. Salsa in Los Angeles became a kind of homing device—for me and for many other Latinas/os living there. Just as many Latinas/os and Latin Americans (who may never have danced salsa before) ground themselves or find themselves grounded as Latinas/os through practices of salsa, I grounded my ethnography of home not in a place where I already have roots but in a practice through which I rooted myself into a new place. Supposedly.

As I suggested earlier, not everyone conceives of salsa in the same way. My way turned out to be the "wrong" way, which jeopardized any easy claim to insider, "native" ethnographer status. And yet even ethnographers who can legitimately claim that they are from a particular dance culture do not fully participate as insiders, because the importance of the ethnographic project can outweigh the importance of success on the dance floor.[8] To what degree, then, am I an insider in this project, a native ethnographer who performs fieldwork at home?

With an increase in transnational and even intranational migration, insider status in a salsa club based on ethnicity, class, nation, or past experience with salsa is neither automatic nor guaranteed. One often is recognized as an insider only after undergoing rigorous salsa (re)training in accordance with local practices. Latinas/os and non-Latinas/os who have never danced salsa before have been able to join the in-crowd in mere months by virtue of their success in L.A. salsa lessons. In contrast, Latinas/os who have danced salsa all their lives may be considered outsiders if, in the context of Los Angeles, their practices are perceived as Mexican *cumbia* rather than salsa. I qualify my insider/outsider status with an understanding that I could not have substituted a study of samba, reggae, or tango for salsa. As a (red-haired) Chicana feminist ethnographer who has been accused of dancing salsa "like a Mexican" when relieved of her "wallflowering," I recognized I was at times implicated as both an insider and an outsider.

I point to my own shifting status as another technique of feminist ethnography. I do so in response to ethnographies in which the body of the ethnographer disappears in the text, only to emerge as a voice that is omniscient and authoritative. As Ruth Behar (1996) writes, a feminist ethnographer draws attention to herself as a vulnerable observer, indicating her bodily presence by revealing her emotions. As she witnesses social injustices, poverty, and death, the vulnerable observer conveys her discomfort, anguish, and fears with the intention of stirring empathy in readers, thereby possibly deepening their grasp of unfamiliar milieus. Behar writes that the vulnerable observer must consider the degree to which she is willing to participate, what to document or leave out, and how to do so without departing from the genre of ethnography when in the midst "of a massacre, in the face of torture, in the eyes of a hurricane, in the aftermath of an earthquake, or even, say, when horror looms apparently more gently in memories that won't recede and so come pouring forth in the late-night quiet of a kitchen, as a storyteller opens her heart to a story listener, recounting hurts that cut deep and raw into the gullies of the self" (2).

One can hardly equate the salsa club anxieties of wallflowering, the turmoil of walking across a room *solita*,[9] and the dread of the unavoidable missteps, miscues, and mistranslations with the horrors of torture, hurricanes, and massacres. Descriptions of these awkward nightclub moments might elicit laughter, an emotional response more conducive to salsa environs than tears of rage or screams of grief. Yet within salsa clubs, social injustice, poverty, and death—the horrors of everyday life that may provoke rage and grief—lurk just below the surface of sequined corporealities.

As club patrons couple leopard prints and hot-pink feathers with smooth techniques, they produce fantastic nighttime corporealities enmeshed in the hierarchies of nation, race, and class of daily life, all (or at lease some) of which they attempt to obscure. Latinas gain higher positions in the nighttime salsa hierarchy by distancing themselves from the bounces of *cumbia* that mark Mexicanness; the drinking of alcohol, which signifies "illegal" immigrant status; and the practice of walking around the club by themselves, which marks the women with "low-class" promiscuity.

Unlike sequins and hair tosses, laughter in a club setting does not disguise these social hierarchies as much as it makes them easier to bear. Patrons joke about each other's daytime struggles and nighttime shortcomings. Yet the stark materialities of death and survival from outside the club often slip past the doorman, cut through the music, and haunt escapist pretenses of unity. When this happens, no one laughs. The moments of humor embedded in the details of my own awkward club experiences highlight the hierarchies and political undercurrents in clubs. At times I've used humor to elucidate the differential vulnerabilities and mobilities among Latinas in heterosexual economies of *latinidad*. I do so, however, with full appreciation of the tragedies that often lie just beneath the sequined surface of the club scene.

My observations and discussions with both longtime L.A. clubbers and newcomers caused me to reflect on how patrons negotiate their belonging in Los Angeles salsa clubs, to ask how they are called in to corporeality amid the conflicting choreographies of *latinidad* already in circulation when they walk into clubs. Through their social practices in nightclubs where Latino expressive culture is centralized, Latina and Latino patrons enact the tensions between Americanness and *latinidad*. During my research, the longer I spent trying to figure out how to get to the dance floor, how to participate within these embattled club choreographies, the more I learned from others that I would have to pay attention to the practices and relationships in the club in order to "make it." Furthermore, even if I made it to the dance floor, I might end up stepping on someone else. Or she might end up stepping on me.

In the spring of 2000 the *salsero* who had recommended El Reino de la Salsa suggested I go to the West Coast Salsa Congress. He said that the congress was an annual event to which dancers come from all over the world, united by their love of salsa. For this salsero, the congress provided a space that transcended histories and social differences. Yet I found that what united the cosmopolitan congress participants from a multitude of nations with the L.A. salseros was the mutual acknowledgment that L.A. salsa was spinning like a whirlwind toward the top of local and global salsa hierarchies.

Acknowledgments

When I told the children at University Hill Elementary School in Boulder, Colorado, that I was leaving them to study dance at UCLA, one of them protested, "But you're already one of the best dancers in the whole school!" She was a dancer from Tumbao, the children's dance group I had created at the school. I wanted to understand more about Mexicanness and dance in the United States, and I had decided to go to graduate school to do so. Uprooting myself from the children and my job as a bilingual elementary school teacher to begin a life in academia was one of the hardest things I have ever done. The love letters sent to Los Angeles from Tumbao's dancers filled my heart and kept me focused.

My adored teachers of *baile popular*, Carmen Nelson and Liliana Valle, attuned me to the politics of dancing. Marta Savigliano, Alicia Arrizón, Susan Leigh Foster, Chon Noriega, and Christopher Waterman, scholars from the University of California, not only generously guided the early dissertation version of this project, but they inspired and critiqued many of the ideas developed in the text. The choreographer Susan Rose from the University of California at Riverside honed my understanding of choreography and moving bodies. During this project, I went to dance clubs in Los Angeles on many nights, sometimes alone and sometimes with friends whose experiences and perceptions have influenced the pages that follow. Thank you to Margit Edwards, Ana Guajardo, María Martínez, Francisco Heredia, Marisol Pérez, and Claudia Brazzale.

This book would not have been possible without funding from the Center for U.S.-Mexican Studies at the University of California, San Diego and the Institute for Advanced Study at the University of Minnesota that supported the various stages of the project. I finished much of the manuscript during a fellowship administered by the National Academies through the Ford Foundation.

I thank my colleagues at the University of Minnesota for all of their support, particularly several from the Department of Theatre Arts and Dance: Sonja Kuftinec, Michal Kobialka, Diyah Larasati, Carl Flink, Margaret Werry, and Ananya Chatterjea. Margaret Werry, Omise'eke Tinsley, and Zenzele Isoke offered their keen insights on portions of the manuscript. Catherine Squires initiated the Faculty of Color Writing Group through the Office of Equity and Diversity, and she and the members of the writing group have been instrumental in the completion of this book. The members of our local Chicana/o Scholars Writing Group—Olga Herrera, Jimmy Patiño, Lorena Muñoz, Bianet Castellanos, Louis Mendoza, and Yolanda Padilla—I thank you for the collective knowledge and enthusiasm you have shared with me.

Many scholars, mentors, colleagues, and friends have passed on their rigorous critiques and encouragement. Lucy Burns has been my most reliable, steadfast critic and fan, helping to sharpen the arguments chapter by chapter. Her knowledge and her sophisticated study of migration and performance have influenced me beyond measure. Sonia Saldivar-Hull supported my work at many points along the way. Ramón Rivera-Servera and Deborah Paredez both pushed my concept of *latinidad* into new directions. Frances Aparicio, whose book, *Listening to Salsa*, gave this project an early jolt and a solid foundation, met with me to discuss her careful, close reading of the manuscript. The work and ideas of fellow dance scholars Anthea Kraut, Diyah Larasati, Harmony Bench, Priya Srinivasan, Raquel Monroe, Ananya Chatterjea, and Melissa Blanco Borelli have contributed much to my own understanding of the political significance of bodies in motion. My inquisitive next-door neighbor, Joan Fritz, did not live to see the publication of this book, but our back porch conversations definitely nurtured me as a writer and a human. I am incredibly grateful for the impact all of these people, whether through Skype conversations, conference presentations, or emails or over tea, have had on this study of salsa.

My parents, Isidro García and Fannie García, and my sister, Amy García, are all storytellers. My father's stories of how the Mexicans and African Americans in his boyhood barrio Chihuahuita were not allowed to go beyond Tenth Street, my mother's stories of her family working in the cotton mill, and my sister's screenplays that depict vivid injustices have profoundly shaped why I write.

I end these acknowledgments with one more child, my daughter, Vivi, whose vivacious curiosity and determination got me through the last page.

Introduction

SALSA'S LOPSIDED GLOBAL FLOW

In his closing remarks after the last performance at the 2000 congress in Los Angeles, the promoter Albert Torres addressed the differences among salsa practices as he elaborated on the meaning of the congress's slogan, "Creating unity through salsa." Projected from the stage, his amplified voice instructed participants to value all styles of salsa. Although we might continue dancing our various styles, he said, we should stop acting as if one style is better than another. In the interest of creating a global community united as salseras/os, he instructed us to dance that night with someone who danced a style different than our own. Salsa, he told us, is "our" common language, an international language that does not belong to any single country or individual; through salsa, we can achieve unity.

The idea of creating unity through the diverse practices of salsa, the harmonious merging of styles under one big tent in a parking lot, purports to bring together all salsa practices under the guise of cultural relativism. In the process of unity, the salsa industry manufactures both the inclusions and exclusions of people, places, and practices to facilitate the consumption of salsa on a global scale.

Each year since 1999 thousands of local, national, and international participants gather for the West Coast Salsa Congress in Los Angeles. Held in the Hollywood Park Casino's parking lot for the first several years, the congress promotes salsa as a global practice and has a recurring theme of "Creating unity through salsa." While throngs of aficionados attend the congress as a leisurely activity, workshop instructors, competitors, dance team members, and choreographers show up each year to mark themselves as salsa professionals. Those who can pay the forty-dollar entrance fee are admitted into the congress's fantasy salsa space, surrounded by a chain-link barrier.

On one of the temporary stages in "Salsa Land," previously selected dance teams showcase three- to five-minute choreographies. On another stage, the musicians hired to provide the live music perform in bands primarily from Puerto Rico, Venezuela, and New York and highlight the Latino and Latin American origins of salsa. However, in 2000, the first year I attended, the abundance of dance teams coming from countries such as Japan, Holland, Canada, and Italy, as well as the relative dearth of teams from Latin America, captured my attention. The dance teams led by directors with Latino and Latin American surnames were predominantly affiliated with Los Angeles, Chicago, and New York.[1] Program notes describing the second annual congress in 2000 made a case for salsa's transnational appeal but did not address the lopsided hemispheric mapping of dance teams and musicians. Salsa had circumvented the globe, taken root in large cities, and selectively crossed hemispheric, national, and socioeconomic borders.

With the unequal leaps and infiltrations that characterize the flow of globalization, the global circuit of salsa congresses largely evaded the global South, such that the supposed worldwide unity through congress-style salsa reinforced a division between the northern and southern hemispheres, between the global North and South. In 2005, between June and December alone, congresses took place in several sites around the world: Paris, Cannes, Philadelphia, Seoul, Hamburg, Sofia, San Juan, Miami, Manhattan, Sydney, London, Monaco, Houston, Vancouver, Tokyo, Oslo, Suriname, New York, and San Francisco.[2] Of the nineteen congresses, only two, those in Australia and Suriname, occurred in the southern hemisphere.[3]

Given the uneven hemispheric participation in the salsa congress industry, the global North has had a lopsided role in defining concepts of both unity and salsa. Salsa practices along the congress network have become codified and homogenized to an extent through congress workshops, exhibitions, and competitions, as many salseras/os from other cities have "refined" their local salsa practices through the incorporation of congress techniques. In this book I consider whether the concept of "unity through salsa" can be stretched to include practices that do not belong within the dominant danced discourses as legitimated by the salsa industry.

That the West Coast Salsa Congress attracted participants from London, Paris, and Tokyo was seen by most as a cause for celebration rather than a testimony to the fact that certain cities in certain nations were giving salsa its new global credibility. The celebration disavowed a number of elements evident at the congress: the erasure of the uneasy relationships among some of the participants, the cities of the global South that had been left off the salsa map, and the omission that salsa and its precursors had been circulating for decades within Latin American countries outside the new global salsa network. As a global city, Los Angeles is not only a metropolitan hub for the integration and dispersal of economic activities within the world capitalist economy but is also a hub for the centralization, standardization, and innovation of global salsa practices (Sassen 2001: xix, 3).

Since the 1970s salsa has flowed across racial, economic, and national borders with an unrestrained exuberance, seemingly unifying Latino and non-Latino practitioners in Los Angeles and across the globe.[4] Salsa appears in urban nightclubs around the world, in contests such as the ESPN World Salsa Championships, and in major motion pictures such as *Along Came Polly* (2004), in which Jennifer Aniston's character shakes it up on the dance floor. With the intense commodification of salsa through international salsa congresses since the late 1990s, salsa has taken root in numerous cities, such as Hamburg, Montreal, and Rome. Salsa appears to embrace diverse movements and moods as it circulates throughout the global North.

When pausing on the live practice of salsa within a specific Los Angeles club, however, nightclub choreographies of exclusion clash with popular conceptualizations of a diverse but united salsa community. In this book, my close analysis of salsa practices demonstrates that corresponding configurations of Latina/o corporealities are hierarchically classified in accordance with U.S. frameworks of racialization. Salsa practitioners contend with the contradictory poles of latinidad produced in

Los Angeles: the sequined, exoticized Latina from an ambiguous Caribbean locale, and the unsequined laboring migrant, usually conflated with "Mexican," in which *Mexican* often serves as an umbrella term for Central American.

What Is Salsa?

This work shifts away from the predominance of salsa narratives that centralize Cuba, Puerto Rico, and New York as sites of salsa origins (Boggs 1992; Concepción 2002; Roberts 1999; Rodríguez 1994) to theorize the social formation of Mexicanness in salsa spaces in Los Angeles. While salsa is historically regarded as Afro-Caribbean, Los Angeles dancers include a large number of Mexicans and Central Americans. I use the term *Mexican* to signify the nightclub practices associated with Mexicans and Central Americans in part because Central Americans in these spaces get indiscriminately lumped together with the Mexicans. I base my interpretations on the social *speculation* of who may or may not be Mexican rather than on sociological data. I am thus interested in the ways that Mexican and Central American movement practices and bodies fall to the bottom of salsa hierarchies, even when the majority of the Latinas/os in Los Angeles clubs are Mexican and Central American. My methodology allows for misperceptions, including my own.

Rather than focus on the figureheads of salsa—the teachers, performers, and contest winners—I attend to the movement practices of people who get identified as dancing "wrong" in Los Angeles salsa spaces: the migrants, the Mexicans, the queers, the ones who are not particularly legible in salsa discourses. As in most Los Angeles partner-dance venues, the salsa clubs support heterosexual couplings. As a (red-haired) Chicana feminist choreographic ethnographer, at times I step away from an analysis of the predominantly heterosexual dance floor partnerships to devote my attention to the interactions among women in out-of-the-way salsa spaces: among wallflowers at the edges of the floor, in women's bathrooms, at the bar, and in cyberspace. These decentralizing moves allow me to consider the nuances of salsa corporealities, hierarchies, divisions, and alliances.

I situate this work within a body of salsa scholarship that challenges racist assumptions about Latinas/os and dance. Fraser Delgado and Muñoz (1997) point to the significance of Latin American social dance in their edited volume

Everynight Life Culture and Dance in Latin/o America. Rivera-Servera (2004) vividly describes salsa dancing as a resistive practice in the queer clubs of New York and Texas. Renta (2004) carefully lays out the history and techniques of Eddie Torres's New York mambo, and Pietrobruno (2006) addresses salsa dance pedagogies in Montreal. Like these authors, I am concerned with the diasporic and transnational migrations of salsa. By studying salsa in Los Angeles rather than in New York, Puerto Rico, and Cuba I am able to address the significations of the dance practices as they circulate translocally to a city and Latino population not historically noted as central to the social performance of salsa. While all of these scholars bring attention to salsa as dance, I broaden this scope to include the movement practices in salsa spaces on and off dance floors. Such an approach emphasizes my concern with analyzing politics in motion and the relations of power between bodies.

I observe salsa movement practices and partnerships among the formally and informally trained, old-timers and newcomers, socializers and dance fanatics. My focus on movement decentralizes salsa scholarship largely concerned with music.[5] Most studies of salsa as a musical genre have made visible a genealogy of African and Spanish roots with its development in Puerto Rico, Cuba, New York, and Colombia (Boggs 1992; Roberts 1999; Rodríguez 1994; Ulloa 1992). Notable in these approaches to salsa is the prolific attention to the musicians, who are primarily men. For example, Willie Colón, Willy Chirino, Oscar D'Leon, and Tito Puente are well-known male musicians often mentioned in salsa discussions. The scholarship on music also tends to naturalize salsa origins stories that reify the Caribbean. Frances Aparicio's groundbreaking work, *Listening to Salsa: Gender, Latin Popular Music, and Puerto Rican Cultures* (1998), detours from this discussion. Aparicio analyzes the *reception* of music, centralizing the salsa listening practices of women. For her, salsa becomes not an object or product but a practice firmly embedded in everyday life social relations. With this approach, she undoes the reification of musicianship and artistry and repopularizes salsa scholarship to focus on "nonspecialists."

This popularization inspires me to ask questions about the relationships between the spectacular and unspectacular people and practices in salsa spaces: How do people attach social meaning to movement and decide who dances salsa "wrong"? What informs the dance-based hierarchies? I take up these questions to make legible the importance of the relations of gender, sexuality, and homosociality, in addition to race and nation, in salsa settings. This book expands previous approaches to consider salsa *practices* deterritorialized from Afro-Caribbean origins stories and reterritorialized in Mexican and Central American Los Angeles.

Some people use *salsa* as an umbrella term to denote numerous Latin American dance genres, including salsa. Others refer to salsa as a genre belonging to a larger group of Latin American dance genres called *baile popular*.[6] When salseras/os and aficionados invoke *salsa*, they usually mean the specific dance rhythm of salsa to the exclusion of other genres. Some share Willie Colón's (1999: 6–7) description of salsa as neither a genre nor a rhythm but a concept, a "social, musical, cultural, hybrid force that has embraced jazz, folklore, pop, and everything else that is relevant or could stand in its evolutionary path." Salsa conversations often reference the *clave* as the rhythmic authenticator (Berríos-Miranda 2002; Boggs 1992), women's hips as the movement signifier (Piedra 1997), resistance to a colonialist past and racist present as the goal, and global camaraderie as a possibility. Scholarly writings about salsa have invoked narratives of resistance and the liberating potentials of dance (Fraser Delgado and Muñoz 1997; Quintero Rivera 1998; Rivera-Servera 2004). In "Rebellions of Everynight Life," Celeste Fraser Delgado and José Esteban Muñoz (1997) theorize the diasporic dancing body as one that can potentially rewrite the colonialist pasts and racial, cultural, and economic marginalizations of the present—the marginalizations of everyday life. As they dance, bodies rebel against hegemonic media representations of "Latinidad as the exotic other to North-of-the-Border rationality and rule" (Fraser Delgado and Muñoz 1997: 26).

Yet close analyses of salsa practices in Los Angeles nightclubs—the obsession with which many salseras/os produce themselves as exotic and cast as "wrong" those who don't—suggest a more complex story. Though salseras/os through their nighttime dance practices may become bodies in rebellion, they simultaneously produce social hierarchies based in part on the exoticisms and marginalizing conditions of everyday life.

When I refer to salsa, I consider not only what are popularly understood as salsa styles, such as mambo, Los Angeles style, or Cuban casino. I also consider other kinds of movement practices, such as where, how, and with whom people travel and affiliate, or distance themselves, while socializing in clubs. In

Salsa Crossings, I focus on the crossings that abound in salsa spaces, such as the crossings of a geopolitical or class border, the crossings of the city, crossover consumers, and the step that curves around and crosses back. In these crossings, I address the ways practitioners exalt and insult one another's style, drinking habits, or country; how they caress, step on, and crash into each other; and how, amid the friendships, romances, and celebrations, they form social hierarchies. I write about salsa as action, but more precisely as *inter*action.

My work depends on observations of moving social bodies. The salsa I write about requires bodies in order to activate it. I could, as in writing a salsa manual, try to pin down the technique of salsa, what a dancer is *supposed* to do. But which technique to foreground? Is it enough to characterize salsa by its footwork, the step-step-step-pause, in order to explain how salsa moves? What happens when salsa is let loose in a social setting? As interaction, the bodies that put salsa into motion determine salsa's legibility. If one dances pause-step-step-step instead of step-step-step-pause, is this the same salsa? Or if another dances step-step-step-pause while crossing behind instead of forward and back, is this still salsa? One forgets to pause, while during that same pause, another invents a backward spin: Still salsa? One pauses to socialize with a bucketful of Coronas and another rehydrates with a bottle of Evian: What does this even have to do with salsa? How to explain the significance of the drinking practices, the music, the emotion, the long pause after your dance partner accuses you of dancing wrong?

The pause in salsa is the most crucial component of the dance—potentially sensual and volatile. The salsa pause takes place between two sets of three beats—right, left, right, pause; left, right, left, pause—following the genre's underlying rhythm repeated throughout the dance, locking the pause into the music. Many newcomers miss the pause altogether, attempting to dash their way through each and every beat as if to emulate the quick-paced salseros who fire off moves in rapid succession. Seasoned dancers know, however, that the dance is not salsa without the pause. The salsa pause is a situated moment, but it is not static. The salsa pause, Liliana Valle has told students, is the choreographic moment at which the tension between bodies is marked by *chispitas en el aire* (little sparks in the air). These little sparks at times signify romance and passion between the bodies of two partners. They also spark within the dancing social body and ignite the salsa wars.

Salsa Wars: Latinidad in Contestation

In his speech at the salsa congress, Torres invokes unity, yet he also indirectly alludes to the salsa wars. The salsa wars are the dance-floor battles in which bodies attempt to claim the authority to define which styles, rhythms, and moves (and thus the bodies that perform them) are to be recognized as the most authentic, sophisticated, "street," or cutting-edge. Is it New York mambo, L.A. salsa, or Cuban casino? Does one dance "on the one" or dance "on the two"? Questions about what counts as dancing salsa "right" extend beyond interrogations about dance moves. To dance "right," should one attend a club on the east side or west side of L.A.? Drink beer or bottled water between songs? Wear shoes with leather or rubber soles? Sequins? Although many in salsa spaces interpret the salsa wars in terms of style, I shift the focus to the larger stakes of dance practices. I consider the ways that people in salsa spaces enact their social membership amid the oppositional pressures of the salsa wars and the ideology of "unity through salsa."

As practitioners engage in the salsa wars, they enact latinidad. The wars over salsa practices are not simply contestations over how to imagine and put latinidad into motion. The wars pit bodies against bodies, determining which bodies matter to latinidad. Which bodies get included and excluded under the umbrella of latinidad in salsa contexts? How do salsa bodies learn to demarcate the practices that fall within the parameters of latinidad and those that do not? How does one gain social status in salsa clubs to move up the social hierarchy? How do moves up and down hierarchies shape latinidad in spaces of leisure?

Latinidad as a nighttime salsa corporeality does not connote a single, stable concept of Latina/o-ness. Aparicio and Chávez-Silverman (1997: 15) theorize that latinidad forms as a process of transculturation, "contestatory and contested, fluid, and relational."[7] Laó-Montes (2001: 8) sees latinidad not as a "static or unifying formation but as a flexible category that relates to a plurality of ideologies of identification, cultural expressions, and political and social agendas." Salsa practitioners negotiate latinidad's legacy of colonialism and imperialism, the homogenization of Latinas/os by the U.S. government (Arrizón 1999), the flattening and reifying of differences through marketing and consumer culture (Dávila 2001), the representations of Latinas/os as exotic others in Hollywood films (López 1997), the patriarchal and heterosexist configurations that cast women and queers as other (Arrizón 1999; Román and Sandoval 1995), and the tensions and contradictions of latinidades formed amid the politics of racialization and U.S. citizenship (De Genova and Ramos-Zayas 2003).

To understand latinidad, Flores and Yúdice (1993) stress the importance of the everyday life practices of Latinas/os. Although I deliberate on the salsa frictions of nightly practices, I also attend to salsa not as utopian but as a possible site of social transformation. Scholars of performance studies have considered latinidad as a space for Latinas/os to potentially come together across differences (Arrizón 1999), for queer Latinas/os to dance out their identities (Rivera-Servera 2004), and for creating relationships, as through memories of Selena Quintanilla Pérez (Paredez 2009). All of these scholars who have theorized latinidad have worked against racist, oppressive constructions of Latina/o identity as static and passive. I continue this challenge, theorizing the way latinidad circulates and morphs in contestation among Latinas/os and non-Latinas/os.

An understanding of a mobile, active latinidad involves choreographically analyzing the everyday practices associated with Latina/o-ness. I envision latinidad put into motion as salsa practices, continuously contested and conceptualized by Latinas/os and non-Latinas/os in salsa settings, rather than an essentialized, bounded race, culture, or ethnicity. Latinidad does not necessarily stick to Latina/o bodies.[8] In the nighttime sphere of salsa dancing, many people, Latina/o or not, enact latinidad.

The cultural globalization of salsa, which often parallels cultural appropriation, occurs as many non-Latinas/os commit themselves to learning, performing, and teaching salsa. The ethnomusicologist Lise Waxer (2002: 3) notes that salsa can be a "gateway to the cultural Other, a fascinating and often exotic world where new selves find liberation from cultural constrictions." Simultaneously many Los Angeles Latina/o salsa practitioners find themselves falling outside of global and local understandings of latinidad. I craft a methodology that makes room for identity perceptions, affects, imaginations, speculations, exaggerations, and desires that circulate the spaces of salsa. I also take into consideration that the latinidades that circulate during salsa nighttimes do not always overlap with the latinidades that circulate by day.

Competing discourses of latinidad emerge in L.A. clubs, sometimes violently. Club patrons often step on, elbow, or bump up against other dancers who compete for the authority to define what it means to belong to latinidad. Thus salsa wars erupt as dancers embody conflicting cultural conceptions of latinidad, often referred to as "differences in style." Hierarchies of styles, as in the valuation of salsa techniques, serve as euphemisms for hierarchies of race, ethnicity, class, and nation embedded in the politics of migration.

Latinos negotiate not only their racialization and homogenization as "U.S. Latinos" but also the terms of their formal and informal citizenship status in Latin America. Further, the mapping of a U.S.-produced latinidad does not acknowledge the ethnonational disharmonies among Latinos. Arlene Dávila (2001: 158) argues that Latino "assertions of cultural differences intersect with dominant norms of American citizenship that give preeminence to white, middle-class producers of and contributors to a political body defined in national terms." As Latinas/os map their belonging in salsa clubs, they do so in dialogue with—and in opposition to—the U.S. parameters of citizenship, with Mexicanness often falling to the bottom of the hierarchy. Yet the mappings of latinidad inside and outside the clubs fall short of belonging to abstract, classless ideals of Americanness.

A Pause in the Global City of Los Angeles

The salsa wars and the calls for unity along the congress network are fueled by the ways that dancers incorporate practices at local levels. In Los Angeles the politics of incorporation converge with the current and historical exploitation of Mexican labor. I pause in Los Angeles to examine the ways the salsa industry and two other local industries, *la limpieza* and the Hollywood industry, intertwine with news media and legislation to impact salsa practices and produce the salsa wars. At the heart of the industries is the war on Mexicans,[9] evident in Los Angeles's history.

In Los Angeles salsa clubs, the war on Mexicans operates in conjunction with political economic structures that allow for the disavowal of the U.S. exploitation of Mexican labor. In the clubs, the performance of Mexicanness (by a Mexican or a non-Mexican) does not propel a dancer to the top of the salsa hierarchy in Los Angeles. And at the core of the more global disavowal is the exploitation itself, based on the fact that Mexicans and Chicanas/os outside the club have long been seen as second-class citizens of the United States as a whole, even in L.A., which until 1848 had been part of Mexico. Los Angeles has remained a city in which Mexicans and Chicanas/os make up the majority of the Latina/o population, although Latinas/os from all over Latin America, especially Central America, live within the city limits. Yet Latinas and Latinos in Los Angeles have historically struggled with low-paying jobs and unemployment, especially as industries have shut down their L.A. factories in order to operate more cheaply abroad.

In the attempt to dissociate Los Angeles from a population of largely working-class Mexican or Mexican American bodies, city elites as early as the late nineteenth century began to appropriate Mexican cultural products such as food and recast them as Spanish. Valle and Torres (2000) offer an example of this effort to erase Mexicanness from Los Angeles while invoking the preferred connection to Europe. In 1912 a traditional Mexican dinner of tamales, beans, and rice was served as part of the "'genuine Spanish dinner'" at the downtown Spanish Kitchen (Valle and Torres 2000: 78). As the city attempted to attract wealthier cosmopolitan citizens, the Mexicans and other Latinas/os disappeared within the "fantasy landscape of Spanish romance" (67). Valle and Torres attribute the city's ability to make its Mexican population less visible to the division of labor. Mexicans and Latinas/os occupied low-wage positions cooking up cultural products in the kitchen while bodies that displayed markers associated with Americanness wrote the menu or set the food on the table.

That practice continues. Globalization in Los Angeles is characterized by the transnationalization of labor, the presence of the global South in the global North, and an increased number of low-wage jobs. Globalization produces economic polarization, such that the outsourcing of unionized manufacturing jobs accompanies the explosion of low-paying jobs in the often informal service industry (Sassen 2001: 9). These sectors include construction, child care, garden work, farm work, day labor, and cleaning. I refer to these services broadly as *la limpieza*, the cleaning industry, a phrase invoked by some nightclub patrons when describing their professions. La limpieza is an insightful construct, as it captures the irony that the exploitation of undocumented migrant labor makes globalization appear seamless.

Mexicans in Los Angeles have long had to negotiate anti-Mexican, anti-immigrant sentiments, laws, and institutionalized attempts to Americanize them, marking their status as second-class citizens. But, as George Sánchez (1993) writes, efforts to Americanize Mexican immigrants and infuse them with Anglo-Protestant values were no longer sustainable once the Great Depression hit. World War I sparked the momentum for Anglo-Americans to incorporate immigrants as low-wage laborers into the workforce and to ensure that their national allegiances were to the United States. While Los Angeles nativists sought to bar immigrants from crossing the border and entering U.S. society, progressive citizens and businesses worked to infuse Mexican immigrants with values and skills that would assimilate them to the industrialized economy. As the economy worsened in the 1930s, those behind the Americanization programs moved to support the U.S. repatriation of thousands of Mexican immigrants to Mexico, thus affirming that even their second-class citizenship and positions as seamstresses and maids, railroad and agricultural workers, were fragile and expendable.[10]

The Mexican government also sought the allegiance of the Mexican emigrants in the United States in the 1920s. In postrevolutionary Mexico, the government endeavored to impose middle-class values on the largely indigenous Mexican peasants in an attempt to create a unified national identity.[11] Efforts to strengthen the nation after the Revolution also included an attempt to Mexicanize emigrants to ensure their return to Mexico after gaining training and skills in the United States that were seen as compatible with Mexico's drive to develop a stronger workforce, a competitive economy, and the image of a racially homogeneous population.

The Mexicanization of emigrants included developing a national loyalty to Mexico among the children of the adult emigrants. In this effort, the Mexican government helped to fund schools that taught the Spanish language and Mexican culture. School texts reflected postrevolutionary Mexico's intent to "civilize" the indigenous population across the border (Sánchez 1993: 117). Mexican government officials observed that former Mexican villagers living in Los Angeles no longer identified with specific rural regions of Mexico but with the nation of Mexico (119).

Although forces of Americanization and Mexicanization worked in opposition in terms of gaining the national allegiance of Mexicans in Los Angeles, both efforts sought to "civilize" and deprovincialize them by training them to enter an industrialized, urban economy as laborers. In the United States, and particularly in California, political debates continue over the extent to which Latino immigrants should be regulated in relation to the post-Fordist economy's requirements for laboring bodies. Lisa Lowe (1996: 160) writes, "Just as the displacement of U.S. workers as well as increased immigration to the United States are an index of global capitalist restructuring, so, too, has restructuring exacerbated both anti-immigrant nativism and the state's 'need' to legislate 'undocumented aliens' and 'permanent resident aliens' who have entered since 1965."

In California voters passed Proposition 187 in 1994 to eliminate undocumented immigrants' rights to public education, social services, and health care. Teachers, law enforcers, social workers, and health care workers would have been required to verify the immigrant status of people, deny services to the undocumented, and then report them. U.S. District Court Judge Marina Pfaezler declared the proposition unconstitutional, stating that legislation regarding the regulation of immigrants should occur at the level of the federal government. In 1998 Proposition 227, the "English-only" initiative, was passed by 61 percent of California voters in favor of dismantling bilingual education in the public schools. In 2004 Governor Arnold Schwarzenegger vetoed a bill that would have allowed undocumented immigrants to test for California driver's licenses. These three California measures call into question the citizenship status of immigrants and those who might be perceived as immigrants, documented and otherwise.

Media representations have supported the configurations of Latinas/os as threatening to the United States and in need of regulation. In an article published in the *Los Angeles Times* titled "Border Agents Warn of Influx," the reporter Scott Gold conceives of Latinas/os as an irrational herd of laborers whose "rush across the Southwest border . . . threatens to overwhelm the U.S. Border Patrol."[12] Gold writes that President George W. Bush's plan to allow guest workers to cross into the United States from Mexico caused the "influx" of border crossers and that "amid the commotion, foreign terrorists might have an easier time slipping into the country."

Not only does this article suggest that border crossers from Mexico may have been plotting a terrorist attack against the United States, but it implies that the disorderly mass of laboring bodies were Mexican, except for the terrorists from whom they were largely indistinguishable. As the news media operates in tandem with state initiatives that support the regulation and interrogation of Latina/o citizenship, it contributes to a structure of feeling based on fear: fear of the Latino body. The laboring Mexican body, which stands in for all Latinas/os in this news article, threatened to devastate the U.S. economy (and potentially homeland security) if unregulated.

Other media representations offer variations on this theme. The Hollywood industry has produced films such as *Dirty Dancing: Havana Nights* (2004) that have tended to depict Latinas/os not as threatening yet necessary to the political economy but rather as threateningly erotic, to be consumed for their hetero/sexuality within a libidinal economy. The erotic Latina/o is most often associated with the Caribbean Latina/o and conflated with blackness. Although before coming to the United States Latinas/os may have distinguished themselves from one another based on differences in class, nation, or ethnicity, within the United States they also have to negotiate mediascapes that racialize them through these two dimensions that mark them as "inauthentic citizens" (Joseph 1999: 3). Representations of Latinas/os as foreign, threatening bodies that are nevertheless desirable for either sex or labor implicate them as outsiders within U.S. frameworks of citizenship and belonging.

In Los Angeles the salsa industry thrives on the Hollywood industry's eroticized representations of salsa-dancing Latinas/os. Although the salsa industry generates income through Latino-based dance clubs, contests, private lessons, and salsa apparel, I am more concerned with the circulation of salsa affects and desires inspired by the Hollywood industry.

Sequined and Unsequined Corporealities

The politics of class and migration significantly impact both salsa affects and dance practices.[13] I introduce the terms *sequined* and *unsequined* to account for the way I conceptualize how the politics of migration and perceptions of social class circulate amid salsa corporealities. Taken literally, the sequined are the highly skilled dancers at the top of the salsa hierarchy who dress in sequins. The unsequined are those whose outfits and dance practices are decidedly less spectacular. The sequined outfits suggest that one's high salsa status correlates with one's social class or experience of migration; however, this is not usually the case.

My theory of sequined and unsequined corporealities addresses the uneasy interplay between the sequined and the unsequined. Sequined corporealities are based on the practices of nightly life within the libidinal salsa economy. This economy relies less on dollars and more on affect, speculation, and desire, as dancers cultivate salsa social status. Unsequined corporealities are more firmly based on the practices of daily life within the political economy. This economy is based in the formal operations of global capitalism that contribute to the exploitation of migrant bodies and people of color in the global North. Success in the political economy can be measured by one's economic and citizenship status; however, one's sequined social status in the libidinal economy of nightly life may not correspond to the unsequined status of daily life. In other words, the adulation of, envy of, and respect for the stars of the nighttime scene often disappear when daytime sheds light on the same bodies working as dishwashers, mechanics, and janitors or even accountants, nurses, and car salesmen.

While the libidinal and political economies operate in tandem, in salsa clubs one primarily gains social status on salsa terms rather than the social terms of everyday life. The way to gain this salsa social status is to keep the libidinal and political economies separate, or at least appearing separate.

In what follows, I use the term corporeality to examine the relationships of power that circulate between bodies as they activate latinidad. In salsa clubs, the identities that patrons choose to enact do not always correspond to the identities bestowed upon them. To account for this, rather than posit the body as an individual agent actively choosing identities, I take into account corporeality, a concept that Marta Savigliano (2001: 10) theorizes as "the body set in culture, the body spoken for." This understanding calls into question the easy conflation of corporeality with "identity." Choreographic analyses of salsa practices can give insight into the corporealities of Mexicanness and Central Americanness in Los Angeles. I am interested in how the spectacle of sequined dancing contributes to the disavowal of the antimigrant violence in Los Angeles.[14] I draw attention to corporeality to point to the ways that patrons claim and are granted differential club memberships, privileges, and mobilities based on the ways that the politics of class and migration interlock with hierarchies of latinidad.

I also analyze the hierarchical distinctions between the sequined and the unsequined as multiply conferred, contested, and performed in terms of status. By status I do not necessarily mean a high-ranking position, but rather the social and economic standing one attains relative to others. While this standing is never static, not everyone has equal access to resources that allow them to compete for a more desired status. People in salsa spaces assign club status to others while negotiating their own. I draw from Sonita Sarker and Esha Niyogi De (2002) to examine how practitioners constantly negotiate and renegotiate their shifting statuses, as well as the terms of their cultural participation. To address the statuses of the club patrons who move back and forth between localities, as in the Mexicans who reside in Los Angeles and travel "home" to participate in another social life,

I employ Sarker and De's theorization of the term trans-status. In these moves, statuses change within each location. For example, someone who occupies an elite position in El Salvador may find herself or himself suddenly Mexicanized within the framework of racialization in Los Angeles.

I apply the term trans-status to latinidad when considering the Latinas/os in the United States and their varied histories of migration. However, when taking into account the history of Latinas/os in Los Angeles, the motion implied by trans- to describe the citizenship status of bodies crossing national borders or migrating within a nation needs to be expanded to include the descendants of immigrants who have maintained a second-class citizenship. As Sarker and De (2002) point out, the motion and instability involved in determinations of status do not necessarily mean that someone has physically moved from one geographical place to another. Legal citizenship in the United States was offered to—or imposed upon—Mexicans who lived within the Mexican land lost to the United States in the U.S.-Mexican War of 1846–48.[15] In this case, the geopolitical border takes on the quality of motion, not the bodies, although the status of their cultural citizenship was unstable. I use the term trans-status to refer to descendants of immigrants two, three, or more generations removed from the act of crossing a geopolitical border or having a border cross them. This sector in L.A. clubs negotiates the ideological shifts, fluctuating cultural statuses, and socioeconomic instabilities seen in the choreographies of globalization.

In chapter 1, "The Salsa Wars," I trace the embattled relationships among three dominant salsa practices in Los Angeles: New York mambo, Los Angeles style, and Cuban casino. I attend to invocations of competing salsa histories, temporary dance partnerships, and impromptu dance lessons at El Reino de la Salsa, recount how L.A. salseras/os made a name for themselves at the salsa congress, and discuss "Cuban Salsa Night" at other Los Angeles venues. An examination of the multiple fronts in the salsa wars elucidates the way that power circulates to form social hierarchies in the salsa clubs. Salsa social hierarchies, I argue, are based on the politics of race, class, and migration. At stake in the formation of these hierarchies are the enactments of latinidad as an uneasy negotiation with blackness.

While I highlight the erasures and exoticizations of blackness in the first chapter, in chapter 2, "Dancing Salsa Wrong," I analyze the ways that L.A. salseras/os seek to define their dance practices in opposition to those who, in their estimation, dance "wrong": bodies associated with Mexicanness, migration, and la limpieza. I discuss how salseras/os erase the light-hearted bounces that could implicate them as workers from la limpieza and begin to elongate their steps to appear more "sophisticated." I offer several accounts of the ways that dancers discipline each other's practices, whether in the middle of a dance or from the sidelines. It becomes apparent that many L.A. salseras/os cultivate techniques of the body that point to a deterritorialized latinidad, seemingly unmarked by any specific geopolitical territory.

I consider the ways club patrons practice their nighttime social identities in relation to the ways that nightclubs manufacture latinidad in chapter 3, "Un/Sequined Corporealities." The sequined salseras/os flash their exotic apparel as they make their way up salsa social hierarchies; the unsequined do not successfully disguise their daytime identities and thus fade to the bottom of the hierarchies, do not get asked to dance, or are not granted entrance due to rigid dress codes that disallow carpenter pants, work boots, and unfashionable jeans. I lay out the tensions between the sequined and the unsequined not as simple opposites but as conceptualizations of latinidad that shift from body to body, club to club, and daytime to nighttime.

I consider the codes of nighttime salsa corporealities in terms of gender in chapter 4, "Circulations of Gender and Power." This chapter reflects on the uneven salsa club mobilities of men and women and how the social codes about how to circulate the club depend on gender. Sustained examination of how salseras/os dance, the people with whom they associate, and how they make their club entrances matter demonstrates that the codes are not the same for women as they are for men. I address several details that women who dance L.A.-style salsa are expected to perfect. I argue that techniques of the arms—she tosses her hair, wrist bent, fingers articulated as her hand shoots above her head—have displaced the hips as central to a salsera's performance. If women wish to move up the salsa hierarchy, details such as the arm techniques allow them to participate in a choreography of display and exchange to demonstrate that they will employ their extensive dance training to help their male partners move up the hierarchy. Both women and men must be recognized as "good dancers" by men in order to gain status in the clubs. I close the chapter with a close reading of the way that social class affects relationships among men and between men and women as they move around the club.

Chapter 5, "'Don't Leave Me, Celia!' Salsera Homosociality and Latina Corporealities," asserts that class hierarchies, often built upon and negotiated through differences in race and nation, test the limits of homosociality among women. Through ethnographic and cinematic bodily analysis, I offer insight into the relationships among Latinas and between Latinas and white women. I perform a close reading of the relationships between the Cuban women and the white American women in *Dirty Dancing: Havana Nights,* arguing that the white protagonist who learns to perform exotic Cubanness displaces the bodies of the Cuban women. A focus on the conditions that support, prevent, and necessitate homosociality allows me to glimpse possibilities of alliance formation among salseras. Fleeting as they may be, these alliances operate both with and against the class-based racializations of Latinas that underlie the exoticized performances of latinidad.

I have centered this study in a global city amid the increasing pressures of globalization and increasing exclusivity over who counts as an American. In Los Angeles, salsa clubs are populated and traversed by Chicanas/os, Mexicanas/os, Latinas/os Americans, Anglo-Americans, African Americans, Asian Americans, and immigrants and tourists from all over the world. In clubs like Copa Cabana West, you might find members of the working class, Mexican Americans, immigrants from El Salvador, Korean models, Anglo business owners, tycoons, movie stars, and European backpackers. My frame accounts not just for the transnationalism of labor and the people in the clubs who do not identify as American but for the relationships among the diverse patrons. This heterogeneous crowd requires a consideration of the socioeconomic, ethnic, racialized, gendered, and national differences among them and an analysis of the tensions over competing discourses of latinidad.

With the globalization of salsa, the pressure to perform exoticized dance moves has impacted the practice of the residual tradition of salsa among Latinas/os and Latin Americans. However, not all Latina/o and Latin American club patrons practice salsa as a residual tradition. Salsa dancing in Los Angeles has become a way in which South Americans, Central Americans, Mexicans, Chicanas/os, and their descendants challenge their marginalized status in the United States. Values of Americanness and Americanized valuations of Latina/o-ness circulate within clubs. Although Latinas/os and Latin Americans might attend clubs with the intention of escaping the daily society in which they are constantly told they do not measure up to the standards of postmodern Americanness, the clubs do not offer them total escape. Through their club practices, they are socially summoned into identities of working-class Mexicanness, exotic Latina/o-ness or classless Americanness. Club patrons articulate their identities as if those identities were unitary and as if cultural differences were apolitical, but they also place Latinas/os into hierarchies of latinidad determined in part by how well they fit—and can be placed by others—into categories of Mexicanness, Latina/o-ness, and Americanness.

CHAPTER 1

The Salsa Wars

One Saturday night at El Reino de la Salsa, as I watched the dancing from the bar area, I introduced myself to a woman who had just ordered a Sprite. Rebecca, a white mambo dancer from New York, said that, since moving to Los Angeles a few months earlier, she usually goes to El Reino de la Salsa on Monday nights, when the "hardcore" mambo dancers, along with some of the best local dance teachers, turn out.

"Who else would come on a Monday night?" she asked. The people who come on Saturday, she told me, typically pick the place simply because it seems like it will be an entertaining weekend spot. They come primarily to socialize: to dine and then to dance, drink, or find someone to sleep with. Her tone of voice showed her contempt. Saturday-night "socializers," Rebecca went on to say, are often not just "beginners" or people piqued by a fleeting interest in salsa, but people who work full-time, labor-intensive jobs Monday through Friday and who rarely go out on weeknights. I thought back to the Saturday night I had sat at an El Reino table with the women from El Salvador, a rare night out for them while the boyfriends stayed home babysitting. Rebecca would probably consider them socializers. An affiliation with the Monday-night crowd allowed Rebecca to assert herself as a serious dancer and not one who associates with Monday-through-Friday workers from la limpieza.

In this chapter I propose that salsa wars make legible the bodies that matter to sequined latinidad. When I use the term *salsa wars*, I mean the sometimes blatant but often hard-to-detect circulations of power involving surveillance, distinctions, erasures, disciplinings, and racialization that form and reform latinidad. Although salsa practitioners often comment on how wonderful it is to dance with others across cultures, races, and nations, dancers often segregate themselves according to their dance practices by time, place, and partnerships. Hence, for all their openness, they are full participants in discrete circuits of power.

For example, Rebecca made it known to me that she was a regular on mambo Mondays at El Reino de la Salsa. The evening I met her, she had separated herself from the dancing by casually drinking a Sprite while waiting around to form a familiar mambo-dancing partnership. On nights like this one, as dancers segregate themselves, they create the illusion of multicultural dance harmonies, as if different dance practices coexist equally and peacefully. Yet as bodies separate themselves based on perceived danced differences, they engage in insults over technique, battles over space, and clashes over timing in the salsa wars. Even those who try to disregard the wars find themselves under surveillance, their techniques critiqued, their toes stepped on, their arms tangled up in someone else's timing. In other words, it is impossible to situate oneself outside of the salsa wars.

Many of the battles are not particularly obvious because dancers fight not with knives and guns but with technique and style. Dancers, however, give their danced differences social meaning that corresponds to class, race, and citizenship status and that underscores configurations of latinidad. Rather than study each dance practice as if it were a static and isolated entity, defined by a list of unique, unchanging characteristics, I consider how the warring factions of dancers attribute meanings to the differences between dance practices. In so doing I analyze the ways that dancers distinguish where the various practices—and the bodies that activate them—fall in the local salsa hierarchy. In particular, in this chapter I am concerned with how L.A.-style salseras/os gain footing in the salsa wars.

In order to destabilize the notion that salsa creates unity, I tell this story by portraying the danced relationships through multiple viewpoints, including the harsh judgments, insults, and misconceptions that fuel salsa war contestations of latinidad. I primarily follow Rebecca, Maricruz, María Elena, and Sarita and their perceptions and surveillances of the salsa practices in Los Angeles. They each detail a multitude of conflicts and tensions that constitute the local salsa wars as they elaborate the relationships between mambo, L.A.-style salsa, and Cuban casino. As L.A.-style salseras/os negotiate the salsa wars, they contend with multiple and overlapping battles to shape latinidad, battles involving class, region, nation, anti-Mexicanness, and the erasure of blackness.

Mambo on Mondays

The only reason Rebecca had gone to the club that Saturday night, she said, was to meet up with her guy friends from the mambo dance company she had recently joined. She said that she'd ask one of them to dance with me when they arrived. As I was still new to the L.A. scene at that point, I welcomed Rebecca's attempt to orient me to the space. She pointed to a couple at the center of the dance floor who also regularly attended El Reino on Monday nights. "Eddie and Giselle teach in Studio City," she said. "They're good dancers technically, but they are L.A. style. All flash and show business." At that very moment, Giselle tossed her head to the side, jumping into Eddie's grip as he captured her momentum, swinging her up to rest on his shoulder. She pinned her arms to her sides and arched her back like a porpoise.

"Hollywood has totally influenced L.A.-style dancers; they embellish all their moves with quick hand and head flourishes and do lots of lifts and high kicks. Anything to stand out from the masses and attract the eye of a casting director," Rebecca stated, interpreting the dance for me. With both feet back on the ground, Giselle bent her knees and went strategically limp, leaning back into Eddie's one-armed embrace. With his other hand behind her hips, he thrust their pelvises together rhythmically three times. Her slack body sprang back to life as she shot an arm into the air like a gymnast.

Through our shared surveillance, Rebecca and I began to articulate our positions in the salsa wars. Neither of us had developed a taste for L.A. salsa, although our reasons did not overlap. To me, Eddie and Giselle performed a stereotype of

Latinas/os as hypereroticized and uncontrollably passionate, a stereotype perpetuated not only by Hollywood film and television productions but also by local dancers hoping to join the casts. Rebecca complained primarily about the predominance of lifts, flourishes, and kicks in commercialized renditions of salsa but did not seem disturbed at all by the racialized gender dynamics. She had sought to distinguish herself from the L.A. salseras/os who take a night of club dancing "too seriously," as if it were an audition for the next salsa movie. Contradicting her earlier effort to contrast herself with the people who come to clubs to socialize and who, in her eyes, didn't take salsa seriously enough, Rebecca remarked, "I rehearse all week, so when I come here, I just want to relax."

Rebecca further distinguished herself from what she called "overly commodified" L.A. salseras/os by pointing out her own involvement in what she deemed artistic stage performances of "authentic" New York mambo. As we filled out our positions, it became evident that, in terms of the salsa wars, I was concerned about the aestheticization of Latinos as sexually violent and dominant, Latinas as promiscuous and submissive, and both as exploitable, while Rebecca's main critique of L.A. salsa was that it left behind authenticity for commercialized latinidad. According to her, L.A. salseras/os constantly invented new moves and even introduced props, such as sunglasses, into salsa, whereas mambo dancers chose a more historically "accurate" way of dancing to the same music, based on techniques she traced back to the Puerto Ricans at the Palladium in New York in the 1950s.

In contrast to her obvious experience with the dance, I had, up to that point, only ever danced mambo unembraced in classes in Cuba and in Colorado, never at a nightclub. In my classes in Cuba, the instructors had placed mambo on a timeline of Cuban music and dance—and, according to them, time had run out for the mambo. Contemporary musicians, they noted, continued to innovate music and had moved on to other forms, like *songo* and *timba*. My instructors in Cuba, Daelyn Martínez and Angel Santos, did not say that people were not practicing these dances anymore, but they stressed their historical importance in the development of contemporary practices, pointing to the tourist shows about Cuban popular music and dance in which performers often dance mambo in a staged history, along with the *danzón* and *son*.

Like Rebecca, I also associate mambo with the 1950s; my aunts from New Mexico have told me about the local dances they went to then, where they danced mambo, jitterbug, and cha cha chá. When Rebecca spoke of her commitment to performing mambo on stage, I imagined a show dedicated to the preservation of the past, and at first did not envision mambo as a contemporary social dance practice that, while drawing its authenticity from the 1950s Palladium, was living and vibrant.

Robert Farris Thompson (2002) writes about mambo emerging in Cuba in 1939, as the Afro-Cuban composer and musician Orestes López recontextualized songs of the Cuban Kongo religion into the orchestration of the danzón.[1] On the dance floor, Thompson says, "couples split in two. Apart dancing in the African manner took over. This, in turn, resulted in wonderful changes in lead. The woman was free to dance around her partner and he was free to dance around her. She circles him. He circles her. She circles him right back. Mambo" (336–37). Thompson asserts, "Orestes López had achieved nothing less than the Africanization of one of the deepest conceits of the West, symphonic music, and the splitting asunder of the Western couple dance" (337).

As Rebecca spoke, she mentioned nothing of mambo's Cuban history but attributed its origin to New York City. I tried to further understand her pro–New York mambo and anti–L.A.-style position in the salsa wars. She said that one of the most notable differences between mambo and L.A. salsa is that "mambo dancers dance 'on the two,' not 'on the one,' like L.A. salseros." She demonstrated the difference in timing between "on the two" and "on the one." "Most people in L.A. begin dancing on the first beat of the music, like this." She counted from one to eight and stepped forward as she said "one" and back as she said "five."

I glanced at Eddie and Giselle, thinking about how they spent so much time spinning, dipping, and thrusting that they did not appear to reference any rhythm on a steady basis. "But mambo dancers," Rebecca continued, interrupting my thoughts, "begin dancing on the second beat of the music." As she performed the basic step—forward on two and back on six—I fell into her rhythm, thinking how similar these movements were to dancing *contratiempo* in Cuba, dancing on the offbeat.

Instead of the forward and back mambo step "on the two," I kept the same timing, but stepped out to the side as in Cuban son, relaxing my torso so I could shift it easily to the side, then let my hip follow, holding it back as long as possible before swinging back to the other side. Then I rounded the steps forward one way and then the other, as in the more contemporary Cuban casino.[2] The contratiempo of Cuban son and casino takes its cues from the rhythm of the clave, although danced interpretations can correlate rhythmically with "on the two." Seeing what I was doing, Rebecca, who had also studied popular dance in Cuba, admitted, albeit barely, that New York mambo dancers might not be the only ones to possess the knowledge of dancing "on the two." She said that when her mambo-dancing friends see anyone performing the torso undulations and swinging hips of what she called "Cuban style," they'd say, "'We don't like that shit.' But I tell them, 'Where do you think salsa comes from?' They are just intimidated by Cuban style because they don't know it."

Rebecca remarked that conflicts often arose among dancers over the most original site of salsa. Yet the mambo dancers from her company erased Cuba from this history. I said, "But mambo is from Cuba too," bringing up the popular line dances of the 1950s. "Well, I don't think they've decided about that issue yet," she responded as our conversation faded.

Since we had both expressed an appreciation for the dances of Cuba, I was curious to see if we danced alike. Even though she identified as a mambo dancer and I did not, I thought that perhaps we used different words to describe similar movements. But then she got up to dance. I was surprised to catch her flicking her leg, flipping her hair, and lifting her arms, hands bent at the wrists above her head—moves I have never desired to incorporate because they remind me of ballroom dancing. She stiffened and lifted her torso, never allowing a lateral sway to creep in, as in son. When her partner whisked her into a low dip, I realized that the mambo from New York that was practiced in L.A., with the elongated arm moves and centered hips, bore little resemblance to the mambo as taught in Cuba, as a line dance.

Thompson (2002: 338) describes the early Cuban mambo danced by Afro-Cuban dancers as characterized by arms held akimbo, with the dancers "blending lindy swing-outs and spins over the pelvic given of the rumba." Mambo from New York as danced in L.A., Cuban son, and casino had the same basic timing but very different qualities of movement. The linear uplifted verticality of the mambo contrasted with the flexed, sideways motions of son and rumba. Yvonne Daniel (1995: 74) notes that the combination of the elongated "Spanish" back and the flexed "African" positions of the rumba-dancing body create a "Cuban creole concept of proper body orientation." What was becoming clear as I interacted with Rebecca was the importance the mambo dancers gave to segregating themselves from practices and origin stories that invoked Cuba.

On the one hand, Rebecca seemed to disagree with her friends' disparaging assessment of Cuban dance practices, but she also appeared to recognize that she could not directly refute it if she wanted to stay in their dance company. Thus the relationship that the salsa wars foster between Rebecca and her mambo-dancing friends necessitated surveillance. As she sought approval from her friends, she had to mask the knowledge she had about Cuban dance practices and histories.

While Rebecca could demonstrate that issues of timing separated mambo from the "less sophisticated" and "overly commercial" L.A.-style salsa, the knowledge she had developed from her experiences in Cuba contradicted that mambo's timing was unique to New York practices. Unable to critique practices they associated with Cuba for improper timing, this group of mambo dancers attacked the movement qualities: the flexed knees, hips, and elbows and the departure from the forward and back basic step. The L.A. mambo dancers thus generated a latinidad that attempted to delegitimize Cuban dance histories and practices.

A Lesson in Smooth(ing Out Blackness)

If you know Jimmy Castillo, who, mustached, was sipping a Corona at the bar while on a break from his Saturday-night bandleader duties, you may have heard him say that he thinks mambo dancers are snobs, because "they only like to dance 'on the two' and won't dance with anybody who doesn't." Just as I thought he was about to counter Rebecca's glorification of mambo and the Palladium, he did the opposite. He told me that he is actually pretty good at dancing "on the two." When he dances "on the one," he has trouble with the turns, but he knows how to execute the mambo turns well. Like mambo, he said, he is from New York.

"I am a Mexican American, but I was raised on the East Coast," he said, maneuvering to distinguish himself from the salsa-dancing Mexican Americans of Los Angeles. According to Jimmy, Central and South Americans and people on the West Coast of the United States dance "on the one," but in New York and Puerto Rico they dance "on the two." Recalling that in Cuba, I had actually observed people incorporate both rhythmic interpretations, depending on the song, I asked, "What about in Cuba? Isn't Cuban son danced to the same rhythm?"

"No," he corrected me, "they don't know how to dance there. All they do is jerk themselves around." He mimicked a Cuban rumba move, stepping to the side and back to his center, exaggerating the "jerky" qualities of his torso and bugging out his eyes in the direction of a couple dancing on the thinned-out floor. "They're still stuck on that old rumba style."

I followed his gaze to notice a black man and woman; they stood out on the dance floor since their pace was slower than that of the other dancers and they seemed more concerned with enjoying the subtleties of the music than with trying to fit a multiplicity of turns into as few beats as possible. As Jimmy mimicked the two dancers, he positioned himself as an adversary of their bodies and practices in the salsa wars. I wondered to what extent he wanted to distance himself from the practice of rumba due to its current and historical association with blackness.

Rumba in Cuba, Daniel (1995: 16–17) writes, "expressed an identification with African-derived elements that make up Cuban culture. . . . It continues to be a dance primarily of black or dark-skinned Cubans, with relatively little participation by mainstream Cuban society."[3] The couple Jimmy and I watched were incorporating variations of rumba into their casino partnership, letting their legs that stepped out to the side carry their weight briefly before returning, their torsos reacting to the opposition until their heads once more reached the center, punctuating the end of the motion before their opposite legs moved to the other side, creating a similar rippling effect. Occasionally they danced embraced, with about six inches of space between their bodies. Their turns took about twice as long to complete as the turns of most of the dancers on the floor, but during the turns the pair incorporated numerous polyrhythmic movements with their shoulders, torsos, and hips. They embodied what Brenda Dixon Gottschild (2003: 15) calls the "Africanist aesthetic" associated with black dancing bodies.[4]

On this front of the salsa war, Jimmy distanced his mambo practice from black bodies performing Cuban dance practices. But historically in Cuba, black dancing bodies were almost always bodies marginalized by social class and segregated by race. David F. García (2009: 178) writes, "The Cuban institution of black working-class social clubs, in which Arcaño y sus Maravillas and Arsenio Rodríguez y su Conjunto developed the earliest styles of mambo music, afforded black dancers and musicians a crucial artistic autonomy in a larger social milieu in which dancing was one of the most segregated cultural activities in Havana." To what extent did Jimmy prefer mambo's New York Palladium origin story because it involved not only black working-class Puerto Ricans but also more upwardly mobile white dance teachers who reinterpreted the moves for other white practitioners?

When the recorded song ended, Jimmy excused himself to go back to lead the band. Drawn in by the couple's dance skills, I went to introduce myself to them and to find out more about them. But just as I drew near, the woman headed outside for a cigarette. So I approached the man, complimenting his dance style. He told me his name was Ramón, that he had come to the United States from Cuba when he was a teenager. Then he invited me to dance.

He led me around him so that we both faced the same direction, a step I had done before. Surprised, he remarked, "Hardly anyone can follow me when I do that turn." This was a step I commonly followed in Cuba, so I assumed that "hardly anyone" at this club had the inclination to dance casino. Ramón incorporated very few turns as he led us on the dance floor and instead focused on holding eye contact, dancing with me and to the music. As we moved, he stepped back, freeing our arms, making room for us to improvise. We leaned forward, bent our knees, and stepped into Cuban rumba. He elongated his torso and allowed it to undulate from side to side, responding to the constant, rhythmic shift of weight from right leg to center to left leg and back to center. When the drums accented a beat, he shook his shoulders, unlike many of the other dancers around us, who held their backs in upright positions, keeping their shoulders still and their weight centered.

In a partnership that seemed effortless, I thought that perhaps the way to make it to the dance floor was to meet up with people who identified with compatible dance practices and to avoid the ones who pointed out your stylistic "flaws"—a sort of unity through segregation. Choreographically this would entail the coexistence of distinct groups that did not interact except to evade those moving differently. To a degree, patrons already adhered to this restrictive movement map, but they failed to completely isolate themselves from each other. After all, El Reino is a social space. Nevertheless, even as I enjoyed the dance immensely, I felt as if we were under surveillance. Even though we danced in the midst of the crowd, an invisible, inimical barrier both segregated us from and exposed us to the judgments of others.

As a fair-skinned Chicana, I found it especially poignant to think about segregation while dancing with an Afro-Cuban man in Los Angeles. While we as a partnership shared an affiliation for similar practices, our partnership performed

Cubanness. In the social space where Jimmy had just caricatured the black bodies performing Cubanness and where Rebecca struggled to hide her knowledge of Cuban practices in order to fit in with her mambo friends, I was struck more deeply by the impossibility of unity through salsa and the social violence that accompanied unity through segregation. Segregation entailed not simply the benign separation of groups according to identified differences but the constant social surveillance involving the social ranking of differences that bolstered salsa hierarchies.

Later that evening at El Reino, I emerged from the bathroom to find that the band had just gone on break. While dancing with Ramón earlier, I had noticed Jimmy assessing us as we danced near the band. He made his way over to chat with me again during his time off but did not explicitly mention the dance with Ramón.

He directed my attention to a couple dancing mambo: "Now, they are good dancers." He dedicated the rest of his break to transforming me into a mambo dancer, giving me an unsolicited dance lesson that, as I was to discover, involved an entire set of its own disciplinary moves. In the end, I regarded the dance lesson with ambivalence. While I had cringed at the presumption that I needed retraining, I also could see that his attempt to educate me about mambo was also his way of integrating me into the scene, to help me assume a higher ranking. Importantly Jimmy invested time in recruiting me as a mambo dancer and smoothing out the "Cuban" moves I had performed with Ramón. I noted, however, that he had not attempted to retrain Ramón or his partner.

Had my skin been black, would Jimmy have dedicated time to retrain me? As an ethnographer, I had decided to pay attention to his cues and criticisms throughout our lesson together, so that I could gain a better understanding of the racial significance he gave to mambo. I interpreted the lesson as his effort to smooth out from my practice any moves that might be associated with blackness; it had been an invitation to join the mambo dancers situated higher up on the salsa hierarchy—if I would agree to excise such moves from my dancing body. But after it was over, the lesson felt like a betrayal of my dance alliance with Ramón and his previous partner; they had watched me dance with Jimmy. In my body, I had felt that I was corroborating the erasure of blackness, and I knew that I would never identify myself as a mambo dancer, even if I could pass as one.

Jimmy began the lesson in conversation, assuring me that dancing "on the two" was actually pretty easy once one learned. He gave me pointers as we observed the couple he had pointed out as exemplary: you have to be smooth;

you have to try to keep the beat on the turns; that's when it is easy for the woman to lose it. I told him I had learned how to dance this timing before, in Cuba, but he ignored my reassurance. Instead he took me to a patch of carpet by the door, teaching me how to start "on the one" and then count myself into "the two." Like Rebecca, he utilized the forward and back basic. We started off in unison "on the one," but to maintain that unison when his counts jumped to emphasize "the two," we were supposed to shift the weight of our bodies at the exact same time. As I was unsure on which count of two he was going to shift, I was not always able to follow him. I told him that it would all work out better if we just started out directly "on two," without undergoing the shift, but he was intent on counting us into it. In order to follow, I tried to tune out the distraction of the counting and listen for cues to both sets of timing within the music.

The different ways dancers learn to interpret rhythms is relevant here. Some people learn to dance in informal interactions, while others take formal lessons. I have noticed that many instructors in the United States focus on counting and incorporate lingo such as "moves" and "styling" to refer to different steps and gestures. Even in formal classes, my teachers in Costa Rica and Cuba rarely counted while they taught; rather they would sing or clap out the footwork in time with the music. Perhaps Jimmy was counting because he was a musician. He may also have been using his formal music training to highlight the physical incompatibilities of dancing "on the one" and dancing "on the two," as well as to impart to me what he perceived as the superiority of dancing on the two.

As I hesitated a moment, Jimmy stopped and again counted us into "the one" and switched to "the two." I thought that if we could just start "on the two," I would be able to follow him by making two basic adjustments to what I already knew: tuning out his counting and imagining that I was dancing son—except that, instead of doing the side-to-side moves, I would need to shift into the forward and back of the mambo. But he insisted on performing the abrupt transition between "the one" and "the two," the crash of rhythmic interpretations that he attempted to smooth over through repeated methodical counting.

I grew tense waiting for the transition and then stumbled uncertainly into Jimmy's New York mambo, trying to accommodate his timing. In order to succeed in his lesson, I had to learn to repress a strong enactment of bodily confusion that resulted from this culture clash, from my forced shift into the performance of a New York mambo. But once I got there, I found that this battle in the salsa war involved more than a shift in timing. This battle involved an elimination of "jerkiness" and the unpredictability that Jimmy had objected to in the night's displays of Cuban dance practices. From Jimmy I learned about the racist eradication of blackness to produce latinidad.

At one point Jimmy warned me that a turn was coming up and that I was supposed to go "that way" when it arrived. I went "that way," but as we separated, I was inspired by the change in the music and turned quickly. He had not yet completed his mirror-image turn, so I decided to turn a second time and finish with him. "You turn too fast," he critiqued. According to him, I was supposed to match his speed so that we could begin and end the turn together. When we tried this again, I refrained from doubling the turn, slowing to his speed. He nodded at me, as if to say, "See what a nice turn this can be?"

Any time I was inspired by the music to add a shimmy of my shoulders, an accent of my hip, or an undulation of my torso, he corrected me, even though I had been following his rhythm, saying that I was not supposed to do those things. Finally, I gave up on an assumption I had made: that if we performed with a common timing and could move without bumping into each other, we shared the same understanding of how to dance as partners. I asked if my torso was supposed to be lifted, recalling Rebecca's techniques. He said yes. To clarify, he said, "It is more graceful that way. No jerking." He stopped to show me the difference between dancing "on the one"—he wrenched his torso from side to side as if in imitation of my dance with Ramón—and dancing "on the two": he lifted his head, straightened his torso, and glided about the patch of carpet.

I decided to forgo the shimmies, accents, and undulations—the moves Ramón and I had used as if playing a game with each other—and danced in a way that I thought was somewhat plain, just to see his response when I incorporated his corrections. I imitated his elevated, "graceful" quality, and he appeared to be encouraged. He raised his eyebrow in pleasant surprise when I remained on the rhythm after a turn, finishing at the same time he did. But even though I could follow him, I began to lose a feel for the music. I realized that I danced "on the two" differently than he did, and I no longer listened for the clave to guide my timing. Confined to following Jimmy's rules, I was not "allowed" to improvise or shift my weight in any manner that he might interpret as Cuban. As I conformed to his smooth mambo style, I felt like a dead woman, heavy and stiff, *un saco de arroz* (a bag of rice). Before he went back to work, he said in my ear, "You've got good rhythm."

Rebecca and Jimmy both referred to the Palladium as a site of mambo's—and therefore salsa's—authenticity. While Rebecca almost reluctantly delegitimized Cuban practices, Jimmy emphatically did so. To what extent might a fear of blackness inform their tastes and their preferred histories of salsa? Accounts of racial relations in the histories of the Palladium may help illuminate some considerations.

In *The Book of Salsa*, César Miguel Rondón (2008: 1–2) writes that in 1947 the exclusively white audiences who attended the Palladium ballroom and who danced foxtrot and tango were on the wane. In order to keep the Palladium running, the manager decided to open the doors for the first time to nonwhites. He would welcome Latinos and bring "the Caribbean to Broadway" by hiring Afro-Cuban bands to play at Sunday matinees for the Latino community, which was largely Puerto Rican.

According to García (2009: 178), Cuban Pete (actually a black Puerto Rican), an early mambo dance innovator at the Palladium, remarked how the professional dancers on the left side of the Palladium "learned" from the real "Latin" dancers on the right side. García writes that "professional dance teachers needed to deem mambo dancing, as performed by 'real Latins from Manhattan' or 'right-side' dancers, as disorganized, undisciplined, wild, sweaty, grotesque, and sexually uninhibited in order to keep intact their desire for a white racial origin and superior Western civilization" (176). Right-siders varied the foot patterns and danced with their whole body (172), making it difficult for left-siders to pick up the practices in a social setting. The left-siders, however, appropriated, simplified, and codified select moves and then taught them to other white dancers. The Palladium thus became a multiethnic space that made Afro-Caribbean popular dance accessible to white dancers. Arguably, black dancers who participated in the space were aware of white fears of blackness, as well as what García deems the fantasies of a white racial origin (177) that were in circulation at the Palladium.

Rondón (2008: 1) points out that, upon considering whether or not to open the club to Afro-Cuban bands and Latinos, the manager feared that "the blacks also would come down to Broadway with, in his mind, all of their bad habits, knives, and unbridled impulses." I should note that Rondón does not make it clear whether the manager was referring to all blacks or was making a distinction between African Americans and Afro-Caribbean Latinos.

I read Jimmy's lesson as a continuation of the early Palladium choreographies to distance mambo from blackness, whether Cuban, Afro–Puerto Rican, or African American. By reproducing mambo's authenticity through bodily techniques that de-accentuated moves associated with blackness, Jimmy effectively perpetuated a latinidad that effaced black dancing bodies.

Special Effects, Explosions, and L.A. Salsa

Stylistic differences attributed to regional understandings of latinidad have influenced the uneasy East Coast–West Coast relationship between L.A.-style salsa and mambo. Despite the mambo dismissal of L.A.-style salsa as inauthentic, L.A. salseras/os have managed to thrust themselves into the salsa wars without wielding an origins story. Although they could reference the historical development of mambo in Mexico in the musical performances of Afro-Cubans living in Mexico City—Celia Cruz, Perez Prado, and Beny Moré (Rondón 1980; Radanovich 2009; Valverde 1982)—they do not. They could sing out the lyrics from Beny Moré's "Bonito y Sabroso": "Pero quê bonito y sabroso bailan el mambo las mexicanas, mueven la cintura y los hombros igualito que las cubanas."[5] They might even trace Cuba's influence on Mexican music and dance back to the *chuchumbé* in the late 1700s.[6] They do not. Cuban music and dances such as rumba, cha cha chá, and mambo were also popularized in the *cabaretera* films produced by the Mexican film industry approximately from the 1940s to the early 1950s (Blanco Borelli 2008; Paranaguá 1995). They could point to this cinematic evidence of salsa's precursors in Mexico, or they could argue that Pérez Prado played mambo in 1952 at the Palladium in Los Angeles. During my ethnographic research, they brandished none of this information.

L.A.-style salseras/os seem to have left the mambo claims—the nods to the 1950s Palladium and the big band orchestras—to the New York dancers. Given these omissions, I suggest that they embrace the notion of the break: a break from the Palladium to the "street corners of New York City's Latino barrios" (Aparicio 1998: 80). The salsa that developed in the 1960s and the 1970s marked a recognizable shift from the music of the Palladium, as it "was music produced not for the luxurious ballroom but for hard life on the street" (Rondón 1985: 16).[7] Further, Rondón characterizes salsa music as a commercial success, as cemented by Fania Records in 1971.

L.A. salseras/os embrace the room for creativity that the break from the Palladium tradition opened up. They mine the possibilities for commercialization in the salsa industry, looking for opportunities to express themselves as dance innovators. Their embrace of innovation pushes their creative and political potential beyond any easy identification with the working-class latinidad of 1960s and 1970s New York or with the marginalizing conditions in the barrios so prevalent in salsa lyrics.

Although L.A.-style salseras/os might ambivalently gesture toward Puerto Rico and New York as original sites of salsa, they insist that innovation defines L.A. style. They develop and execute difficult, technically over-the-top moves that tend to catch more attention than do sophisticated mambo steps, moves that seem static to L.A. salseras/os. As part of this innovation, they constantly search out new material every year to challenge the *mamberas/os*, both locally and at salsa congresses. Despite the reliance on innovation, however, L.A. salseras/os simultaneously make their practices recognizable as salsa to the mamberas/os. They employ some of the same dance practices that mamberas/os do, such as taking private lessons to master technically difficult moves, choosing dance partners who will separate them from "the masses," wearing "serious dancer" apparel such as leather-soled shoes, and performing at salsa congresses. Crucially, though, they both activate a practice that carefully circumvents blackness.

Back at El Reino de la Salsa, as I alternately observed the mambo of Rebecca and her partner and the L.A. salsa of Eddie and Giselle, I noted that New York mambo and L.A. salsa shared some common techniques, despite Rebecca's attempts to completely distinguish the two. Both couples appeared to have participated in extensive training in order to acquire a repertoire of embellishments that mark each style. Rebecca and Giselle both focused much of their energy on the precise performance of brushes, flips, taps, and tosses of their fingers, hair, toes, and heads. They both tended to straighten their torsos and immobilize their hips, thus reining in the undulating spine and hip rolls so frequently associated with blackness.

L.A.-style salsa, so well-performed by Eddie and Giselle, was singular in its direct references to the sexual objectification of women and the amount of space required to execute the dips, lifts, and kicks. In contrast to the salsa dancers, the mambo dancers that night focused on moving their bodies in a linear back-and-forth pattern. They did not usually incorporate jumps, lifts, and other tricks that would cause their bodies to change levels, although they tended to indulge in the dip. For Rebecca, these details, in addition to the "on two" timing, marked mambo dancers as more sophisticated interpreters of salsa music than L.A. salseras/os.

Maricruz, an avid practitioner of L.A. salsa whom I met at The Legend downtown, offered additional insights and a different perspective on the relationship between L.A. and New York styles. Maricruz said that the battle between dancing "on the two" and "on the one" developed in the context of the salsa congresses:

> The "on two" people say that dancing "on two" was the original way that mambo dancers at the New York Palladium danced. They say it is more authentic than dancing "on one," because salsa was invented in New York. Eddie Torres revived mambo dancing in New York over the last several years, but when New Yorker Albert Torres tried to introduce dancing "on the two" in Los Angeles in the 1980s, he decided instead to teach "on one," because Los Angelenos had difficulty with the timing.[8] At the salsa congresses, people from different parts of the country could see each other's styles and an East Coast–West Coast rivalry got started. The dance team Fuego from San Diego did a whole choreography at one of the congresses, where dancers battled between one and two. I don't think that one style is more right than the other; you just have to feel your own style and decide what is right for you. The problem is that the "on two" people act like they are better dancers, and now a whole generation of dancers in Los Angeles will only dance "on two."

Even though Maricruz maintained that Los Angelenas/os have difficulty learning the "on two" timing, dancing "on one" is not essentially easier. By the time mambo "on two" came to town, Los Angelenas/os already had a cultural history of dancing salsa and other popular dance forms "on one," which is more common in most Latin American countries and the United States. Learning how to hear music differently in order to dance "on two" requires considerable practice if one has always and only danced "on one."

Though the reverse also holds true, local L.A. practitioners, even those who dance "on one," assign more prestige to the skill of dancing "on two." Jimmy and Rebecca, like other mambo dancers I have spoken with, described "on two" dancing as more sophisticated, more complicated, and more authentic than dancing "on the one." Dancing "on the two," they said, takes a lot of training, and very few people can actually discern the rhythm. Jimmy's and Rebecca's perception that dancing "on two" is more difficult operates in conjunction with the perception that most dancers in Los Angeles learn to hear and dance "on one" as a cultural practice rather than in a dance studio with specialized instruction. Dancing "on one" thus becomes devalued as "common" knowledge, as if it is a natural ability that requires no special training.

Though Maricruz said that the congress exalts Puerto Rico and promotes a Puerto Rican–inflected L.A. salsa, the congress has also provided L.A. salseras/os with an international forum in which to develop and showcase an "on one" salsa unique to Los Angeles. If, as Maricruz said, the East Coast started the salsa wars by disparaging West Coast practices as inauthentic and unsophisticated, then the West Coast dancers responded by innovating their salsa routines and practices with more tricks and Hollywood imagery. Maricruz said that at the congresses,

> the West Coast routines always get bigger reactions because we are more creative. We play more with the music and don't dance to the same song all the way through like they do on the East Coast. The West Coast cuts and pastes music from twenty different songs together for one two-minute piece. We add special effects and explosions. We dress up as characters from Hollywood blockbuster movies, which the East Coasters used to snub at first, calling it superficial. They may have the original "on two" style, but now the East Coast dancers borrow moves and ideas for routines from L.A. They are starting to copy the style that has become authentic to Los Angeles. The discrimination against us has gone on too long, and now a lot of L.A. dancers are actually proud to dance "on one."

Practitioners of LA salsa thus shuttle between their aspirations to embody values of the "sophisticated" East Coast–Puerto Rican styles and their aspirations to stake their own local claims on cutting-edge salsa innovations.

L.A. salseras/os, she went on to say, choreographed their version of salsa in response to a hierarchy that positioned New York Latinas/os above Los Angeles Latinas/os, the group with whom she, as an immigrant from El Salvador who moved to Los Angeles when she was seven, identifies. New Yorkers looked down on salseras/os in Los Angeles, primarily because many of the dancers who have contributed to the development of L.A. salsa have been Mexicans and Mexican Americans. Mambo dancers in New York and in L.A., Latina/o or not, have associated themselves with Puerto Ricanness, distinguishing themselves from L.A. salsa, Los Angeles, and Mexicanness.

As Maricruz described this East Coast–West Coast hierarchy, she noted that even at the West Coast Salsa Congress in Los Angeles, Puerto Rican salsa music, and any dance groups directly from Puerto Rico for that matter, were typically given "major status, like the Puerto Ricans own salsa." Thus the association of salsa's authenticity with Puerto Rico or Puerto Ricans in New York does not remain confined to East Coast but is also evident on the West Coast. Even though

Maricruz resides on the West Coast and practices L.A. salsa, she does not identify easily with a latinidad that reifies Puerto Rico, however. To various degrees, L.A. salseras/os like Maricruz have internalized that their enactments of West Coast latinidad fall to the bottom of the hierarchy.

The L.A. salseras/os who come from Mexico and Central America articulate an ambivalent desire to identify Puerto Rico as the source of their West Coast practices. In their eyes, identifying with movements marked as Puerto Rican delegitimizes their practices as Mexicans and Central Americans in L.A. To authenticate themselves as contenders in the salsa wars, L.A. salseras/os innovate moves danced to Puerto Rican salsa. Simultaneously their innovations break away from the practices of Mexico and Central America and resignify West Coast latinidad.

"We aren't salseras!" Authenticating Caribbean Casual

As L.A. salseras/os innovate a style that dissociates them from Mexico and Central America, they also retain the historical effacement of black dancing bodies. As such, they continue the imperfect process of salsa segregation by keeping themselves away from spaces, times, and practices designated as Cuban, which is conflated with blackness. The night I danced with Ramón at El Reino, there were just three of us casino dancers,[9] and at other clubs they were also relatively few in number. In the advertised "Cuban Salsa" room at one club in Culver City, a deejay spun Cuban timba hits like La Charanga Habanera's "Lola, Lola" and Los Van Van's "Temba, Tumba, Timba" while no more than four or five patrons wandered in to dance at any one time.

The deejay on the main floor played primarily Puerto Rican–based salsa and had previously alternated sets with the deejay who played Cuban tunes. When the club patrons complained that they could not dance to the Cuban music, the promoter moved the Cuban music into another room. The club eventually canceled the Cuban music altogether because it did not make a profit. The number of dancers attending "Cuban Salsa Night" increased at a couple of other clubs, but only slightly. Like mambo dancers, practitioners of Cuban salsa composed a relatively small group in comparison to practitioners of L.A. salsa.

Additionally, like mambo dancers, dancers of "Cuban salsa" claimed that their dance practice was the most authentic. While the word *salsa* may have originated in

New York, antecedents to salsa—son, cha cha chá, and mambo, for example—were Cuban. Most casino practitioners in Los Angeles tied their practices to a history of Afro-Cuban repression and resistance against colonialism in Cuba. Although heterogeneous in terms of ethnicity, this crowd was composed of many non-Cuban university-affiliated dancers who outnumbered the local Cubans.

The outside positionalities of these L.A. practitioners contrasted sharply with their nostalgic narrations, which reified an abject yet revolutionary Afro-Cubanness. According to Sarita, a regular at "Cuban Salsa Nights," relatively few of the Los Angeles Cubans who turned out for weekend festivals showed up during the week, unless it was to celebrate someone's birthday. Explaining why, she told me, "A lot of the Cubans are working class and have to get up early to get to their jobs during the week." Afro-Cubans like Ramón, a working musician, was an exception. Most of the Tuesday- and Thursday-night practitioners have not been Cuban but American: European American, Asian American, U.S. Latina/o, and African American.

In contrast to spaces where mambo and L.A. salsa reign, L.A. spaces of casino attracted a larger proportion of black dancers, specifically African American dancers. This is not surprising, given that, as I have argued, spaces of mambo and L.A. salsa do not welcome practices associated with blackness, particularly when black bodies perform them. Leila, an African American grad student, confirmed this when she told me of her experiences at The Legend. She said that when she goes to L.A. salsa clubs like The Legend, she rarely gets asked to dance. She prefers to go to one of the Cuban dance nights, where blackness is desirable as a sign of authenticity. In Cuban dance spaces, Leila hardly ever sits down.

Like Leila, many of the casino dancers are affiliated with local universities or are professionals who have been to Cuba for research, dance lessons, or pleasure. Because limited authorization is granted to U.S. citizens to travel to Cuba (for research purposes, for example), U.S. practitioners who have gone to Cuba have gained cultural capital among other L.A. aficionados of Cuban salsa. They not only learned dance moves that they attempted to replicate in Los Angeles, but some also came back with stacks of dance videotapes that marked them as serious investigators of dance practices. Practitioners emphasized that their status in Cuba had not been that of the common tourist but that of researcher, and that they had gained rare knowledge when they engaged with culture. In this way, they sought to authenticate their dance practices of casino in Los Angeles.

Unlike the L.A. salseras/os and mambo dancers, these casino dancers tended to "dress down." Instead of the stunning sequins, heels, and exotic leopard prints associated with L.A. salseras, casino dancers are among the unsequined, often dressing in cotton fabrics, denim, and flats. One woman, Arlene, dancing in sneakers told me that in Cuba, many of the women put on sneakers when they dance, not high heels. Distinguishing her casual style of dress from that of the L.A. salseras, she said, "In Cuba, people just dance in whatever they are wearing. Clothes don't matter." I disagreed with her assessment that clothes did not matter to the Cubans in Cuba, suggesting instead that her interpretation of Cuban outfits informed her own dancewear choices in the effort to recreate Cuban "authenticity." Sarita generalized that dancers on "Cuban Salsa Night" dress more casually than L.A. salseras but emphasized that the look was "casual Caribbean." "When the Cubanos come out, they look pretty sharp in their *guayaberas* or tank tops, jeans, and high heels. It's a very clean look with lots of white. Some of the non-Cubans come dressed a little too much like slobs," she said, in a critique that extended to women like Arlene dancing in sneakers. Sarita went on to say that she and her women friends at the club would never wear sneakers but would rarely wear anything too "glitzy" or "sequined" in their efforts not to come across as "salsera," the name they use to specify women dancers of L.A. salsa.

In her account of casino dancers' preferred style of dress, Sarita articulates her detection of and sensitivity to the racism directed toward black bodies in L.A.-style salsa spaces. She appears to dissociate herself from salsa crowds that shun black bodies as she romanticizes Afro-Cuban bodies, aestheticized as casual Caribbean on the dance floor. Her unsequined identification with an Afro-Cuban black dancing body perhaps cites her affiliation with black Cuban bodies as revolutionary and subaltern.

As Sarita spoke the words *salsera* and *glitzy* with distaste, she used the same tone Rebecca used when she slighted L.A. salseras/os for being too Hollywood and superficial. Their two critiques suggest the importance of a latinidad based in origins stories rather than on mainstream blockbuster representations of latinidad. Perhaps both expressions of distaste for the sequined and the mainstream also suggest that sequins and other over-the-top L.A. salsa practices fail to convince the artistic mambo and university casino practitioners that L.A. salseras/os perform anything other than working-class tastes. As mambo and casino dancers perceive L.A. salseras/os as lower on class hierarchies, they locate themselves as part of an elite crowd. Sarita emphasized that when salseros came to the Cuban club, none of the women wanted to dance with them. "We get mad at them when they try to make us dance L.A. style to the Cuban music, and they look really stiff and awkward," she said. "We aren't salseras."

Sarita's disavowal of being a salsera calls attention to her discomfort with the salsera/o effacement of Afro-Cuban practices and bodies. I have never seen L.A. salseras/os incorporate the basic curving steps or the turn sequences of casino; however, I have infrequently seen them reference Cuban rumba on stage and on the dance floor. Maricruz, a successful competitor at L.A. salsa competitions, said that she and her dance partner incorporated the basic step from a kind of Cuban rumba called *guaguancó* as a momentary highlight in their routine: "We might do the step from guaguancó to show it off as part of our repertoire. We would only do it once in a competition because you don't want to repeat things over and over." She demonstrated how she performed guaguancó, which incorporates steps similar to the rumba moves that Ramón and I had danced, but Maricruz quickened her side-center-side movement, accentuating the direction change without rolling into it with her torso and hips and keeping her weight more evenly centered.

Maricruz explained that, socially, people sometimes repeated the step twice in one dance, but that it was important not to repeat moves even outside of competitions, since such repetition would imply that the leader had a limited repertoire. In contrast, when Ramón and I danced, we repeated the side-center-side movement numerous times, and not because he had a limited repertoire. We had both enjoyed playing with many variations within that single sequence.

By momentarily citing Cuban rumba, Maricruz and her partner demonstrate their ability to appropriate it on their terms, the terms of L.A.-style salsa. By eliminating the undulations and keeping their bodies as centered as possible, they draw upon a latinidad marked by an element of blackness while simultaneously distancing themselves from that blackness. And in doing so they further situate themselves as innovators in the salsa wars.

My interactions with Sarita, Maricruz, Jimmy, and Rebecca alerted me to the meanings they ascribed to some of the locally practiced dance techniques and informed my understandings of the thorny relationships of mambo, L.A. salsa, and Cuban casino. These practices constituted a three-way battle in the salsa wars. Mambo dancers distanced themselves from dance qualities they associated with Cuba, preferring "smoothness" over "jerkiness," ascribing each of these two qualities of movement to a style, either mambo or Cuban; to a place, either New York or Cuba; and to a particular kind of latinidad: Puerto Rican or Cuban.

L.A. mambo dancers referenced mambo's development among Puerto Rican Latinos in New York City. They subtly tied differences in timing and values to groupings of people to make a distinction between the "on two" dancers and the majority of L.A. dancers they said danced "on one." They grouped "on one" dancers as nondancers, new dancers, and socializers, as well as Cubans, Mexicans, Central Americans, South Americans, (U.S.) West Coast dancers, and (nonmambo) L.A. salseras/os. In response, practitioners of L.A. salsa developed techniques meant to displace the dominance of mambo by overshadowing it with "innovation."

The relationship among the three styles is fraught with contradictions as practitioners generate three disparate images of latinidad. Yet mambo and casino dancers nevertheless held overlapping beliefs. While L.A. mambo dancers maligned techniques of (Cuban-like) casino dancers, the two groups both sought to distance themselves from L.A.-style salseras/os. Although L.A.-style salsa has the largest number of practitioners in Los Angeles, and probably the most international visibility and highest rate of commercial success, mambo and casino dancers consider the innovations in L.A.-style salsa to be too "mainstream," "phony," and "tacky." They see L.A.-style salseras/os as gathering moves and ideas for moves from multiple pop-cultural sites, dance genres, and movies. To distance themselves from the L.A.-style salsera/o obsession with developing blockbuster dance routines, mambo and casino dancers authenticate their practices with narratives of the origins of the forms tied to nostalgic images of bodies and places.

The L.A. mambo dancers I spoke with look back to the 1950s for their Palladium-style moves, while the casino dancers travel to Cuba. While many of the practitioners of L.A.-style salsa are Mexican or Central American immigrants and their descendants, their salsa practices are not recognized within the dominant, tightly framed narratives of mambo and casino; Mexicans and Central Americans are not recognized as the kind of Latinas/os with the authority to shape salsa dance traditions.[10] L.A.-style salseras/os, however, turn to the break: a break with practices associated with the Palladium, a break that propels them into sequined visibility. While interacting with dancers of each practice, I found that they shared a common value: la limpieza and migration, when associated with Mexicanness,[11] did not fit within their formations of latinidad.

CHAPTER 2

Dancing Salsa Wrong

In a booth at Chuck's Grill in the City of Commerce, I sat waiting for María Elena to arrive. It was only 8 o'clock in the evening, but since the Sunday afternoon lesson started at 3, early-bird dancers, drinkers, and diners filled the floor and the stools along the bar that spanned the length of the restaurant-turned-nightclub. *Extreme Makeover: Home Edition* noiselessly flickered on the television screen above the bar, flashing new Sears appliances, but people directed their attention to the dancing on the small dance floor wedged in like an afterthought.

A few newcomers practiced moves they must have learned at the class taught earlier. They clutched each other tensely, unsuccessfully attempting to appear effortless and fabulous as they swung about haphazardly across the floor. In contrast, a very skinny man (who later asked me to dance), Felipe from Mexico, led his partner with a touch so light, it appeared as if he had no bones in his arms. His partner responded uncertainly at first, but then more assuredly as she became accustomed to the slightness of his finger signals. Without any sort of pressure between their bodies, they did not gain momentum, but puttered in place. An older man and woman closed their eyes and cuddled. Others danced with the lateral sways of Cuban son, comfortably on tempo, minus the uncontained hoopla of the newcomers.

One couple stood out from the others in the club; they were injecting speedy dips and spins into their moves, layering gestures such as head rolls and neck drops. With precision and velocity, they incorporated these techniques—techniques that professionals and amateurs have developed in the context of L.A. salsa competitions and congress exhibitions—into their social dancing. They lifted, lunged, and raised their arms into the air, triumphant like acrobats. He snapped his fingers and slicked back his hair, while she swished her skirt. They effectively distanced themselves from, and occasionally bumped into, those who practiced less spectacular techniques, the contained sways, the jerking, bobbing, overzealous exertions of the newcomers and the boneless arms of the more informally trained. The newcomers teetered closer to the edges of the floor, giving up space to the ones who danced L.A. salsa. Together on the same dance floor, they signified their differences dancing in and out of each other's spaces.

This description of the practices among dancers at Chuck's Grill highlights the relationships between L.A. salseras/os and the "socializers." While L.A. salseras/os, mamberas/os, and casino dancers clash with each other in the salsa wars in clubs across the city, they do not include the socializers as credible competitors in the wars. Nor do they extend salsa congress appeals for "unity through salsa" to these socializers. On one front, L.A. salseras/os blatantly pit themselves against casino and mambo dancers in the salsa wars, although often wielding subtle competitive techniques. In order to be recognized as adversaries in these more overtly discussed wars, L.A. salseras/os also continuously distance themselves from the socializers on a more obscure front. From the perspective of the salsa warriors, socializers dance salsa "wrong."

The ways L.A. salseras/os distinguish themselves from the socializers intertwine with the politics of migration and the determination to not be linked to la limpieza while in the dance clubs. Whether or not Latinas/os work in la limpieza, they are often interpreted as doing so in everyday life. In everyday life, many Latinas/os battle a suturing together of la limpieza, Mexicanness, and migration. Salsa dancing offers a chance to undo the tightly woven components that undergird anti-Mexican, anti-immigrant violence. Yet the unraveling of la limpieza,

Mexicanness, and migration, along with the distancing of these from salsa, often means stepping on others in order to activate a latinidad that disavows the socializing practices associated with la limpieza, Mexicanness, and migration.

Since many of the L.A. salseras/os and those who developed L.A. salsa were Mexican American or Mexican migrants, the anti-Mexican, antimigrant sentiment expressed among practitioners at first seemed ironic.[1] I suggest, however, that many L.A. salseras/os internalize these violences and reproduce themselves not as Mexicans, migrants, or workers of la limpieza but as exoticized (nonblack) Caribbeanesque Latinas/os, a representation produced and mediated by the Hollywood industry.

In discriminatory observations, the L.A. style dancers most strongly decry practices associated with Mexicanness, migration, and la limpieza: cuddling, making out, beer drinking, bouncing and bobbing, dancing salsa to any kind of cumbia music—but especially Mexican cumbia—and, possibly worst of all, instead of the linear forward and back of mambo and L.A. style, performing a basic step that circles behind and crosses back. L.A.-style salseras/os, attempting to legitimize themselves as salsa bodies in the larger salsa wars, often consider and label these practices "wrong." At times their accusations are direct. More often, however, they tend to assess a socializer as untrained, unsophisticated, and unsexy, masking indirect evaluations of citizenship status, class, and nation hidden under the language of "technique."

I interpret salsa clubs as what Lisa Lowe (1996: 172) calls "regulating sites," locales where patrons claim and bestow social membership based on the evaluation of dance practices.[2] In such spaces, dancers negotiate their social demarcations as "citizens" or "immigrants," a distinction that drives conceptualizations of latinidad. In salsa clubs, then, practitioners can become "citizens" or get marked as "immigrants" through their dance practices. Instances of dancing salsa wrong can be understood as moments in which the ones who exercise discipline demonstrate their affiliation with local standards of belonging while also ascribing outsider status to others. As dancers embody their differences and affiliations, they compete with each other to define and place themselves within the parameters of latinidad.

My close analysis of salsa practices demonstrates that practitioners contend with the contradictory poles of latinidad produced in Los Angeles: the exotic Latino (re)produced by the Hollywood entertainment industry and the laboring migrant from la limpieza. To move up the salsa social hierarchy, local salseras/os perform the exoticized L.A.-style salsa that distances them from practices associated with undocumented Mexican laborers. For as dancers learn that practices perceived as embodying Mexicanness are devalued in the clubs, they also learn that the perception that one is Mexican almost always accompanies the assumption that one is also undocumented, a status that quickly lands Latina/o bodies at the very bottom of both socioeconomic and salsa club hierarchies.

Within a U.S. framework of racialization that polarizes Americanness and Mexicanness, salseras/os configure this danced latinidad. Latinas/os in the United States often have to navigate the opposition of Americanness with Mexicanness, no matter where they come from. More precisely, they navigate the hegemonic appeal of Americanness and disdain for Mexicanness. As they internalize the anti-Mexican wars of everyday life as well as nightlife, they begin to activate themselves in danced discourses of latinidad.

As the media and the global salsa network popularize L.A. salsa, it displaces other salsa practices from the category of salsa. Indeed practitioners even begin to forget that other practices of salsa exist or existed. One can thus interpret the tensions between Americanness and latinidad, between dancing salsa "right" or "wrong," through the lens of trans-status latinidad and the multiple histories of Latina/o migration and citizenship. The tensions over the varied performances of salsa in Los Angeles correlate with the destabilization of identifications with the social, economic, and cultural practices from another homeland, due to emigration or shifts in geopolitical borders. As the excessiveness of L.A. salsa becomes hegemonically enacted, L.A. salseras/os and socializers battle over cultural memory and forgetting.

The socializers embody the reminders of the violence that the L.A. salseras/os dance to forget. The practitioners who do not remember the actual act of crossing the border, the act of migration, the act of leaving a place behind, recall it in the stories told to them by those who physically moved from one place to another. They are the ones removed by one or more generations from the physicality of transnational or cultural displacement. They re-create salsa and latinidad in conjunction with those immigrants who have experienced displacement, who want to break away from the haunting memories of war or poverty, the marginalized conditions of daily life in the place they live in now, and the abject bodies that the people in the new place might interpret them to be.

Joseph Roach (1996) considers forgetting an "opportunistic tactic" in the project of whiteness. To those who have more access to representation, it is meant to "displace, refashion, and transfer those persistent memories into representations more amenable to those who most frequently wield the pencil and the eraser" (7). The ones who refashion memories of dance into Hollywood salsa practices, developing complex vocabularies with which to classify moves and describe nuances, raise their salsa status within the clubs as they become L.A. salseras/os. This process of recreating latinidad through salsa cannot be so complete as to stamp out that from which L.A. salseras/os try to distance themselves. L.A. salseras/os depend on the presence of the unsequined socializers whose dance practices remind them of marginalized conditions they want to leave outside of the club. The L.A. salseras/os continuously confirm their higher social positions by performing in a way that asserts they are not socializers. Through this acknowledgment, the L.A. salseras/os and the socializers collectively disrupt economies of latinidad that also disavow the Latina/o bodies at the bottom of the hierarchy. And yet the larger-than-life L.A. salsa stifles the stories and practices of the ones who cannot and do not want to forget, the ones accused of dancing salsa wrong. As on many dance floors throughout L.A., these enactments of latinidad occur in and between spaces at Chuck's Grill, through techniques, affect, and timing of dancing salsa wrong.

The Great Migration

At Chuck's Grill I noticed that the distinctions on the dance floor also involved a physical separation of space; those who had worked themselves to the top of the L.A.-style salsa hierarchy removed themselves altogether from the company of the dancers in the restaurant. At about 10:30 that night, the sequined dancers headed across the restaurant and into a room on the other side of the lobby. María Elena and I followed the struts, swaggers, and sashays of these dance migrants past the lobby and into a spacious banquet hall, where couples spun to quicker tempos on the long floor that stretched down the length of the room—a perfect setup for seeing and being seen. María Elena, born in Mexico and raised in Los Angeles, called this departure "the Great Migration."

Historically the Great Migration refers to African American migration from the rural South to urban centers in the North, Midwest, and West. This migration has often been valorized as a move toward upward mobility and racial integration despite considerable backlash from the European American working class and further racial segregation.[3] María Elena's invocation of the Great Migration as a metaphor in this salsa setting also calls to mind the northward migration of Mexicans and Central Americans to Los Angeles. In this distinctive historical context, many of the Mexican and Central American migrants have also moved from rural spaces to U.S. urban spaces. Many with dreams of upward mobility have instead been met with antimigrant policies and the racialized violences of everyday life. In the leisure space of Chuck's Grill, María Elena deems the banquet hall the ultimate site of arrival. The performance of patrons there also suggests that they belong as upwardly mobile Latinas/os in a southern California context. Belonging in both contexts, the banquet hall and southern California, does not occur without racialized distinctions and segregations. In daily life, successful acts of undocumented migration across geopolitical borders partly depend on one's invisibility to protect one from the violence of thirst, rape, unscrupulous coyotes, MinuteMen, and deportation. Once a person arrives, his or her ability to remain undetected is crucial. María Elena's description, "the Great Migration," suggests that L.A. salseras/os resignify the criminalized act of migration by making themselves as spectacular as possible.

"See that guy who just walked in, with the sunglasses and long leather coat?" María Elena asked, staring at a thin *Matrix*-type guy with spiky, gelled hair and shiny white shoes. "He just bleached out his hair. It was black last week." She alerted me to the kind of attention that the banquet hall salseras/os seek in order to keep their salsa-dancing personas dramatically fresh. His leather coat opened like wings as he strode right through all the dancers up to a Latina in a cheerleader skirt whom he spun into a neck drop. The couple that had stood out in the restaurant earlier that night danced next to them, but now they blended in with the other banquet hall dancers.

A white woman captured our attention as she threw her head back orgasmically. She tossed her very straight, medium-blonde hair up into the air with her hand. The strands fell to cover her face, and she allowed them to slink back into place instead of pushing them away from her eyes. María Elena and I exchanged glances of subtle amusement and mild disgust. Back in the restaurant, María Elena had expressed her annoyance over the way white women misinterpreted salsa and tried to pretend they were Latina.

María Elena's boyfriend, Aldo, commented that the guy dancing with this woman was from "el D.F." (Mexico City) because of the way he bounced occasionally and truncated his steps. "But you can tell he has taken lessons in Los Angeles, because he accents the music with head gestures and he never lets his partner stay in the basic too long without performing a trick. See how he keeps turning her and dipping her?" We looked back to the couple. The man pulled his partner's thigh over his hip to support her as she arched her back. He released his hold on her back as she dropped lower, and then caught her to bring her upright. He double-dipped his partner, releasing the pressure on her back a second time before tugging her back upright.

When the song ended, the double-dipper caught my overly interested ethnographic eye and extended his hand in my direction from several feet away, much to my alarm. I shook my head and mouthed a "no thanks." But he wasn't taking no for an answer. We repeated the whole process a few times, each hand extension, headshake, and mouthed refusal more vigorous than the last. Finally, he approached my chair, and I agreed so as not to make a scene. "I'll make it smooth," he said; I wondered if I looked like a mambo dancer to him or if the offer to dance smoothly simply meant that he would not throw anything like neck drops my way.

Without any extraneous hair flipping, I followed his clear lead, which was devoid of any double-dip signals. Confirming Aldo's guess that he was from Mexico City, he said he learned to dance salsa, not cumbia, in Mexico before coming to Los Angeles and taking lessons here. He told me that his salsa was more sophisticated and smoother than that of the other Mexicans in Mexico City, because he had also taken ballroom lessons. He had been a dance teacher in Mexico, he said, but lately had been financing cars at a used-car lot in Pacoima.

I rejoined Aldo and María Elena when the song ended. "Mexicans from Mexico City are the best salsa dancers," Aldo informed me. María Elena corrected him: "You mean the ones who learn in L.A." Aldo agreed.

Once the flashy L.A. salsa dancers had evacuated the restaurant, traffic into the banquet hall slowed. María Elena was not the only one to detect this social choreography of the Great Migration, in which those daring enough and who had developed the proper skills crossed over to the larger space, with supposedly better music, more room to move, and more opportunities to dance with the ones who danced "right." She remarked that the banquet hall dancers primarily identified themselves as first-, second-, or third-generation immigrants with ties to a Latin American nation: El Salvador, Peru, Mexico. But importantly, they also identified themselves as Los Angelenas/os.

Many of them took private lessons and spent several hours a week rehearsing with a dance team for the next competition or performance. They contrasted themselves with the dancers in the restaurant area, whom they considered more recent immigrants, limited not only by the "provincial" styles they brought with them to Los Angeles but by their association with la limpieza. In incorporating double dips, head rolls, and neck drops, the banquet hall dancers differentiated themselves from those who danced wrong in the restaurant. The crowds in the two rooms tended not to mix, and both recognized as dominant the dance techniques practiced in the banquet hall. Although many of the dancers on both sides of Chuck's Grill brought with them diverse knowledge of how to dance salsa, what happened in the banquet hall made apparent the homogenization of practices into a codified repertoire of acceptable moves and techniques.

Globalization is often associated with a homogenization of cultural practices into standardized commodities; however, the forces of differentiation work together with homogenization in these enactments.[4] Practitioners of L.A. salsa homogenize and codify dance practices according to an aesthetic that dissociates latinidad from Mexicanness,[5] but some practitioners who get lumped together as "immigrants," "low class," or "Mexicans" do not retrain themselves to perform the dominant local moves. In conversations with these club patrons who constitute the socializers, I found that they consciously refuse to incorporate L.A. techniques. Like the mambo and casino dancers, they do not identify with L.A. salseras/os. The mambo and non-Cuban casino dancers, however, appear to be more established socially and economically outside of the club than either the L.A. salseras/os or the socializers. Practitioners of L.A. salsa juggle the forces of both homogenization and differentiation as they select certain practices to include under the umbrella of latinidad and exclude ones they attribute to the socializers.

In the restaurant some of the socializers described L.A. salsa as too flashy, too Hollywood, too much like a competition, critiques that corresponded with those made by mambo and casino dancers. Their reasons for their critiques differed, however. Rafael, a Colombian immigrant who worked at a used-car lot in Long Beach, characterized L.A. salsa and its Latina/o "fanatics" as typifying what Americans think Latinas/os are like. Not only did many working-class Latinos share his concern over this "diluted" latinidad, but a handful of upwardly mobile, university-educated Latinas/os I spoke with on the restaurant side echoed this sentiment, expressing a predilection for a more "authentic" salsa.

Sarita, who identified as Chicana and is a university student, clarified what she meant by this. While she realized that there was no one authentic salsa, "the people on the restaurant side are a little more relaxed. They haven't turned salsa into a spectacle." A couple of newcomers who aspired to become L.A. salseras/os confessed that they were too intimidated to dance in the banquet hall, but that they would as soon as they took a few more lessons.

The socializers, many who self-identify or are identified by others as migrants, workers from la limpieza, or Mexican and Central American, accuse L.A. salseras/os of no longer being Latina/o. The socializers view them as contaminated by Hollywood influences, a sign of Americanness, and as perhaps having rejected their pre-migrant familial, social, and cultural connections. These assumptions and accusations hinge upon a complex web of desires interlaced in practices of migration. Not all migrants to the United States wish to change their citizenship status and become incorporated as Americans. Although they may want to reside in the United States and have the right to participate culturally and politically, some may not wish to give up the rights they had in the countries from which they emigrated: the right to own property, to participate in elections, and to return, for example (Sassen 1999: 146). As trans-status corporeals, they may also affiliate more strongly with people, events, and sets of practices from within their previous localities. Dancing salsa "wrong" in this context signals a desire to maintain ties with the places from which they emigrated, while dancing salsa "right" suggests a desire to more fully incorporate into the dominant local formations of latinidad more closely aligned with Americanness.

In Los Angeles salsa clubs where performing latinidad has become a commodity, one does not move up the club hierarchies through the performance of white Americanness. Since most practitioners claim salsa as a Latino- or Latin American–based practice, they value the performance of latinidad as distinct from both black Americanness and white Americanness. Nina Glick Schiller's (1999) analysis of the process of Americanization offers some insight into salsa club categorizations of racialized belonging. According to her, European immigrants in nineteenth-century America regulated the social perception of their citizenship status by differentiating themselves from other immigrants. This included trying to distance themselves from the more "provincial" regions from which they emigrated and identifying instead with their nations of origin, a more sophisticated affiliation. But becoming American, Glick Schiller argues, was ultimately about becoming white, and immigrants accomplished this by performing whiteness. The European immigrants defined whiteness in terms of practices that were not associated with blacks, Mexicans, Chinese, or Japanese (17–18). This process of whitening thus entailed the social identification of practices considered un-American and a subsequent distancing from them. Yet, in the Los Angeles salsa clubs, belonging depends not on one's ability to perform whiteness but on one's ability to perform a U.S. latinidad. The L.A. salseras/os at Chuck's Grill co-create latinidad out of their varied experiences as Latinas/os in the United States.

However, practitioners do not all imagine and enact the performance of latinidad in the same way and do not define whiteness and Americanness in a binary relationship to latinidad. Rafa, the dancer from Colombia, said that he resented the banquet hall techniques because they were "too Hollywood," that is, Latino only in the eyes of Hollywood. Sarita connected those same L.A. salsa techniques—techniques that conjure up the "passionate," "uncontained," and "sexually promiscuous" Latinos we often see dancing on movie and television screens—to the exoticized tropes of latinidad. The dancers in the banquet hall cultivate dance techniques that correspond to these predominant, stereotypical images.

Yet even if the banquet hall dancers do not perform whiteness, they incorporate the kinds of practices that many non-Latina/o dancers desire to consume and perform themselves. Banquet hall dancers value bodies trained to exaggerate passionate, exotic Latinoness, disciplined to suppress moves that they would consider a lack of technique, moves that call to mind the other, less desirable stereotypes of Latinos: Latinos making up the hordes of working-class immigrants, uneducated and sexually undesirable.

To what extent does the move to the banquet hall *dis*locate practitioners from criminalized acts of migration and second-class citizenship to *re*locate them as L.A. Latinas and Latinos? Irena, a Puerto Rican mambo dancer whom I met at the salsa congress, did not acknowledge the difference between the restaurant socializers and the banquet hall salseras/os. Without making any distinctions among the dancing bodies at Chuck's Grill, she warned me against going there because "it's a meat market without any good dancers, just showy ones doing L.A. salsa. It's a really rough crowd, with a lot of immigrants who live on the east side or in Long Beach." She said the same crowd goes to The Legend downtown, Valentino's on the east side of Los Angeles, and Alexandre's Isle in Koreatown. She preferred to go to El Reino in East Hollywood and Juanita's in West Hollywood, places María Elena decried as upper-class clubs with "way too many Anglos" and snobby Latinas/os.

Despite Irena's "snobby" interpretation and indiscriminate lumping together of dance practices at Chuck's Grill, the club remains a sort of training ground, a home base where L.A.-style dancers train their bodies to perform techniques recognizable as salsa to the dominant players in the wars and migrate up the hierarchy of latinidad.

Training, Retraining, and Street Training

At Chuck's Grill, L.A. salseras/os segregate themselves in space, literally distancing themselves from those they perceive to be migrants. With the city's proximity to Mexico, "dancing like a migrant" is often conflated with "dancing like a Mexican," even if the Mexican in question is actually from the United States or another Latin American country other than Mexico (e.g., El Salvador, Ecuador, Guatemala, Colombia). If a person fails to pass as an L.A.-style salsera/o, and the crowd appraises him or her as a migrant, that person may be accused not simply of dancing salsa "wrong" but of "dancing like a Mexican." At work in these accusations are specific techniques and connotations associated with Mexicanness and specific ways that dancers learn to identify others as "wrong." That is to say, dancers train, don't train, retrain, and street train their bodies to perform a latinidad in opposition to anti-Mexican, antimigrant violence.

One Sunday afternoon I met up with Sook, a friend from UCLA, her boyfriend, Danilo, and their friend Manrique. We were all headed to The Marina, a club off the Santa Monica Pier, to go dancing. "I lived in Costa Rica until I was seven before moving to Los Angeles," Manrique told me. He never cared about dancing salsa until two years earlier, when he started taking lessons. When I asked where he was taking lessons, he repeated that he had taken lessons two years earlier and had mastered the technique. He was now a professional instructor. He had recently appeared as a featured dancer in a promotional salsa music video, he told me, enthused by the opportunities available to him as a salsero.

While I regard two years as an exceedingly short time to go from dancing in beginner's classes to teaching and performing as a professional, this is not all that unusual for many L.A. salseras/os. Many believe that mastery is quite possible in that time frame. They often reproduce the language used to advertise locally produced dance videotapes that guarantee "mastery" of salsa in just a few lessons. Considering Manrique's boast, I was skeptical that one could gain a set of standardized salsa skills via the television set or that one could ever claim a mastery of salsa within two years of one's first lesson. But perhaps budding L.A. salseras/os' level of commitment to frequent and private lessons, as well as their appearance at salsa clubs just about every day of the week, helped them fulfill their hopes for professionalization.

Sook had been encouraging a reluctant Danilo to learn salsa and thought he might like to take the club's 3 o'clock lesson for beginners. She had also previously asked if I would show him a few steps, sensing that he would learn more readily from someone who was not his girlfriend. When we arrived at the pier, we noticed several Latinos standing in the sand and peering in at the salsa lesson in progress through the bars of the glassless club window. "Quick, quick, slow; quick, quick, slow," called the salsa instructor from within the club. By the time we made it inside, the lesson was almost over, and Danilo preferred watching the end of the class to jumping in late. "Quick, quick, slow," chanted the instructor again. Her amplified voice carried this ballroom methodology to her students,[6] who awkwardly followed her directions and received praise for their accomplishments: "Cross right, cross left, and pivot. That was beautiful!"

Daylight streamed in over the heads that peeked through the window, lighting up details that made clear how different this club was from others in Los Angeles. With its afternoon hours and beach location, the club invited a more casual clientele: those who had been sunning on the beach or riding the Ferris wheel on the pier and heard the salsa music and stopped in to try it out for the first time. But once the lesson ended, the floor filled with mostly Latinas/os who seemed to enjoy the club's early hours (3 in the afternoon to 10 at night), possibly because they had to work Monday morning. They came dressed in an assortment of outfits: some in T-shirts, jeans, and sneakers and others in fancy Italian shoes and shiny button-down purple blouses. A couple of dancers brought their young children. They pivoted, spun, and shuffled, grinding stray grains of sand into the gritty floor.

Manrique took off to dance while Sook and I got to work on Danilo. Hesitant to even step onto the dance floor, he seemed intimidated by the loud music and the other men who appeared to know exactly where and how to stand when they were not dancing, as well as how to navigate the lack of empty space. Sook and I coaxed him into the most secluded corner of the floor, the corner blocked by the stairs, farthest away from spectators, in order to begin our lesson. Recalling my own training as a dance student at Merecumbé in Costa Rica, I suggested we start with three basic steps (from the point of view of the leader's feet): stepping forward with the left and back with the right; stepping left foot side, center, right foot side, center; and crossing back toward the left side and then to the right. In Los Angeles these are referred to respectively as the mambo or L.A.-style basic, the Cuban rumba basic, and either the cumbia basic or "wrong." In about half an hour, Danilo could recognize the rhythm and was practicing moving between the first two basic steps as he led Sook.

As Danilo worked on transitioning from one basic step into another, Manrique approached. He expressed alarm as he watched Danilo and Sook. Danilo led Sook into the basic that alternated sides crossing in back, but before he could practice the transition to the next basic, Manrique interrupted. "No, Danilo, that's Mexican! This is what you are trying to do," he said. He then pulled Sook from Danilo and led her into a step that crossed in the front instead of the back. Since he had not been part of the teaching process, he did not realize that Danilo was figuring out how to connect the steps he had just learned, not add new steps to his repertoire. I felt my skin prickle in annoyance as he comfortably installed himself as the new instructor, one who vehemently shunned a step he associated with Mexicanness.

Danilo looked uncertain as we watched Manrique demonstrate an "un-Mexican" step with Sook. I told Danilo, "Don't worry about it. That's not what we were working on."

Manrique turned to me, exasperated, and said, "But you were showing him cumbia. You can't do cumbia to salsa music. That's Mexican." Each time he said "Mexican," his eyebrows crinkled together, his nose wrinkled, and his upper lip curled back in disgust.

"I was showing him one of the basic steps of salsa from Costa Rica," I tried to explain. Manrique did not care to discuss this further and slipped back into the crowd to dance.

To understand the confusion around this single step, I had to tease out the connections between the techniques I had learned in Costa Rica and the techniques associated with Mexican cumbia. I have observed that practitioners of Mexican cumbia and Central American salsa have the crossing-back basic in common. While dancing cumbia, a practitioner might flick a foot forward during the pause before crossing it to the back. This flick was not as prominent among salsa practitioners who crossed back. Manrique seemed to classify the crossing-back basic as cumbia only, flick or no flick. The classification of the crossing-back basic as nonsalsa was crucial for Manrique, even at this most relaxed, beachy dance space.

For Manrique, the crossing-back basic signified cumbia, and in Los Angeles salsa clubs cumbia and salsa have a strained, sometimes volatile relationship. Salsa is considered more of a "crossover" genre than cumbia, meaning that it has more appeal to pan-Latina/o and non-Latina/o consumers. Yet in relation to Mexican genres of *ranchera* and *banda*, cumbia is considered more pan-Latino, marketable to larger audiences, and more cosmopolitan. In contrast to cumbia, ranchera is identified with a working-class, rural, Tejano or Chicano population. Among Chicanas/os and Mexicans, to practice cumbia indicates upward mobility, cosmopolitanism (Peña 1999), and an identification with Latinoness rather than solely Chicanoness or Mexicanness.

Manuel Peña (1999) points out that the incorporation of cumbia has contributed to the upward mobility and international success of Chicano (Tejano) recording artists, such as Selena. She gained success internationally once she began to perform cumbia and salsa at her concerts, not solely the ranchera that informed her earlier repertoire. But in Los Angeles salsa clubs, cumbiaesque elements indicate a more rural, working-class, Mexican or Chicana/o aesthetic. In the film and television productions from Los Angeles, characters dance salsa, not cumbia, to indicate an association with latinidad. A hierarchy emerges among the genres, with salsa at the top, cumbia in the middle, and ranchera and banda at the bottom. When elements of cumbia show up as dance techniques in salsa clubs or in the movies, they locate bodies as Mexican.

Manrique's insistence that the crossing-back basic is cumbia, and therefore Mexican, supports the dominant local narrative that discounts salsa's historical or present basis in Mexico. While I am not suggesting that salsa has stood out as a prominent dance in Mexico, I do find that Los Angeles salsa origin stories negate salsa's transnational circulation to cities associated with non-Caribbean Latinas/os. The translocal music and dance practices that have influenced salsa have also helped establish salsa's foothold and regionalized interpretations in Mexico City, as well as in cities in Central America, such as San José and Panama City. The codification of salsa in Los Angeles dance clubs and classes elides these regionalized interpretations.

Some days later, I told the story of Manrique to Pati, a Chicana who recently stopped going to salsa clubs because guys would tell her she danced too much like a Mexican. She responded with a story about a conversation she had overheard among three white women listening to a salsa band at the Autry Museum:

> One of the women said she went to this club in Universal City, but when she went, they were playing cumbia, not salsa. She said, "When I walked in after paying for my valet parking and like a lot of money to get in, I look around and they were dancing . . ." She stops to think up the best insult she can. One of the others interjects, "The wrong, the wrong, the wrong . . ." Then the first woman says, "There were all these Mexicans dancing with their cowboy hats to cumbia!"

For the women in Pati's story, cowboy hats and cumbia signify Mexicanness, the wrong kind of hat, dance, and Latina/o. The anti-Mexican sentiment expressed by Manrique and present in Pati's story echoed my own family's accounts of the discrimination they have encountered throughout their lives for displaying signifiers of working-class Mexicanness in a southern New Mexico town, for example, speaking Spanish and living in a barrio in an adobe house with two rooms and eleven children. It resonated with the (anti–cowboy hat) stereotypes of Mexicans as poor and provincial expressed by non-Latinas/os and Latinas/os of the non-Mexican or non–Mexican American kind, as well as by some L.A.-salsa-dancing Mexicans themselves.

At Valentino's, Carlos, an L.A.-style salsero, explained how he had responded to the anti-Mexicanness that circulates in Los Angeles salsa spaces. He told me that he had been dancing salsa for years in Mexico City, but when he moved to Los Angeles two years earlier, he learned that he had been dancing salsa wrong all that time. He imitated his former practice, with short, stilted steps that crossed behind, bobbing his head up and down as his hands twitched at midtorso to the one-two-three-pause rhythm that underscores both salsa and cumbia. He told me, "I used to dance like this. When I got to L.A., I found out I had been dancing cumbia, not salsa. Salsa is supposed to be danced like this." Then he demonstrated his more recent salsa training, elongating his forward and back stride, moving quickly to inhabit more space, smoothing out the bobbing. Stopping, he commented, "Much more elegant. I can never go back to dancing the way they do in Mexico." The contempt for Mexicanness was recoded in dance terms.

This dancer's internalization of local L.A. salsa standards and his apparent readiness to dismiss what was socially referred to as "salsa in Mexico" is striking. He spent considerable time retraining his body to perform L.A. salsa. What exactly had prompted his retraining? Had he spoken with one of the local club promoters who criticized Mexicans and Central Americans for their dance practices? Clearing up what he considered the biggest misconception about salsa, one promoter had said to me, "Mexicans and Central Americans think that people in Los Angeles dance salsa too fast. I tell them it's not too fast. They get confused by all the turns and tricks, but I show them that if they just watch what salseros do with their feet, half the time they move their feet even slower than dancers in Mexico and Central America." Dancing too slowly, bobbing, and crossing back into the basic implicated one as Mexican and were all signs of a "provincial" body that "lacked training" in Los Angeles.

In contrast to Manrique and Carlos, who both explained the ways they had to train or retrain their bodies to dance salsa in Los Angeles, Gerardo asserted that he never needed a lesson: "Salsa is in my blood." After a trip to the El Reino women's bathroom on my first night there, I had wandered back over to the table to talk to my friend Jan, who was deep in conversation with Gerardo, a regular at the club. As I dragged an empty chair over to join them, she introduced us, saying that Gerardo was from Venezuela. "Did you know that Alexa McBeal's secretary is here?" he asked me, tipping his slicked-back head in the direction of a woman in fuchsia sitting at a table near the wall.

Just then, a cha cha chá came on and Jane Krakowski, the actress who played Elaine on the primetime television show *Ally McBeal*, popped up to dance with one of the men at her table. Her partner hung his head down to watch his feet shuffle along to the unfamiliar rhythm, but she danced on the beat a pace away, with an uplifted posture and very lengthy strides. As he danced in place, she turned herself around with perfect timing and then continued her back-and-forth cha cha chá basic step. According to Gerardo, she was a good dancer. "But you can tell she learned how to dance in a class." He continued, "People who take classes learn how to dance by counting out steps, not by feeling the music. I never had to take lessons. I learned naturally. Salsa's in my blood."

Gerardo's observations exemplify a perception among many salsa dancers that non-Latina/o bodies can dance salsa only because of training, while Latinas/os dance salsa naturally, without training. This sets up an unwieldy binary that pits the trained against the untrained, with several twists. Gerardo critiqued the trained body of Ally McBeal's secretary because salsa is not "in her blood," essentializing salsa as a racial characteristic that Latinas/os possess. Gerardo, in his description, classifies salsa as a thing, a feeling Latinos are biologically equipped to recognize and perform. For Gerardo, the untrained body is the Latina/o body that does not need formal training in order to dance salsa. Non-Latina/o bodies must undergo formal training so that they can approximate the ability to dance, an ability that remains always out of reach. Gerardo's judgment ties an authentic knowledge of salsa to the Latina/o rather than the white, non-Latina/o body. His view simultaneously upholds media representations that racialize Latinas/os as exotic others, unable to contain their "natural" salsa prowess.

Gerardo's claim that salsa is in his blood has more than just essentializing connotations. Latinas/os in salsa clubs often use blood as a metaphor to indicate that they did not have to labor to belong to a culture where people learn to dance informally. They invoke the metaphor not to argue that Latinas/os are biologically prone or physically more equipped to dance than non-Latinas/os but to acknowledge that salsa techniques have been culled from cultural practices of Latina/o bodies, practices that have been standardized, fetishized, and commodified.

When I asked one experienced white salsera (who happened to be a former rock star) for advice about how to make it to the dance floor, she emphasized the differences between ballroom and "street training" and the importance of proper training:

> FORMER ROCK STAR: When I go out, I don't go for the "social" reasons. I just go to dance. I usually wear my leggings and T-shirt and I get asked to dance all night long. You want to know how to make it to the dance floor? I'll tell you how to make it to the dance floor—you take a class, that's how. First, you go to a studio and get a really good teacher. Not a ballroom teacher, but a street teacher. The next class you take is conducted in a club, which is the clue to everything. Before some clubs open, there's a class for beginners. After the class, the deejay begins playing around nine o'clock, and all the beginners know who each other are and dance among themselves. Then you go to the next level, learn the moves, graduate, and go to the next one.
>
> ME: But what about if you're not really a beginner? What if you've been dancing salsa all your life, say in Mexico, but you don't dance like they do here?
>
> FORMER ROCK STAR: You take a class to learn the new style. This is L.A.; you dance L.A. style.

Her method of learning through street-training classes differs markedly from Gerardo's explanation of dancing "naturally" in the "Latino way." To belong in Los Angeles salsa clubs according to her logic, which is indicative of the dominant logic, one must street-train in L.A. salsa, even if one already knows how to dance. She contends that newcomers must "refine" the moves they learned somewhere else if they want to fit in. In fact, according to her, dancing "right" falls somewhere in between dancing "naturally" and dancing too ballroom. Practitioners dance right when they demonstrate street training in order to appear as if they learned naturally, while simultaneously exhibiting evidence of their rigorously trained bodies.

The street training that so many salseros attempt to "master" to move up the salsa hierarchy does not actually take place in the street. And showing off street training involves more than simply knowledge and practice. It costs money and takes time to learn. The reference to blood is an attempt to make visible that in salsa clubs, Latina/o bodies are not expendable and that they possess a cultural knowledge that cannot be either commodified or acquired—no matter how much training. The rationale is that, even with time and money, one can never completely purchase the complexity of a culture that one hasn't been born into.

In Los Angeles practitioners tend to value the oxymoronic street training, a combination of the refinement, or whitening, of selected techniques and the stylization of la limpieza. In the former rock star's description of street training, *street* is a code word for an urban latinidad. Even non-Latinas/os can take classes to perform this kind of latinidad. The L.A. salseras/os who use this terminology contrast a highly trained "urban" body with a provincial or rural body. Even though practitioners like Carlos often come to L.A. from the large urban center of Mexico City, L.A. salseras/os still mark them as provincial because of the crossing-back basic.

White dancers at the top of the salsa hierarchy, dancers like the former rock star, express a preference for immersing themselves into an urban latinidad that has been aestheticized to produce, reproduce, and update the codified moves of L.A. salsa. Urban aestheticization involves a sanitization of the material realities of la limpieza or imaginations of latinidad on the "street," complete with crime, sex, drugs, fights, gangsters, and poverty. This stylization of poverty is similar to the codification of dance practices at the historical Palladium, in which the practices from Latina/o bodies were gleaned and "cleaned" so that white bodies could learn them in classes. Without the right kind of Latina/o bodies present to authenticate salsa practices for non-Latina/o practitioners, salsa becomes "ballroom," a code word for "white," or is implicated in la limpieza. Latinas/os and non-Latinas/os who dance L.A. salsa collaborate to produce this aestheticized street-trained latinidad.

The Trouble with Dancing Salsa (Really Well) to Cumbia Music

Dancers train and retrain their bodies to perform L.A. salsa, but to move up the hierarchy of latinidad requires more than a highly skilled body and a separation of space. L.A. salseras/os rely on the timing of their performances to distinguish themselves from those marked as migrant, Mexican, or workers of la limpieza. More specifically, they refine the timing of their relationships to cumbia.

When the band played a cumbia at The Legend, a large number of dancers vacated the floor. An older couple sprang through the departing crowds to lightheartedly bounce out cumbia, as if they had been waiting all night for this song, this moment. A bow on the woman's head tied up her gray curls that bobbed up and down to the rhythm. With an occasional series of intricate turns through the arches of their arms, they didn't miss a beat. They never looked around to see who was watching but were oblivious to all but the swing of the music and each other. Nevertheless they were aware of where they were in relation to the other dancers, who left a cushion of space around them. Though they did not take up any extra space, no one took space away from them, either.

Very few bands and even fewer deejays play cumbia music on a regular basis in L.A. salsa clubs. My own identification with the cumbia dancers' exuberant performance jolted me out of the easy interpretation that the dominance of L.A. salsa has obliterated the presence of other genres that fall under the rubric of Latin American popular dance: cumbia, merengue, bolero, and punta, for example. And yet when I looked around for someone to dance cumbia with, I realized that no one else was tapping their toes at the edge of the floor. No one seemed interested. With the centralization of salsa, I wondered if others had forgotten how to dance these other genres, had never wished to learn them, or had been disciplined not to demonstrate their connections to rhythms associated with expressions of a less desirable latinidad as defined by L.A. salsa. Salsa, not cumbia, had come to constitute the selected tradition in Los Angeles.

Not everyone at The Legend responded to the cumbia music in the same way as this couple. Their two bodies always remained vertical, in contrast to those of other dancing couples, who appeared not to realize that the music had changed; they still danced salsa. Most likely newer to salsa, some of these dancers attempted single turns and unsteady dips on the thinned-out floor in front of the band. When partners lost track of one other or the rhythm, they sometimes stopped and restarted. A few couples, however, dipped, dropped, and turned with the quick, dramatic energy of L.A. salsa. They broke with the rhythm to pose, a woman's thigh wrapped around her partner's waist as he supported her diagonal tilt.

The flashy salseras/os expanded the dimensions of their partnership, their bodies carving into the space around them not just vertically but also horizontally and diagonally. They distinguished themselves from the beginning as salsa dancers as well as the cumbia dancers—but to their own detriment. They may not have noticed that another group of salseras/os, the dancers at the apex of the club hierarchy—the teachers, contest winners, and longtime practitioners—left the floor when the cumbia music started; they neither danced cumbia, nor did they dance salsa to cumbia music. The salseras/os who showed off their salsa moves to cumbia not only revealed their lack of musical knowledge but also inadvertently distanced themselves from the top dancers, who sat sipping water or took off for bathroom breaks during cumbia music.

I felt a little embarrassed about the untimely bravado of the salsa dancers who seemed overeager to prove their worth, but I was elated as I watched the cumbia dancers outdance everyone during this momentary musical departure from salsa. The cumbia dancers pointed out that not all skilled dancers preferred salsa and that a system for evaluating cumbia existed beyond the parameters of salsa. Were others in the crowd repressing their knowledge of cumbia to distance themselves from a system that valued cumbia?

As I assessed the scene, I realized that if it had not become apparent in the course of this ethnography that the difference between L.A. salsa and cumbia mattered, I would likely not have learned to feel embarrassed on behalf of the salsa dancers who danced salsa really well to cumbia music (the right dance to the wrong music). I would have regarded them as the ones against whom the beginners and cumbia dancers were ultimately judged, without noticing that those who chose not to dance to cumbia performed their belonging to the dominant group at the club by merely walking off the floor the moment they recognized the music as nonsalsa.

Although salsa music and cumbia music have distinct instrumentation, the similarity in their rhythms has been known to confuse beginners who do not have a previous knowledge of the differences in the qualities of the sounds. Yet dancers who do possess an understanding of the musical differences often dispute the movement practices that might accompany them. While some dancers include moves associated with cumbia into their expressions of salsa, others insist that such moves are not compatible with salsa.

Maricruz, who took private lessons in L.A. (street) salsa, gave me some insight into the codifications that local salseras/os reinforce when assessing whether a dance qualifies as salsa. Like many of the salseras/os I spoke and danced with in Los Angeles, Maricruz classified a dance as salsa only if the dancers work from the "standard" front and back basic: stepping forward with the left foot, back to center to join the right foot, and back with the right foot, then back to center to join the left foot. I asked her if she considered the crossing-behind step (which was cumbia for Manrique) and the side-center, side-center step as salsa. "Of course," she told me, naming them the "cumbia break" and the "guaguancó," respectively. But when I showed her a videotape of salsa from a stage performance of Merecumbé, a dance company in Costa Rica, she did not recognize what they did as salsa. "They're dancing to salsa music, but they don't have the basic step," she said, meaning the forward and back basic.

We watched the dancers move through the choreography of steps that Maricruz called cumbia. "In salsa," she said, "we only use the cumbia step to break out of the basic and into something else, like a turn or a trick." In this case, the cumbia break acted as a transition step, not a point of focus. She compared it to the ballroom-based cross-body lead that many salseras/os use to set up turns; however, the cross-body lead was not the basis for an entire dance genre like cumbia. "You use cumbia to break from salsa, and only for eight counts or it gets boring. Some people do sixteen counts, which unfortunately starts to look like they are dancing cumbia instead of using a cumbia break as a transition within salsa," she explained.

She again appraised the predominance of the cumbia basic in the video and said, "They don't work from the salsa [front and back] basic. They're dancing cumbia, not salsa." Just then, the dancers in the tape switched to the front and back basic, and I noted this aloud. When the dance eluded Maricruz's classification as cumbia and nonsalsa, she amended her opinion. "Well, people in Los Angeles are a lot more strict about what they count as salsa."

The "right" way to incorporate what L.A. salseras/os classify as cumbia is as a break, a moment of transition to prepare for the next opportunity to "shine." In a single dance, the break connects the elements that identify the dance as L.A. salsa. In the larger social choreography of the club, the break between sets of salsa music might also be called a cumbia break, a chance for the L.A.-style salsa dancers to cool off, rehydrate, reapply lipstick, wipe off perspiration, and, after performing their exodus from the floor, to remove themselves from direct association with cumbia. The night I was watching the older couple dance cumbia, when the cumbia music ended, the recharged salseras/os at the top of the hierarchy took their places back on the dance floor, ready to garner attention through their salsa moves.

Maricruz told me that L.A. salseras/os do not like cumbia because they think it is too jumpy. Although she will occasionally dance it, she said, it is not her favorite dance because "it is not as seductive, passionate, and sexy like salsa. In cumbia, there's no caressing, no dips. No romanticism. It's just bouncy and happy. That is probably why a lot of people don't like it. At some clubs dancers complain, 'They play too much cumbia here!' and they'll stop going there. I don't know if they think lower-class people do it. . . . I don't really think they are being classist. It's more that people have different musical tastes."

I am drawn to Maricruz's first hesitant analysis associating cumbia with the lower class. She articulates a dominant club pattern of ascribing a low-class status to happy, cumbia-dancing Latinos and opposing it to passionate, salsa-dancing Latinas/os. Notably she quickly attributed differences in aesthetic taste to the particularities of culture and to personal taste. She thus dismissed her own very accurate (in my opinion) assessment of classism and the presence of la limpieza in the club.

Dancing salsa right includes spacing, training, and timing that deterritorialize latinidad from la limpieza, Mexico, and migration. In Los Angeles any dance practices associated with Mexico almost always get labeled as "wrong." Therefore salseras/os in L.A. generally strive to situate themselves and their salsa practices within Los Angeles, while infusing them with U.S. pop-cultural injections of a highly trained, codified, exoticized latinidad. By recrafting their dance practices, they in turn refashion enactments of latinidad so as to be desirable within the United States—weighing the implications of dancing "on the two" and "on the one," of performing with and without gymnastic tricks, of performing with sustained, undulating, or bouncy qualities, and with stepping forward and back, side to side, or crossing behind. They thus negotiate Americanness and latinidad, creating more bearable spaces for themselves as Latinas/os in the United States.

The virtuoso cumbia performance at The Legend, however, momentarily exposed the imperfections of breaking away from Mexicanness as a strategy for moving up the dance hierarchy. Maricruz acknowledged the difficulty dancers face in trying to move up this hierarchy. "You don't get to place yourself in the hierarchy; you get placed into it by everyone else." According to her, at the top are a handful of world-class teachers who travel the globe, visiting Japan, Switzerland, Germany, Greece, and North Carolina to give workshops all year long. Next are the competitors, then the ones who perform with a dance team, then the intermediate dancers considering joining a group, and last, the beginners and the now-and-then dancers (the ones who know how to dance but haven't learned the latest moves).

Maricruz's hierarchy does not include the cumbia dancers and the others who have been disciplined for dancing wrong in L.A. clubs and elsewhere. Yet the moving bodies of the cumbia dancers at The Legend challenge the totality of the break with Mexicanness, contradict the logic that L.A. salseras/os use to evaluate good dancing, and hamper the ability to completely erase their proximity to and memories of the wrong kind of latinidad.

Although Mexican and Central American immigrants and descendants represent the majority of the Latinas/os in Los Angeles, dance practices associated with Mexico and Central America occupy the bottom levels of club hierarchies. What becomes evident is that dancing salsa wrong disrupts globalization's effect of erasing place—not place as an abstract concept but the specific locations of Mexico, the U.S.-Mexican border, and la limpieza. Identifications with and implications concerning these locations tie latinidad to Latinas/os as abject, laboring bodies, referencing painful memories of war, poverty, and death. Without place, memories of violence, sadness, and beauty become lost in a deterritorialized pan-Latina/o nostalgia—a much more commodifiable form of latinidad within the economies of the salsa industry.

CHAPTER 3

Un/Sequined Corporealities

Behind me in line outside of Valentino's on salsa night, a well-dressed Latino in a black pinstriped blazer asks me if I know why the wait is so much longer than usual. "Trouble with the fire marshal is what I heard," I tell him. It is almost midnight and we are not allowed in until someone inside leaves.

"I've been coming here for thirteen years and this has never happened before," he says. He usually drops by Valentino's right after work to have a drink, staying for twenty minutes and then leaving. He has to get up at 6 tomorrow because he has staff meetings on Thursday mornings, and he can't be late. Maybe he will have to skip Valentino's this week, he considers, because he still has to drive all the way home to Long Beach.

"Where do you work?" I ask. Beaming, he opens up one side of his coat to reveal a Universal City Nissan patch on his white button-down shirt. "I can help you upgrade your car," he offers, handing me a business card that reads "Frank Flores, Sales and Leasing Consultant." He lets his jacket fall back over the patch that marks his position as a car salesman in daily life. "Call me anytime," he says. The details of employment embedded within the mini sales pitch and the awareness of building fire codes call into question the disparity between the sequined, exoticized latinidades produced by salsa clubs and unsequined Latina/o corporealities of everyday life. Yet both sequined and unsequined Latina/o corporealities are intimately intertwined with the regulations and demands of a capitalist economy.

In this chapter I consider the interconnectedness of latinidad and the capitalist economy. I theorize the failed attempts of dancers and nightclubs to disentangle the latinidad produced in the libidinal salsa economy—the economy that circulates affect, desires, and identities—from the political economy. Nightclub economies such as those circulating at Copa Cabana West and The Legend that attract a mix of Latinas/os and non-Latinas/os disrupt imaginations of the unsequined latinidades of the political economy (marked as Mexican, migrant, and workers of la limpieza). They do this by creating the conditions conducive to producing a sequined latinidad in the libidinal salsa economy.

Such a sequined latinidad circulates profitably, desired and consumed by both Latinas/os and non-Latinas/os. In collaboration with these club economies, salseras/os capitalize on the erotics of latinidad and work to disguise any references to themselves as laboring, poor, or working-class bodies. Salseras/os thus move to separate the libidinal from the political economy—an impossible maneuver. Since the latinidad produced in salsa libidinal economies is always intertwined with the political economy, salsera/o attempts to separate sequined from unsequined corporealities is temporary at best.

A club promoter once told me that salsa clubs are places in which Latinas/os "reinvent" themselves and that his job is to facilitate and profit from this transformation. In my observations, Latinas/os reinvent themselves as exotic (as with pinstriped jackets, sequins, or feathers), to cloak the social and economic marginalities associated with Latinas/os in everyday life, or to disrupt the imaginations of those who would otherwise locate them among the working class regardless of their social status. Outside the salsa clubs, working-class Latinas/os struggle to survive and find niches within the global economy. This is not an easy accomplishment, according to the Latinas/os I have met in salsa clubs who have revealed their daytime positions as mechanics, maids, waitresses, repairmen, hairdressers, and car salesmen.

Upward mobility has become largely a fantasy of the past, as the flailing

U.S. economy takes its toll,[1] especially on working and lower-middle classes, and hampers the accumulation of capital for all but the very rich. Salseras/os strive toward another kind of upward mobility. In libidinal salsa economies that flourish after dark, patrons toil to gain status on the dance floor by attempting to detach their class positions from the sequined corporealities of Copa Cabana West and The Legend.

The dancers do not create this economy alone. Salsa practitioners and promoters co-create utopian libidinal spaces in which desire for the performance and consumption of a sequined latinidad flourishes. Patrons can move up salsa hierarchies based on the performance of desired Latina/o corporealities that the club economies manufacture. By refining dance moves and disguising the working body with their outfits, salsa practitioners can mask the socioeconomic status of their daily lives and accumulate salsa club capital.

In clubs working-class Latinas/os potentially become more desirable when they convert themselves into fetishized, dancing bodies rather than reminders of the outside-of-club laboring bodies that perform the groundwork for others to attain their desires. Yet, as the sales and leasing consultant I met in line at Valentino's did, patrons also sometimes opt to tactically reveal their out-of-club occupations to generate opportunities to increase their capital outside the club. By revealing his identity as he did, Frank Flores not only defused the possibility that I might classify him as a construction worker or a day laborer—common occupations for men making up the primarily working-class clientele of Valentino's—but he also did not lose the chance to gain a commission from a potential customer.

To a great extent, however, salsa practitioners and promoters endeavor to segregate nightly life from daily life, the sequined from the unsequined, and the libidinal salsa social economy from the political economy. The political economy, based on the accumulation of capital, and the libidinal economy, based on feeding desires, converge with and challenge each other, even as the erotics of sequined latinidad camouflage the mechanisms of the political economy. Although patrons attempt to untwist economic interests from libidinal interests, they labor at accumulating both salsa club capital and dollar profits within what Marta Savigliano (1995: 1–2) theorizes as the "political economy of Passion," an economy in which the libidinal and the political economies intersect through the production and consumption of the exotic.[2]

In L.A. salsa clubs, the exotic is configured through a latinidad that deterritorializes salsa practices from Mexico, migration, and la limpieza and reterritorializes them through exoticized practices of L.A. salsa. The libidinal and political economies operate simultaneously to exploit and rank bodies as desirable through their seemingly classless performances of sequined latinidad in the clubs or through their execution of cheap labor in la limpieza. More precisely, the commodification of salsa-dancing Latina/o corporealities in local clubs reproduces the uneven mechanisms of globalization that exploit Latina/o bodies in both daily and nightly life.

The nightclub consumption of salsa configures latinidad in an entangled libidinal-political economy. When sliding money across the counter to satisfy an admission fee, patrons act as clients who pay for the club's operational expenses and build profits within the political economy. Although the consumption of salsa occurs within business establishments with the primary goal of making a profit, clients prefer to imagine that they engage with salsa in a purely social economy, one that does not rely on the circulation of money, let alone the commodification of a dancing Latina/o corporeality. To mask the profit-based economy that serves as a backdrop to the salsa wars, they invent narratives that romanticize latinidad and mystify capitalist operations by reifying the intersection of latinidad with the libidinal.

Of course, like other businesses, nightclubs need capital in order to serve their clientele. They must pay rent, taxes, insurance, and fines if they violate the occupancy limitations set by the fire marshal. They employ a number of people, both seen and behind the scenes—managers, promoters, marketers, accountants, valet parkers, security guards, ticket sellers, doormen and women, bartenders, bands, deejays, bathroom attendants, and custodians—who assist in the production of the fantasy latinidad. And to generate more capital beyond that needed for their mere operation, the businesses amplify the libidinal to such a degree that it elides even as it makes possible the behind-the-scenes dollar profit of the owners.

Not all clubs produce and profit from the same kind of latinidad, however. Each club, working with and against dominant representations of exotic latinidad, commodifies its own variation. And clients perform their desired nightclub corporealities through their affiliations with competing club promotions of latinidad. Mirroring similar productions across L.A., these identifications intersect with the tensions between the political and the libidinal in three nightclub economies stratified by class across the city: Copa Cabana West, Las Feliz Edades, and The Legend.

The "Crossover" Market at Copa Cabana West

Every time I go to Copa Cabana West, someone points out the celebrities present: Jennifer López, Kareem Abdul-Jabbar, Mario Van Peebles, Jimmy Smits, a couple of guys from Days of Our Lives, Freddie from Welcome Back Kotter (played by Laurence Hilton-Jacobs), to name just a few.[3] Copa Cabana West has become known not just for the appearance of Hollywood film and television stars, some of whom identify as Latina/o, but also for the juxtaposition of the rich and famous with the most strikingly flamboyant and accomplished salseras/os in Los Angeles.

The owners created this club so that wealthier Angelenas/os from the west side could enjoy Latina/o music and dance from the east side without having to cross into a part of town associated with poverty and Spanish-speaking gang members, according to Olivia, a Mexican American from Orange County who occasionally attends Copa Cabana West. She prefers to go to Chuck's Grill on the east side and criticized Copa Cabana West, calling it "too Americanized. It's trying too hard to be a crossover space—that's what their website calls it. I mean, just look where the location is. It's as far east as most of the white people on the west side will venture and not too far west so that Latinos on the east side will come to make it 'authentic.'"

By "crossover," Olivia did not mean the jovial union of L.A. east-side and west-side bodies as they enjoy Latina/o dance and music but rather the carefully designed "cleaning up," relocating, and repackaging of the product of salsa within the glossy, Hollywood aesthetic of latinidad—a deterritorialized, ahistorical, and hypereroticized latinidad manufactured for mass consumption. More precisely, the emphasis on the circulation of the product seems to outweigh concerns over the unity of practitioners, who have little contact with each other during the day. At Copa Cabana West, owners and promoters produce latinidad in order to profit from the dollars of non-Latina/o and middle- and upper-class Los Angeles west-siders.

The location of the club between the east side of L.A. and the west, but closer to the west, means that, rather than an east-sider–west-sider crisscross in which the patrons cross over into each others' spaces, the meeting is more like a temporary assembly of two crowds coming from opposite directions. Their subsequent dispersal at the end of the night is such that they rarely cross over into the other's geographical or economic territory.

The daytime class and racial tensions that prevail between the populations associated with each side of town challenge promoters to find ways to capitalize on the nighttime desires and considerations of each crowd. For example, some salsa aficionados from west-side clubs have indicated that they prefer to dance on their side of town rather than travel to east-side clubs. Libby, a white woman who had just finished a beginning-level salsa lesson at another club in Santa Monica, said that she had been to The Legend downtown and thought that the crowd was "too ghetto" and that the neighborhood was "too sketchy." She regarded the mostly upper- and middle-class crowd in Santa Monica as more "diverse" because more white people and Asians went there, which "balanced out" the Latinas/os. Responding to this kind of concern, the Copa Cabana West promoter engages in a balancing act to ameliorate west-sider fears of working-class east-siders by drawing in only the Latinas/os complicit with the exoticization of salsa and its detachment from associations with the Latinas/os perceived to constitute the working poor.

The Latina/o dancers from the east side do not need Copa Cabana West to reproduce a space for the social activity they already practice in locations such as Valentino's and The Legend, but Copa Cabana West needs them. The club economy thus provides opportunities for east-siders to network with celebrities and west-siders, chances to profit from the capital and connections of the rich and famous. The promoter acts as a broker, concocting (at least) two different campaigns in order to lure the east and west sides of town together under the roof—and onto the floor—of one business.

Some promoters are more successful than others at coaxing Latina/o bodies through club doors with dancer-friendly business strategies. The promoter at Copa Cabana West collects the phone numbers of those who produce a sequined latinidad and invites them to the club each week, offering to put them on the guest list. The phone call and the free admission for the sequined helps Copa Cabana West edge out other nightclubs in competition for the spectacle of L.A.'s flashiest salseras/os, which include dance team choreographers, teachers, and contest winners (i.e., the professional class of dancers). Such salseras/os thus do not directly contribute to club profits, as they usually do not pay to get in. In addition, they do not spend money on pricey, watered-down alcoholic beverages. West-side clients are quick to associate the consumption of alcohol by Latinas/os with immigrants from la limpieza. Guest-list salseras/os drink water instead, marking themselves not only as something other than workers of la limpieza but also as more than casual dancers.

The patrons not on the guest list, those who come to the clubs wishing to view the most over-the-top salsa moves, pay the bills. According to Mauricio, a former club employee, these are often the Anglo middle- or upper-class clientele from the west side, who hang out buying drink after drink at the bar because they are too intimidated to dance among the agile, acrobatic salseras/os. For white non-Latinas/os, a drink in the hand signifies the luxury of being able to afford it, as well as the privilege of operating outside of class-based associations that many Latinas/os encounter in the clubs.

A VIP entrance enables people willing and able to pay the forty-dollar entrance fee, instead of the standard twenty-five, to enter ahead of the long crowd trailing down the sidewalk. Copa Cabana West not only has a VIP front-door entrance, but it also has a VIP backdoor entrance. I think you have to be at least slightly famous, rather than simply rich, to warrant the security guard's walkie-talkie hailing of the manager, who then greets the backdoor guests. He leads them up the backdoor staircase into a closely monitored hallway that leads to a special vip section with tables and chairs, elevated and roped off from the standing-room-only crowd.

On a night I was waiting in line for about a half hour to get into Copa Cabana West, I observed a group of five Latinas/os emerge from a Honda Civic. One of the three men, the one with a sequined vest, high-fived the security guard and led the group to the vip entrance. Instead of paying forty dollars each, however, the sequined salsero and his carload of followers got in for free, since the salsero's name, Manny Valencia, was on the guest list.

Champion of another club's recent salsa competition, Manny Valencia had joined the ranks of the most recognizable salseros in town. The addition of his name to Copa Cabana West's no-pay guest list was a move on the club promoter's part to generate revenue. One of many Latinas/os who preferred the less expensive east-side clubs where all the best salseras/os went, Manny would change his routine when club promoters personally invited him to be a guest.

Flanked by the carefully selected members of his posse,[4] Manny performed his salsa celebrity status as he expertly hugged, back-slapped, high-fived, and secret-handshook club doormen and other salsero acquaintances. The small parade erratically slowed, stopped, and started with each greeting, jamming the easy flow of traffic up and down the stairs. By the time they entered the dance space, they had garnered the attention of a number of bystanders. Manny had arrived.

This easy entrance to Copa Cabana West belies the work it takes to maintain status among the elite dancers and sought-after club guests. If salseras/os like Manny want to maintain their noteworthy positions as highly skilled dancers, they must practice their moves ahead of time so they can execute them flawlessly during the weekly spectacle. In this way, the salseras/os provide the club with their surplus labor, as their dance skills draw financially stable spectators who generate the economic capital that keeps the clubs in business. Copa Cabana West does not directly exchange money with dancers for their expertise, outfits, bodily training, or rehearsal space. Salseras/os independently finance their own transformation into the sequined bodies—the bodies of the ones who dance "right"—that increase the club's profit. Practitioners sculpt themselves in accordance with the club's economy, an economy that profits from the conjunction of the salsa industry and latinidad. And the club's economy runs on the dominant practices of salsa in Los Angeles, involving the exoticization of dance practices and especially the fetishization of the dancing Latina body.

The high-caliber dancers on the Copa Cabana West guest list lure other Latinas/os and non-Latinas/os who aspire to attain guest-list status. This group includes students of guest-listers, those who dance salsa really well to cumbia music, and the ones who compete as amateurs in the club competitions. They actively seek the attention and expertise of the salseras/os, who have been known to pass out business cards along with offers of group and private lessons or choreographic services. Mauricio told me that, with a few exceptions, non-Latinas/os who take enough classes to become highly skilled are unlikely to make the guest list, since they are not the ones the west-siders and future salseras/os wish to pay to consume. But the earnest Latina/o members of the amateur crowd move up club hierarchies when the elite salseras/os recognize them by inviting them to dance or inviting them to join their parties at the vip guest entrance, where they can enter for free at the discretion of the salsero.

Unlike Frank the car salesman from Valentino's, the Copa Cabana West salseras/os who pass out business cards advertise only the business of salsa, even if they earn a daily wage elsewhere. The top Latina/o salseras/os attract students by never allowing themselves to be located outside of the salsa economy. In giving lessons, some earn an unpredictable income that supplements their daytime wages, and some earn enough to transform salsa instruction into full-time jobs. Many of the salseras/os, however, benefit primarily within the libidinal economy of the club by drawing on the temporary nighttime club capital. The club's acknowledgment of their selectively developed dance techniques (which they may have spent months practicing and paying private instructors for) yields them high status among their peers. Annual club-sponsored competitions also provide a stage for average dancers to become salseras/os and for salseras/os to stun the crowd with innovative choreographies, moves, and costumes.

Contest champions such as Manny move up club hierarchies through their guest-list entrances, staircase promenades, and contest appearances, but once at the top of the salsa hierarchy at Copa Cabana West, they have only a few ways to surpass the other top salseras/os in club capital. One way is to become a Hollywood celebrity, or at least to associate with one. Hollywood celebrities who aren't skilled dancers don't need to dance well; they already stand out in the crowd and are considered desirable dance partners. A person's out-of-club occupation allows him or her to supersede the highest salsera/o position within all elaborate ranking systems in place at the club. The outside-the-club position of celebrity is nearly the only one whose revelation is valued and valuable inside the club; the presence of known actors contributes to the libidinal mystique of the club. If patrons spoke of their less glamorous daytime lives, as Frank Flores did with me, they would break the spell that allows latinidad to remain seemingly disconnected from the political economy.

The market at Copa Cabana West cultivates a "crossover" fantasy space in which non-Latina/o patrons can consume a "passionate" latinidad and meet with the sequined on the less threatening west side. The east-side unsequined-by-day temporarily enjoy being the stars of the evening, desired and admired for their dance skills rather than avoided because of their (perceived) status as exploitable labor. Such dance liaisons "unite" patrons across the differences of race, class, and sides of town that segregate them by day, creating an apparent "unity through exoticization."

La Misma Historia, Except for the Details at Las Feliz Edades

"Nicaragua, Guatemala, Honduras, Méééééxicooooo!!!!" called the deejay at Las Feliz Edades, pulling these nations together through the microphone repeatedly throughout the evening. He did not summon Peru, Chile, Colombia, Venezuela, Ecuador, Puerto Rico, or Cuba into his conceptualization of latinidad for the crowd. By grouping together a particular set of nations, he restricted the constituents of latinidad to the region-specific area of Mexico and Central America. This move grouped together the people of Mexico and Central American nations in the United States while differentiating them from the Caribbeanesque latinidad manufactured in clubs like Copa Cabana West. In contrast to patrons at Copa Cabana West, patrons of Las Feliz Edades did not attempt to deterritorialize latinidad from Mexico and Central America.

A club economy that attracts migrants from Mexico and Central America, Las Feliz Edades draws a different kind of "crossover" crowd than does Copa Cabana West. The crossover crowd at Las Feliz Edades consists primarily of patrons who have recently crossed national borders and who negotiate their nighttime corporealities in dialogue with their often unstable daytime positionings. Many patrons I have spoken with at Las Feliz Edades seem to have an ambivalent relationship to living in the United States and are unhappy with the way that they are viewed as "illegal," expendable labor in Los Angeles.

Las Feliz Edades offers them a space in which to socialize and form networks of support without exposing them to the kinds of surveillance and segregation practiced in clubs like The Legend or Chuck's Grill. Las Feliz Edades emerges as a sort of refuge from the violence directed at the undocumented, allowing them to socialize almost invisibly. Even the club's blinking lights on Sunset Boulevard in Silver Lake do not capture the attention of Americans, who seem to have only rarely heard of Las Feliz Edades.

Brokers of the salsa industry consider Las Feliz Edades an example of what salsa clubs are not. Las Feliz Edades does not produce L.A. salsa and sequined latinidad and does not attract speakers of English; it only comfortably consumes the latinidad it does produce. The waitresses, deejays, emcees, and patrons speak Spanish and do not cater to an English-speaking clientele. Without the brokers to lure in a wealthier class of Americans or the professional class of Latinas/os in attendance to act as translators between non-Latinas/os and the migrant class, Las Feliz Edades remains a pocket of Mexican- and Central-Americanness within Los Angeles. If, as Willie Colón (1999) writes, salsa "has embraced" everything that is "relevant," those who cannot pass through the doors of The Legend or make it on the guest list of Copa Cabana West seem to be irrelevant to the salsa industry. Those whom the salsa industry rejects are largely the same dancers that Las Feliz Edades welcomes night after night.

Patrons of Las Feliz Edades go to "the club," not "the salsa club," and they do not refer to themselves as salsa dancers or even dancers. They go to the club to socialize, which includes, but is not limited to, talking, drinking, flirting, and dancing. No genre of music outweighs another in terms of airtime, although younger dancers have begun to pack the floor when a reggaetón set is played. Unlike Copa Cabana West and The Legend, the Las Feliz Edades economy does not depend on the centralization of salsa. For L.A.-style salsa dancers who have limited their training to salsa, the variety of music genres at Las Feliz Edades would be difficult to keep track of, especially without any club contests to standardize danced interpretations.

Las Feliz Edades patrons regard the singular focus on the minutiae of dance techniques an Americanized obsession. Some members of the crowd have articulated their dismay over the Latinas/os who perform sequined latinidad—the latinidad they link to American fantasies of Latinas/os. In response, they dissociate themselves from those who practice L.A. salsa and criticize them for taking on U.S. values, including the value of upward mobility for the individual at the expense of others.

Lorenzo, an immigrant from El Salvador, explained to me one night that at Feliz Edades, the people are more respectful of one another. They do not go to the club to compete with each other based on local standards of good dancing or to cover up the unpleasant, sad, and sometimes violent memories and events of daily life. Rather, as I witnessed one night, men pour salt and squeeze lime into their Coronas in between dances and vividly recount the horror of crossing the border, a walk across the desert, the death of family members, and the anguish of leaving others behind. They thus constitute latinidad in relation to specific out-of-club places and displacements in the political economy rather than blurring them with quick, slick salsa moves. Such a nighttime articulation of latinidad, however fleeting, contrasts with the latinidad homogenized as exotic in the Hollywood Industry.

The first night I went to Las Feliz Edades, I went alone. As the petite women in halter tops, miniskirts, fishnets, and stilettos streamed into the club from the parking lot, I immediately realized that I was going to stand out. At the salsa clubs, I tended to get lost in the crowd, but here I had the feeling that things would go differently. Not only did my body look entirely white American (freckled, pale, and tall) in comparison to most of the other clients, but my Fashion of Echo Park pants, black boots, and long-sleeved lacy dress were out of place; as a woman, even on a cold and rainy December night, I was wearing too much.

I paid the thirteen dollars to get in, just missing the "mujeres gratis" before-10 deadline. As I walked up the stairs of red carpet into the club, the deejay called out over the music, "Guatemala! Nicaragua! Honduras! Méxicooooooo!" People packed the dance floor, working out some reggaetón moves,[5] and others filled the tables that circled the floor and lined the bar area. On the other side of the room, away from the dance floor and the bar, a small group celebrating a birthday had pulled together several round tables and tied balloons to the back of one of the chairs. Except for the birthday partiers and a few couples here and there, not many people filled this section.

In salsa clubs, empty tables and chairs are hard to come by, and when they are available, they are reserved for vip clients. But people at clubs like The Legend had made it clear to me that Las Feliz Edades was not a salsa club, so I suppose I should not have expected things to be the same. "It's where the Central American and Mexican immigrants go," they said. Further distinguishing these spaces, they said, "They don't really dance salsa there. They care more about drinking and getting laid than dancing." They suggested that salseras/os at The Legend had a specialized dance knowledge that the ones at Las Feliz Edades lacked, and that migrants from Central America and Mexico danced "wrong." Their disdain created distance between the self-proclaimed serious salseras/os at The Legend, who identify up in relation to their class and ethnonational status, and the socializers at Las Feliz Edades.

My own observations at Las Feliz Edades would corroborate not the derision of the salseras/os but some of the content of their statements. Central American and Mexican migrants did appear to make up the majority of the crowd: 90 percent, Ignacio estimated later that night. In contrast to the dominance of salsa music played in clubs like Copa Cabana West and The Legend, salsa was no more special than any other genre of music at this club. The mix of music resonated with the music and dance pasts of the different clusters of migrants, who were primarily from Mexico, Honduras, Nicaragua, Guatemala, and El Salvador. While some of the urban nightclubs in each of these nations play salsa, the clients at Las Feliz Edades told me that Mexican and Central American clubs do not limit the rhythmic repertoire exclusively to salsa.

At Las Feliz Edades they did dance salsa, and also merengue, pachanga, punta, reggaetón, and cumbia. What they cared about more, beer, sex, or dancing, I cannot say, but I can tell you what I think they cared about most. I can tell you about how I socialized for almost four hours at two little tables with five men who each shared with me things that mattered to them. Or at least they shared things they thought would matter to me. Even though we sat side by side, they had to shout out their stories that were almost drowned out by the music.

Before I met Ignacio and the others, I had wound my way through the crowd, walking back and forth across the room, searching for the best place to observe. The empty tables were too far away from the dancing, and I paused behind a wall of men who were watching the dance floor. The manager, who must have noticed that I was not one of the regulars, came over and asked if I had come solita and wanted a place to sit. He offered to seat me at a table of puras mujeres, which I happily accepted, touched by his thoughtfulness. At no club I have attended is it a practice to seat the guests. Others had come into the club after me and seated themselves, so my case may have been an exception. It crossed my mind that I could interpret his gesture as a disciplinary measure, meant to round up and contain all the women roaming about unaccompanied by men. Even if that were true, the measure doubled as the perfect opportunity to do what I hoped to do that night: talk with some of the women.

But things didn't go exactly according to my hopes. Moments later he returned to suggest an alternate scenario. His good friend Lorenzo was there and had invited me to join his table, and that was where I also met Humberto, Manuel, Jorge, and Ignacio. Lorenzo, who was about forty, introduced me to the other guys, all twenty-three. This happened mostly through nods and smiles since we couldn't hear much above the music. The minute I sat down, Jorge pulled the last beer from the bucket, placed it in front of me, and we all held our bottles up to toast.

Sitting right across from me, Lorenzo was curious about what I was doing at this club. When I told him I was doing research on salsa clubs and latinidad in Los Angeles, he described it as a very respectable place, the kind where, when it was crowded, the manager found you a place to sit at a table. Affirming the significance of the manager's earlier gesture, he went on to say that this was one way that Las Feliz Edades was unlike salsa clubs like The Legend downtown, where the few tables fill up early and too many people are left wandering around, without any place to settle. At those clubs, he said, people competed for space, but at Las Feliz Edades people offer to share the space, squeezing closer together to accommodate one another.

As I spoke with him, I realized that what Lorenzo thought were respectful practices were in opposition to the practices that Latinas/os like the ones in salsa clubs had taken on in the United States. The only one at the tables who had ever been to The Legend or Copa Cabana West, he considered those clubs to be harsh places where people skipped social formalities and did not take time to socialize with or get to know each other. Rather, in his opinion, they used each other for their dance skills. The kind of graciousness Lorenzo attributed to the patrons of Las Feliz Edades accompanied rather than covered up discussions of the violence in their everyday lives and memories; at Copa Cabana West and The Legend, patrons did not speak directly about their past and present struggles but rather stylized violence through their dance moves.

At Las Feliz Edades, Lorenzo stood out from the rest of the men at the table because he expressed the importance of keeping quiet his relatively successful position in daily life. An immigrant from El Salvador, a local restaurant owner, and almost twice the age of the others in the group, Lorenzo said he did very well financially but didn't ever tell the other guys that because he wanted them to think he was one of them. I suspected that they knew. Lorenzo was the one who paid for the buckets filled with ice-packed Coronas that kept coming all night. All the men held Lorenzo in high esteem. Even if he had not mentioned his success in business, his display of generosity earned him club capital. Like Manny, Lorenzo occupied a high position within the club hierarchy, but he did so even as he overtly recognized other patrons' experiences of migration and displacement. As a migrant who came to the United States as a young man, he had successfully crossed over and through multiple economies without becoming a salsero.

Jorge, also from El Salvador, was a bit intoxicated. He cut into my chat with Lorenzo to ask about my salsa project and to invite me to dance. "I'm a dance teacher," he explained, hoping to lure me to the floor. He wondered if I knew how to dance, and I mentioned that I would love to dance cumbia. It turned out that his favorites were merengue, salsa, and reggaetón, and even though I said we could dance to one of those instead, he waited for the next cumbia set before leading me out to dance. Like some of the other couples around us who had incorporated kissing and groping into their dance techniques, Jorge was more interested in making moves on me than in keeping track of the rhythm of the music; while he pulled me closer, I gently lodged an elbow between us.

When the song ended, I thanked Jorge for the dance, and we headed back to the table. I picked up my conversation with Lorenzo, hoping to stave off any misunderstandings with Jorge. But Jorge kept interrupting to shake my hand, saying, "Soy Jorge. Mucho gusto." He looked to Lorenzo and said, "You probably don't even know his name."

"Lorenzo," I answered.

"He probably doesn't even know your name then," Jorge said. Lorenzo did. As Lorenzo began telling me that he grew up with his father and never knew his mother, Jorge stood up next to him, yelling and gesturing toward me with his hands. Though I did not hear every word, I think he said, "I was the one who offered her a beer. . . . I am the one who invited her to dance!" And then he walked off. I had been in the club for only a half hour before this essentially one-sided altercation occurred over who had a more legitimate claim on me.

I tried to ask about Jorge and apologize for my part in the incident, but none of the guys would connect his outburst to me. They said things like, "This happens with Jorge every week" and "Don't worry. It wasn't you" and "He drinks a little too much and gets angry." Ignacio had followed Jorge to check on him and returned without him; he had left the club. Although nothing was scandalous about the romantic hookups that the club economy allowed for, Jorge's friends recognized that his behavior toward me, a woman who had been entrusted to their care, had been inappropriate and they had carefully tried to shield me from the incident. Manuel tipped my half-empty Corona upside-down in the new bucket of beer and set an ice-cold full one in front of me. He held up his own beer above the center of the table, and we all clinked our bottles together. When I first learned that Jorge had left, I thought that maybe it was time to check up on the table of puras mujeres, but as we toasted one another I decided to stay.

After Jorge's dramatic exit, each of the other guys broke from their conversations at their end of the table and rotated into the empty spot next to me. My presence in the club and at their table bewildered them, and asking question after question they tried to get me to explain what I was doing there without making me feel unwelcome. Americans don't really come here, they said. Especially an American woman. Alone. Who ends up at a table with men she does not know.

Otra cerveza? I answered all of these questions five different times, explaining my project to each one in turn.

While patrons at Copa Cabana West and The Legend would excitedly speak for long intervals about dance practices when I asked them their views on salsa, at Las Feliz Edades my questions about salsa did not generate much conversation. Had they ever been to The Legend? What did they think about L.A. salsa? Neither The Legend nor L.A. salsa held meaning for anyone but Lorenzo, who had been to several other clubs in Los Angeles. Ignacio told me that if I wanted to know more about salsa, I should talk to the good salsa dancers, the ones from Cuba, Puerto Rico, and Venezuela. "Van a otros sitios," he said, but did not have a name for any of these places. "Bailamos salsa también, pero no con tantos movimientos."[6]

When salsa music blasted through the speakers, the people on the dance floor continued dancing, switching rhythms and maintaining a laid-back energy. One guy in a gray blazer strutted alone at the edge of the dance floor, crossing his legs and untwisting them into spins like Michael Jackson. No one seemed to pay any attention to him. Eventually he worked his way to finding a dance partner. I had seen the woman he had chosen dancing earlier—she had been very comfortable and versatile on the dance floor—but now she hesitated, not sure what to do when her partner broke off into an extended solo.

I wondered if this smooth dancer also attended The Legend, where men told me that they'd select a dance partner based on the quality of her moves or shoes. Fernando, a Mexicano salsero at The Legend, explained to me once that not all the people there were serious dancers, so he would ask a woman to dance only after he had assessed her shoes. If she wore the kind of dance shoes made for professional dancers, ones with low heels with suede bottoms, rather than high-heeled street shoes, then he would consider asking her to dance. He evaluated the rest of her clothing too, to be sure that she would be able to move comfortably; pants or loose skirts, in his view, were "clothes that let you move." He would not ask a woman in a tight skirt and spiky high heels, signs that she cared more about attracting men for socializing and sex than dancing. The men who asked these kinds of women to dance, he said, were interested only in the status that comes from dancing with a sexy woman or in having sex with her. "But," he added, "if she can dance, sexiness is a plus."

Fernando had made a great effort to distance himself from the people and practices that he specifically linked to the working-class immigrants of Las Feliz

Edades. The guys I sat with at Las Feliz Edades did not articulate or enact such an extensive selection process. And, though I can't be absolutely certain about this, none of the women dancing was wearing shoes with suede soles. Instead they wore street shoes or boots, with and without stiletto heels, to accompany their jeans, miniskirts, dresses, halters, and tank tops. While the guy in the gray blazer had scoped out his potential partner by first watching her dance, the guys I sat with went about it in a more neighborly fashion, asking me and the women at the table next to us to be their partners. In fact at the same time that they connected with the women at the next table, the solitary guy at the women's table invited me out to the floor.

As we danced salsa at Las Feliz Edades, I noticed that neither my partner nor many of the others danced consistently on the beat or to a shared beat. The dancing was much more casual than at The Legend or Copa Cabana West. No one was ruffled by those who interchanged the one-two shuffle of merengue with salsa's triple-step pause. Even when two partners slipped in and out of time with each other, they did not complain. I realized that at Las Feliz Edades, it would be disrespectful to correct someone's dancing or to take up too much space in order to execute maneuvers that required sudden horizontal and diagonal charges. Instead partners kept their steps small and adjusted to each other's irregular weight shifts.

At Copa Cabana West and The Legend, dancers typically separate practices that connote respeto from the competitive drive to move up nightly social hierarchies. If a woman does not accurately follow the lead and does not respond to the quick timing of a serious salsero, she is subject to correction or even dismissal. Couples at salsa clubs often collide with adjacent dancers (and sometimes musicians, waiters, and spectators) as elbows strike, heels stab, and heads crash at relatively high velocities. At Las Feliz Edades, in contrast, contact with other couples—the unintentional but unavoidable rubbing of backs, brushing of shoulders, and bumping of butts—is less physically disastrous and not regarded as invasive.

The patrons at Las Feliz Edades demonstrate a willingness to inhabit the limited space together by decreasing the size of their movements rather than carving out larger areas for themselves with acrobatic moves like dips, jumps, and lifts. At Las Feliz Edades, such movements, which physically force surrounding dancers to relinquish the space around them, would be signs of disrespect.[7] Dancers at Las Feliz Edades tend to blend into one another so that few bodies stand out from the group. In contrast, the L.A. salseras/os at The Legend and Copa Cabana West compete for space on the floor in which to perform an exoticized latinidad. And they move up the club hierarchy by marking themselves as individuals with the "right" skills and the right to take up space, as Manny Valencia did with his grand entrance.

The willingness of dancers at Las Feliz Edades to absorb the overlapping of bodies is a practice that falls under the rubric of Lorenzo's description of respeto.[8] I interpret this deep regard for respeto as the kind of generosity formed when one has experienced violence and grief through acts of migration. If dancing on the crowded floor gets dancers elbowed or stepped on, their casual acceptance also gestures to a desire to become absorbed into the crowd. As such, the crowd cradles those dancing within it. A bump between bodies might ripple through the crowd and dissipate, but in the wake of this ripple the connection between the bodies dancing so closely together strengthens.

After returning to our table from the dance floor that night at Las Feliz Edades, Ignacio shifted into the spot next to me to talk not about dancing but about what had relevance for him. I learned that he worked for a tropical fish company that sold saltwater fish to pet store clients. Unlike the others, Ignacio spoke English, because, he said, he had been in the United States since he was fifteen. He had gone to school here. His dad had left Mexico to live in California when Ignacio was very young and died soon after he arrived. His mother died in Mexico when he was fourteen, leaving him an orphan in Mexico.

As he told me the details of his teenage years, the band's trumpet player began tooting into the microphone to accompany the deejay's merengue. Ignacio raised his voice almost to a scream so that I could hear him. After his mother died, he said, he had no one to take care of him except a sister who lived in Los Angeles. He moved up here to live with her and go to high school, but the transition to the new school and to the United States was tough. He said, "We always thought how great it would be to live in the United States, but they never tell you how hard it is to come here. The ones who leave Mexico and go back to visit . . . they don't talk about the racism, or the language barriers, or the conflicts with other Latinos over culture and even how we speak Spanish differently. We had so many fights in school." He shared with me details of the conflicts among Latinos. In the very next breath he continued, "Pero mira, somos dos Mexicanos, dos Salvadoreños, y un Nicaraguense, todos en la misma mesa, amigos. Todos somos Latinos."[9]

Humberto, from Nicaragua, rotated into the chair beside me after Ignacio finished. He had attended college for a little while in Nicaragua, studying marine biology, but he left because of the poor economy and the few job opportunities. He had been in the United States for only three months. He migrated on his own, without legal documentation, traveling up through Mexico for a month, and then walking for six days from Nogales into the United States. "If I had money to pay someone to help me," he told me, "it would have only taken two days."

He said that, in general, Mexico is more desperate than Nicaragua, since the economy there is so much worse. "There are thieves everywhere," he said. On his way north he was robbed a couple of times. Once, someone held a gun to his head just to steal his belt, all that he had had left of value. Now he lived and worked as a mechanic in Inglewood, and although he lived in a city bordering the ocean, his dream of becoming a marine biologist was less sustainable in the United States than it had been in Nicaragua.

He came to Las Feliz Edades every Saturday night with this group of friends who also lived in Inglewood. Having been in L.A. only a short time and without relatives to help smooth his transition, Humberto especially valued his friendships with the guys at his table. Without transportation of his own, he was included in the group's carpool to the club. Although he could not have overheard Ignacio's conversation with me, he repeated what Ignacio had said, turning it into a kind of mantra: "Somos dos Mexicanos, dos Salvadoreños, y un Nicaraguense, todos en la misma mesa. Tenemos la misma cultura latina, el mismo idioma."[10] He delivered these lines as if he barely believed them, as if he had to keep saying them or else the fragile bond among them would evaporate.

He seemed to know the irony of his words, though. In each of the countries he listed, the men at the table had been accustomed to identifying themselves against each other in terms of their different nationalities. In Mexico, El Salvador, and Nicaragua, they had long-standing, local understandings of their relationships to the people of other nations in the region. In the United States, however, Humberto and the others tried to make sense of finding themselves socializing together as Mexicanos and Centroamericanos. A Los Angeles–based latinidad allowed him to reimagine his corporeality in conjunction with the men at his table and in relation to Latinas/os of other regions as well as non-Latinas/os in the United States. He employed the concept of latinidad to explain the strangeness of suddenly being identified by the club economy as belonging to a group of people with such different histories, who now shared a similar displacement and social space in the United States.

When I had spoken with all the guys at the table, including Manuel, a Mexicano who worked at the same company as Ignacio ("If you want freshwater fish, I'm your guy"), Ignacio maneuvered his way back over to me. He asked if I had heard the same story over and over again throughout the course of my research, as well as at their table that night. He followed up by saying, "Cada uno, cada lugar tiene sus propios detalles, pero siempre es la misma historia."[11] At Las Feliz Edades the patrons connected with each other through their memories of the places from which they had migrated, but with neither nostalgia nor ambivalence. Ignacio marked his ties to Mexico by reference to his memories of the absence and death of his parents. Yet he no longer had family there—no one left there to belong to—and he never wanted to go back. The sense of belonging he ascribed to that place, however, grounded his affiliations with the other trans-status migrants in the club.

What bound them together at this club, he summarized, was that they had left behind the problems they faced in Latin America to come to the United States, looking for the "opportunities and freedom" that they would never have had had they not come to this country. What he liked about the United States, he said, was the idea that "anyone can get a college education," even though such an opportunity had never been among the possibilities available to him. Although he had had difficulty sustaining a livelihood in Los Angeles, his options in Mexico might have been more determined, predictable, and, most important, limited to the networks already established by his family. While his invocation of the equal opportunities promised by the American Dream contradicted an earlier expression of disillusionment with the racism prevalent in the United States, he nevertheless stressed the possibility of success, pointing to Humberto's unexpected job opportunity as a mechanic, a job for which he had no previously developed skills. In his own case, the knowledge he developed as a student of marine biology had not gained him access to anything other than the low-wage positions in la limpieza, positions that were reserved for the undocumented.

The Las Feliz Edades economy created a space in which patrons socially conceptualized their relationships to each other and to latinidad. The space virtually lacked any sign of the American or Americanized Latina/o L.A. salseras/os that were integral to the mixed space of The Legend. Las Feliz Edades thus allowed a social intimacy to emerge on and off the dance floor among the most recent immigrants, the ones most vulnerable to anti-immigrant violence and exploitation in the United States.

The desires of Ignacio and Humberto to unify the men at the table, men they had to compete with for limited resources outside the club, persisted despite the political and economic stakes of their differences. This made evident the fact that, amid the socializing, an unsequined, unstylized concept of unity informed latinidad, as patrons learned from one another how to survive, where to live, where to find jobs, and how to send money back home to relatives. As Ignacio explained, the divisions among Latinas/os can impede their survival in the United States. Disunity can mean death.

Profiting from Latinidad at The Legend

The Legend—on its website, on a phone recording, and at the doorway—announces the requirements one must meet in order to access the club economy:

> No baggy clothing, no corduroys, khakis, overalls, carpenter pants, painter pants, flannel shirts, white t-shirts, tank tops, shorts, athletic wear. No industrial or hiking boots. No athletic shoes or sandals. No baseball caps, skull caps, or bandanas. No vests or jackets with t-shirts. Fashionable jeans only (no ripped jeans). Men are required to wear collared shirts.

In short, you will not get through the door if you do not make an effort to look like a salsera/o. The detailed list rejects those who look too much like a member of a gang or a worker from la limpieza; this exclusion thus dovetails with practices that reject the "wrong" kind of latinidad at Copa Cabana West.

West-siders new to salsa, not accustomed to being denied access to places because of their clothing, can be outraged at the seemingly arbitrary rules when they have been turned away. Willow, a UCLA student I knew who had tried to gain entrance, was barred from entry because she was wearing jazz shoes, the kind used in practice sessions and classes. Considered "athletic" shoes, her footwear revealed her familiarity with dancing in a studio and also her unfamiliarity—or nonidentification—with salsera dress codes. Salseras take exorbitant care to distance themselves from the labor of dance training that they undertake outside the club. Once they step inside the club, they take the libidinal stage, and studio shoes are not part of the costume. If one cannot sport an acceptable outfit, one is disqualified from the next two stages of entry: the metal detector and the cashier.

Much like Valentino's and Chuck's Grill, The Legend welcomes and profits from the patronage of as many people along the salsa hierarchy as possible;

patrons just have to be able to make it into the club. The largest salsa dance venue in Los Angeles, The Legend actively manufactures L.A. salseras/os. The club provides weekly classes and, most important, houses an annual "world" salsa competition. Judged by figures prominent in the local salsa context, the contest determines who has most convincingly mastered sequined latinidad.

Architecturally the space supports the nuanced hierarchical divisions among the sequined and the unsequined. As I leaned on the railing overlooking the dance floor one night, I observed the way the dancers spatialized themselves in the club. From my vantage point, I could most easily view the flawlessly sequined L.A. salseras/os who occupied the highest positions on the salsa hierarchy: the teachers, contest winners, and couples and teams who performed at salsa congresses. Nearest the band and still on the uplifted stage, they danced until the song came to an end. The bodies of the sequined women suddenly disappeared, as their partners swept them into low dips for the big finish. The sequined L.A. salsa couples at The Legend frequently integrated speedy, gymnastic lifts, dips, and turns—a set of techniques that blurred their associations with the wrong kind of latinidad. These were the high-level dancers that often made the guest list at Copa Cabana West.

One step down from this upper stage danced the newer or less skilled L.A. salseras/os, dancers with solid technique who occasionally missed crucial opportunities to separate themselves from the unsequined through timing. The dancers on these first two tiers refer to themselves as salseras/os who go to the salsa club to dance, not socialize. Off the stage and on the general floor danced everybody else: the unsequined with their socializing tendencies. Beyond the dance floor, socializers packed the bar area and the tables, occasionally stepping out to dance on the floor farthest from the band.

Some of the patrons at The Legend fit the criteria of the patrons at Las Feliz Edades. They may also be from Mexico or Central America, but instead of aiming to forge bonds based on shared experiences of migration in a noncompetitive social space, they pursue networks and friendships in a salsa economy that commodifies sequined latinidad. Their commitment to sequined latinidad may allow them to move up The Legend's salsa hierarchy, but their social status in the club's economy may not correspond to their social class outside the club. Like the migrant patrons at Las Feliz Edades, patrons at The Legend also forge networks with each other, but the broader spectrum of social classes at The Legend increases the chances of interactions across class differences.

A familiarity, friendship, or romance might determine whether a woman will be someone's maid or will be able to hire her own maid. In this way, going to the salsa club is like going to the casino: nothing is guaranteed except the possibility of meeting someone who might set one up with a job, a place to live, transportation, a cell phone, a set of friends, sex, a free drink, or a dance that places you higher in the salsa hierarchy. But good fortune is unpredictable: you might be offered a job but have no transportation, encounter a potential lover only to discover she has picked your pocket, or get a discount through a friend at a department store but have no income because your teaching certificate from Mexico City is not valid in Los Angeles.

With uneven opportunities and uncertain acquaintances, potential profits can get mismatched and rarely fulfill all of a person's desires for latinidad in the libidinal and political economies. As much as the workers of la limpieza do not want to be criminalized or seen as abject by wealthier west-siders, the upper classes do not wish to recognize the astounding social and economic gaps among the patrons. By making it into The Legend, the workers of la limpieza increase their probability of making connections with the fully loaded patrons by performing sequined latinidad and masking class differences. The wealthier patrons, often seen as west-siders who desire to hook up with these sequined dancers, cooperate by misrecognizing their mechanic and nanny and by allowing deeper understandings of the ways they contribute to the exploitation of latinidad to bounce off the shimmery sequins.

The economy at The Legend especially values patronage from a small sector of the unsequined: the upper-middle- and middle-class Latinas/os, either migrants or longtime U.S. citizens, hailing from New York, Puerto Rico, and South America as well as Mexico and Central America. They are doctors, business owners, university professors, scientists, engineers, university students, accountants, museum curators, nurses, and teachers. Often the sole member of their working-class family to attend university, they also search for networks of stability to help anchor them within their new places. They too can be considered trans-status corporeals, but unlike many migrant Latinas/os they have become socialized within U.S. educational institutions where English is the language of instruction. When they cross national borders, it is usually with a valid visa for business, education, or vacation. These factors, along with U.S. citizenship, have increased but not guaranteed their chances of upward mobility. Like many of the unsequined migrants, the unsequined nonmigrant Latinas/os have crossed a border—not a national border but a socioeconomic one.

As Latinas/os who have succeeded within the U.S. economy, they embody neither the stereotype of the exotic Latina/o nor that of the poverty-stricken criminalized immigrant Latina/o. With no legitimate category to account for their identification with latinidad within U.S. frameworks of class-based racialization, they often find that, as socioeconomically successful Latinas/os, they have become subsumed into the generalized category of American. Attending salsa spaces such as the restaurant side of Chuck's Grill or off-stage sections at The Legend—spaces that do not attract the highly trained L.A. salseras/os—they thus challenge their erasure under conceptualizations of latinidad.

Inside the club they eschew practices of L.A. salsa and sequined latinidad and instead associate themselves with other socializers: their Latina/o and non-Latina/o class peers as well as working-class Latinas/os. Shuttling between the two classes, they act as translators, mediators, guides, and liaisons, linking working-class Latinas/os and the non-Latinos desiring to access a more "authentic," rather than sequined, latinidad.

Brought together by their scorn for L.A. salsa practices, both classes of the unsequined become allies in their refusal to conform to the flashy "Americanizing" aesthetics. The shuttlers at The Legend often characterize L.A. salsa as "tacky," "cheesy," "Hollywood," "overly commodified," and "inauthentic," class-based characterizations that point to their own aversion for what might be seen as lower-middle-class tastes. The desire of the more economically successful unsequined to affiliate with the working-class migrant socializers in spaces not occupied by L.A. salseras/os disrupts the presumption that Latinas/os will become "assimilated" through eventual identification with a white Americanness. So too does it disrupt the assumption that an identification with Americanness is part of an upward, linear progression from working class to upper class, from untrained provincial to "street-trained" urbanite, from unsequined to sequined.

The upper-middle- and middle-class Latinas/os do not need to perform sequined latinidad in order to mark themselves as upwardly mobile in the U.S. economy because they already are successful outside the club. At The Legend, however, they attempt to mask their superior class positions by distancing themselves from the L.A. salseras/os, the ones considered upwardly mobile in the club's libidinal economy.

Although they break with The Legend's cultivation of sequined latinidad, their masking of their class positions contributes to the appearance that latinidad is separate from capitalism and class inequities. Outside the club the upwardly mobile Latinas/os have much less leeway to break with the rules of the political economy if they want to maintain their status in the white-collar, professional class. Inside the club their affiliation with what Libby, the white woman I met at Copa Cabana West who had disdain for The Legend, called the "sketchy" crowd helps to produce latinidad as more accessible to tentative west-siders, making unsequined latinidad less "ghetto" and sequined latinidad more desirable.

Another, even smaller group of upwardly mobile Latinas/os at The Legend are the ones who act as brokers. They not only attend the clubs, but they also own and manage them. They judge local salsa competitions, promote salsa events, and support sequined L.A. salsa couples at salsa congresses. The brokers fashion salsa to be consumed by non-Latinas/os and Latinas/os. This group has the authority to exoticize salsa and simultaneously whiten salsa with ballroom considerations, such as line and extension, all the while becoming more and more savvy about the aspects of latinidad that local and global markets desire. They recognize success among themselves when they attract Latina/o and non-Latina/o Hollywood celebrities to their clubs and events or when salseras/os they have molded become part of Hollywood productions, a sign that salsa has become more associated with the alluring bodies of a sequined latinidad than with the abject bodies of la limpieza.

The sequined salseros/as, socializers, shuttlers, and brokers learn to navigate the "invisibilized" class disparities within the social parameters of the libidinal club economy at places like The Legend. Nightclubs that foster a clientele marked by their class disparities, however masked, along with fantasies of consuming exoticized latinidad, also foster the potential success of another class of "invisible" people: pickpockets. Unlike the salseras/os who hone their ability to be recognized by as many people as possible, this relatively unknown group of improvisers forgoes nightly status recognition in favor of being undetected by all but unsuspecting newcomers from the west side. They maximize their dollar profits by exploiting west-sider desires for sequined latinidad. And they do so by performing their own elaborate improvisation sequences: pick up, pick out, pass off, pilfer, and replace.

The biggest scam I heard about in the clubs went something like this:

Dulce spotted the rubber-soled shoes the moment the wayward west-sider stepped onto the dance floor at 8 o'clock that evening for the dance lesson. Alone and a little bit nervous, he pretended that he was enjoying trying to figure out the rhythm as he paired up with women also taking the lesson. Dulce noticed that, one by one, the women in the class seem relieved when the instructor told them to change partners and they got to move on to more relaxed partners.

When the lights dimmed and the lesson came to a close, the self-conscious neophyte considered his options: leave before it gets any worse or have a drink to loosen up. Dulce, dressed in fishnets and hoop earrings, slid out of the booth in which she had been sitting and approached the newcomer for the first step in her dance: pick up.

She casually started a conversation with the man, who by now was standing at the bar, tossing back the last of a scotch. He believed that he was seducing her just as she was seducing him. When he asked her to dance, she accepted, complimenting his style and ignoring the squeak of his shoes and the abruptness of his leads. Flatter, beguile, move closer: those were her next moves. Move close enough to reach into his pocket and pick out his wallet and keys without his noticing.

Dulce excused herself to go to the bathroom and then passed the loot to the silent and most invisible third partner in the dance, her boyfriend, Osvaldo. He wasted no time casually heading for the parking lot and racing to the address on the driver's license nestled in the unsuspecting west-sider's wallet. He let himself in with the keys, pilfered the apartment, and loaded the car's trunk: vcr, dvd player, tv, stereo.

When Osvaldo returned to the club, he returned the wallet and keys to Dulce, who replaced them into the pockets of the man who could hardly believe that his salsa club fantasies were coming true. When he asked her to come home with him, she said maybe next time; her brother was there and would not allow it. That's when Osvaldo cut in and twirled Dulce expertly as they danced out the door to drive away with the loot. The abandoned west-sider pulled a twenty out of his wallet to buy another scotch at the bar. End improvisation.

Dulce, Osvaldo, and a number of eager west-siders executed this dance as a trio. The scam worked well enough for Dulce and Osvaldo for a while, increasing their income periodically, yet without bumping them up to the middle class. But when they began to attract too much attention with their skillful, twirling, parting moves, they were unable to maintain the low profile necessary for the pickpocket dance. Instead of continuing, they ditched their aliases, invested their pawn-shop money in private lessons, and transformed themselves into world-renowned, financially successful salsa teachers, performers, and choreographers. They became true players in the global salsa congress network.

Ditch, invest, transform. The libidinal and political economies intersected in the actions and transformations of Dulce and Osvaldo, who successfully turned themselves into the kind of exotic Latinas/os desired within the economies inside as well as outside the club. They are among the very few financed by promoters as figureheads of the salsa economy, having severed their current high-profile salsa celebrity status from their working-class past as underground thieves. Whether or not this scam story is true, its occasional circulation in the club demonstrates that salseras/os develop a sophisticated knowledge of the ways that latinidad gets marketed, produced, and consumed in both the libidinal and political economies.

Salsa economies that produce sequined corporealities find multiple ways to profit from latinidad. Copa Cabana West lures in highly trained L.A.-style salsa-dancing east-siders to create a heightened Hollywood performance that feeds the desires and garners the dollars of west-side clientele. The Legend manufactures L.A. salseras/os from an incredible mix of patrons who do not necessarily start out as skilled dancers but who must dissociate themselves from la limpieza and a criminalized latinidad in order to meet the minimum requirements for entry. Las Feliz Edades and its patrons do not cooperate with the economies of sequined latinidad that attempt to separate the political from the libidinal. Instead the patrons articulate a latinidad held together by their experiences of migration, displacement, and experiences of everyday life that ground their social relationships.

Club economies based on sequined latinidad, however, correlate with globalization's erasure of the politics, economics, and specificities of place. The sequined salsa economies obscure the interconnections between club practices and the unequal accumulation of capital. Yet within the salsa clubs, patrons occasionally disrupt the economies of sequined latinidad and call attention to their ties to other places and practices. For example, Frank Flores, the sales and leasing consultant, conjured up images of himself bound by the timelines, freeway commutes, and desires related to the economy of his daily life. The shuttlers I observed rebuffed L.A. salsa and socialized with the unsequined at the bottom of the club hierarchies. At The Legend, the Chicana university student Sarita told me that the last time she had attended the club, the deejay surprised the crowd by playing a rare punta:

> In little pockets across the club, some dancers, including some of the flashy salseras and salseros, broke out with these amazing, beautiful punta moves. They were smiling and shouting out to each other, happy to recognize that they weren't the only ones who knew how to dance punta. You could see who all the Hondurans and other Central Americans were, because everyone else looked lost, tried to fake it, or sat down. It was like a brief reclaiming of a punta. I had no idea they could dance like that. Then salsa came on and everything went back to normal.

For the length of one song, the punta dancers identified with each other across the segregated spaces at The Legend, through a dance that seemed typically irrelevant in the sequined corporealities of latinidad.

CHAPTER 4

Circulations of Gender and Power

A woman walks up to a bar and says, “Bartender, I’ll have a rum and Coke, please.” A guy who had been leaning against the bar watching the dancers turns his attention to the woman. “Can you dance, or are you new here?” Caught off-guard, the woman pauses, considering whether to respond to the inquiry, and then says, “I’m new here, but I know how to dance.” He says, “I’ll decide if I want to dance with you after I’ve seen you dance with someone else first.”

The punch line does not wittily reframe his objectifying proposition because the guy at the bar was not joking. Neither was the woman, who told me about it not long after the incident. The exchange highlights that club habitués configure hierarchies of belonging that entail the inclusion of those who learn to become desirable within the dominant club economy and the exclusion of those who do not.

Yet even if patrons bestow nightly membership on selected bodies, not all of those included share equal status. Belonging and belonging at a high position in the club hierarchy are not the same, especially if you are a woman. Each club economy dictates different gendered sets of rules for how to move around the club, how to belong, how to actively move up the club hierarchy, rules that circulate as part of club choreographies. As patrons navigate salsa hierarchies, they negotiate differential memberships, privileges, constraints, and mobilities based on choreographies of gender, such that the relationships between masculinity and femininity are highly interdependent.

In the previous chapter, I analyzed how five immigrant men at the working-class club of Las Feliz Edades negotiated their classed and raced positions as newcomers to the United States. In this chapter I call attention to their masculinity. Although outside the club their opportunities to move up class hierarchies were limited, inside the club their performance of masculinity allowed them to circulate the space in ways that femininity cannot. To a large extent, men determine which women to include in the club economy, the degree to which those women may participate, and the terms of their participation. Women negotiate this heterosexist choreography as they move around the spaces—on and off dance floors, on the way to bathrooms, in the bars, and in designated smoking areas. They also both reinforce and challenge the practices that put the hierarchy into motion.

I do not intend to essentialize club masculinities and femininities through this gender analysis. However, within the choreo-economic structures of salsa clubs, men and women continually re-create the heterosexual gendered divisions as if gender consisted of two cohesive and opposite identities. Women who have been accused of being "too masculine" and men of being "too feminine" must disrupt and navigate heterosexist responses to queerness very carefully if they wish to participate in predominantly heterosexual club economies.

The hierarchies of nation, region, class, and race that are at stake in the salsa wars and in dancing salsa "right" and "wrong" also challenge and reinforce the dominant performance of gender as binary. The performances of nightclub masculinity and femininity therefore play out in conjunction with stratified configurations of latinidad. This involves not just the racialization of gender but also the analysis of gender in relation to migration and class.

In seeming contradiction to the globalizing pressures to conceptualize a world without borders, differences in nation, race, and class intensify with increases of transnational labor in the United States. How do trans-status Latina/o migrants and other Latinas/os who identify with the economies of more than one nightclub or locality theorize gender and gendered relationships in Los Angeles nightclub economies? How do different understandings of gender overlap and conflict with the circulation of power in the nightclubs?

Many women at the different clubs know that, since club economies manufacture a choreographic structure that presumes and supports male dominance, they enter the clubs under the scrutiny of men who are accustomed to ranking women according to desirability within the economy of a specific club. Marta Savigliano (2003: 189) interprets the economy of Buenos Aires *milongas* as a game in which *milongueras* gamble their femininity as "they risk waiting for a male dancer to identify them as desirable." Milongueras who do not actively desire to dance—an essential component of what Savigliano calls "wallflowering"—are removed from the dance-focused economy of the tango club (167). The gambling framework also applies to salsa club economies, although women who do not desire to dance in Los Angeles salsa economies might still be identified as desirable dance partners and be asked to dance.

Clubs with a high degree of class stratification, like Copa Cabana West and The Legend, allow for the coexistence of patrons with different kinds of desires. Patrons less interested in moving up dance hierarchies might dance to try their luck in the pickup scene for a number of sex-, romance-, and economic-related reasons. In this case, women's bodies may become situated outside the dance economy of latinidad and tangled up in the meat market. Men too might find themselves valued—or not—for their potential as dance or sex partners. Yet unless they choose to interact directly with someone, men who go to a club can avoid direct communication with anyone the entire night, no matter where they sit, stand, or walk, if they so choose. This is not usually the case for women, who balance the possibilities of a night of wallflowering with an onslaught of unwanted but persistent invitations to dance the minute they walk through the door.

This is the story of a night at Copa Cabana West where I observed that exaggerated performances of gendered latinidad generated unequal profits within the club's libidinal economy. A small hubbub of activity erupted near Luis and me as we noticed that two men, actors from *Days of Our Lives*, were standing near us at the edge of the floor, near the band. They were directing their gazes past Luis and me and toward a single female go-go salsera atop a wooden box at the edge of the stage, in front of the band. She was bent forward with her feet apart, swinging her hair through the air. Then she shimmied her hips in a figure-eight pattern, her hands clasped behind her head, elbows stretching toward opposite walls.

While captivated by this spectacle, the two men had garnered the interest of a number of dance-floor salseras and salseros, who edged closer to them with each rotation of their bodies. Desiring to interact with the soap actors, the salseras/os simultaneously attempted to refrain from appearing star-struck. They did their best to be seen by the daytime dramatists, displaying their most outrageous, eye-catching, practiced moves, as if willing the duo to initiate interaction with them.

A short, stocky salsero and his partner were particularly eager to draw the eyes of the stars away from the go-go salsa dancer. Inching toward the actors with each spin and dip, the salsero continually turned to see if the men had noticed him and his partner. They had not. Then, in a quick move, he propelled his partner into the arms of another salsero and stole away the petite salsera with whom he had danced in competitions. After executing a few more moves, he ran out of patience, abandoning his subtle attempts to catch the attention of the actors. He tapped one of them on the shoulder. "Hey, watch this!" he said, at last winning their attention.

He spun the featherweight salsera behind him, reached back to hoist her above his head, and turned her upside-down, her legs in a jumping-jack split with feet pointing toward opposite corners of the ceiling. She balanced there briefly before she tilted forward, dropping toward the floor. The salsero caught her with a palm at the back of her neck. With his partner's heels dragging across the floor, he lunged toward the base of the go-go box and craned his neck to peer up the skirt of the salsera on top. With his dance partner firmly maintaining the almost horizontal slant of the dip, he froze in his one-legged crouch.

His eyes brazenly dared the go-go salsera to react, to retreat, but she casually peered down at him without breaking her routine and continued her figure-eights. Her job required that she seduce the clients with her performance of sequined Latina femininity, not hop off the box every time someone overtly exercised his power to scope out her body. The leering salsero prolonged the pose, giving spectators ample time to glimpse his maneuver, then whipped his partner back into the rhythm and away from the dancer on the box. He abruptly ended the dance before the song was over to confer with the celebrities. He did not invite his partner to join in the conversation.

Whether or not he moved up the salsa hierarchy with this performance of sequined Latino masculinity and physical proximity to the actors, the salsero demonstrated his knowledge of navigating the Copa Cabana West economy: in order for men to move up the club hierarchy, they need to prove themselves to higher-ranking men. Men facilitate their inclusion within high-status circles of other men through brief partnerships with women who are complicit with practices of Latina femininity. Like the two salseras in this partnership, women might prove themselves to be desirable dance partners for other men to use for their social climb, but they do not gain entry into the homosocial networks of men as peers.

Regardless of the economy in question, men usurp and are given the authority to perform a choreography in which women are supposed to desire to become objects of male desire. The choreographies of most clubs are such that, if women do not desire the attention of men or attempt to remove themselves from this economy, however temporarily, they risk drawing negative attention to themselves. If women desire the company of other women, for example, either socializing at a table or dancing with other women, they must rely on their own ingenuity rather than structures already in place if they wish to keep from being splintered into heterosexual dyads without hostile repercussions.

On another night, this time at Las Feliz Edades, Enrique, a twenty-year-old who had arrived in Los Angeles from Guatemala three months earlier and with whom I was dancing, kept looking over at two women, Anaís and Roxana, who danced punta next to us on the dance floor. "¡Son locas!" he told me. "¿Por qué?" I asked, glancing their way. "Son lesbianas," he said.[1] Then he shouted at them, "Hey!" He poked the woman in the ruffled pink skirt in the arm and shook his head disapprovingly at her when she glanced up.

Like many of the other women present at Las Feliz Edades, Anaís and Roxana had long hair and wore lots of carefully applied makeup, big hoop earrings, high heels, and short skirts. But the two did not pass as heterosexual women when they danced. It is possible that Enrique and others in the club read their bodies or dance practices as lesbian because they danced a little more closely than other women couples or they focused on each other and not outwardly, as if expecting to be asked to dance by a man. They appeared to be a couple, dancing closely together; yet they did not touch, as did many of the couples who performed heterosexuality. A few of the heterosexual couples had abandoned the dancing and simply made out on the dance floor.

Performing an act of transgression—dancing so closely together in this space—the two women also seemed to have learned how far they could push the boundaries of club conceptions of femininity. They did not dress themselves in the pants and button-down collared shirts that an acquaintance of mine, Teresa, wears when she goes dancing at another club on its designated "queer salsa" night. With her spiky hair in a neat crew cut, Teresa calls this her androgynous look and says she will not venture into a club like Las Feliz Edades because she does not feel safe in a heterosexual nightclub environment. Unlike the women at Las Feliz Edades, Teresa is a middle-class, fair-skinned Chicana, born and raised in California. By dressing like most of the other women at Las Feliz Edades, Anaís and Roxana, in contrast to what Teresa might have experienced in the same space, minimized but did not eliminate the risk of their participation. They may not have been thrown out of the club, but they had to endure Enrique's assault.

The dynamics of these club economies bring to mind Judith Butler's (1995: 31) notion that "the act of renouncing homosexuality thus paradoxically strengthens homosexuality."[2] Butler does not culturally situate gender in her argument, but gendered performances of latinidad in Los Angeles nightclub economies intertwine with desires marked by the politics of culture, race, class, and nation. The anthropologist Jeff Tobin (1998), who theorizes the performance of exaggerated masculinity and femininity in tango clubs, critiques Butler for universalizing gender, leaving it unmarked. He writes, "According to Butler, straight people's hyperbolic gender displays . . . result from the denial of same-sex desire" (99). When taking into account the multiple social dimensions of local gendered identities in L.A. salsa clubs, male exaggerated performances of masculinity and female exaggerated performances of femininity, rather than, or possibly in addition to, a homosexual desire for love or sex, complicate Butler's idea in several ways.

At Copa Cabana West exaggerated sequined Latino masculinity and Latina femininity are commodified within the club economy. Patrons compete with each other in spectacularized gendered performances of this sequined, gendered latinidad. The Copa Cabana West salsero, in his over-the-top performance, demonstrated a desire for the approval of same-sex patrons. He specifically desired the recognition of the two celebrities, men he would not have access to outside the club. Women also attempt to out-Latina each other in order to gain access to high-status men.

At Las Feliz Edades, where dancing is a part of socializing, women compete with each other but not through salsa or temporary nighttime exaggerations of sequined Latina femininity involving elaborate costuming. The two women who danced punta together at Las Feliz Edades appeared to be a couple, but, dressed in ruffles, short skirts, and heels, they attempted to fit in at the club rather than call attention to themselves. In this case, it seems that the opposite of Butler's theory was enacted: the exaggerated femininity of a lesbian couple, not a straight couple, with regard to their choice of outfits, signified female homosexual or homosocial desire. If, conversely, the two women were straight, even though Enrique interpreted them as lesbian, their attention to one another would support Butler's theory that exaggerated femininity signals a denial of same-sex desire. Their woman-to-woman focus and intimate-without-contact moves indicated, however, that they did not deny their desire for one another but rather had limited that desire in a negotiation with gendered club politics.[3]

Butler's theory does not neatly account for either scenario, since in the context of Las Feliz Edades, ruffles, short skirts, and heels are not considered to be exaggerations of femininity. Rather the Latinas at Las Feliz Edades regard their nighttime apparel as standard to the Latina femininities that many of them duplicate in daily life. Unlike Teresa, Anaís and Roxana are not from the United States or the middle class, where butch and androgynous femininities are more common, especially in alternative spaces such as Valentino's on queer salsa night. Latinas such as Anaís and Roxana, who blend in with expressions of femininity at Las Feliz Edades, identify with the Latino or Latin American aesthetics of Latinaness at the club.

After speaking with Denise, a Chicana who regularly attended Valentino's once-a-month queer salsa night before the club was turned into a sports bar, I began to discern that some trans-status Latinas more fully value a femme aesthetic than an androgynous or butch aesthetic. I suspected that Valentino's attracted more middle-class Latina patrons with sexual values more inflected with Americanized standards of how to perform "lesbianness." I had observed that queer Latina working-class migrants who tend to frequent clubs like Las Feliz Edades identified more with other working-class migrant Latinas/os than with middle-class Latinas/os who identify with U.S. ideologies of gender and sexuality.

The queer Latinas I met and observed seemed to prefer a femme aesthetic, partly because it allowed them to participate socially in a crowd unfamiliar with or threatened by female androgyny or butch aesthetics. Many of the Latina migrants at Las Feliz Edades avoid clubs attended by middle-class Latina/o and non-Latina/o Americans because they find themselves interpellated as the "wrong" kind of Latinas in terms of socioeconomics and possibly undocumented immigrant status. Neither Valentino's middle-class lesbian space nor Las Feliz Edades's queer-unfriendly immigrant space, then, is especially welcoming to working-class, migrant Latinas performing queerly.[4]

At Las Feliz Edades, Anaís, in her pink ruffles, and her partner, Roxana, kept dancing punta and ignored Enrique, perhaps the most transgressive aspect of their performance. Unlike some of the other women who danced together, they did not invite the company of men. Not only did they remove themselves from circulation within the heterosexual economy, but they also denied men the opportunity to gain cultural capital through their performances of masculinity in relation to women who desired them. Despite and because of their disinterest in the attention of men, Enrique saw a chance to assert his masculinity through an unwanted, though not surprising, disciplinary intervention. The poke in the arm signified more than a homophobic lack of tolerance. When a woman becomes unavailable to men in this economy, the men lose the chance not only to generate capital through their display of her dancing body but also to compete for the capital that she gains through her exchange from man to man.

Unlike Copa Cabana West and The Legend, Las Feliz Edades does not capitalize on the commodification of sequined latinidad, the deterritorialized, exoticized expression of Latinaness so dominant in Los Angeles. Femininities upheld and disrupted among the working-class, migrant Latinas at Las Feliz Edades contrast with the femininities honed and contested within salsa clubs. How do Latinas within economies of sequined latinidad negotiate the gendered, social pressures to incorporate techniques of sequined Latinaness?

Los Detalles de la Mujer: A Call to Arms

The boom box shook out a faint, tinny salsa as Hector led me into the new combination: from the basic, a half turn, then a full turn, in which I orbited Hector before returning to the basic, back where we started. We managed without any problems—no bumping into one another—both still on the same beat. Nonetheless Geisa gazed at us, frowning. Although Hector regularly attended the lessons in Geisa's living room twice a week, I had just popped in for a single lesson after meeting the two of them one night at Delicia's, a club in Downey that mostly attracted socializers. Geisa and her friends were among the few who were interested in polishing their dance technique.

Hector and his friend Marco, who work together as mechanics, are the only other students besides me. All three, Hector, Marco, and Geisa, came to the United States from Mexico as adults and had learned—or were learning—how to switch from cumbia to salsa in Los Angeles. Geisa asked Hector and me to do the sequence again. This time, she specifically frowned at me. She told me that I had the timing and could follow the lead, but that I was missing *los detalles de la mujer*, the details of the woman that were supposed to make me look like a better dancer.

Geisa taught me to make my turns less open; I needed to stay closer to the man's body as I twirled, because "es mas preciso" (it is more precise). She told me to incorporate *tango ochos*, a step I had been surprised to see linked with salsa in the clubs. I should do this, she said, when the man holds his arms open, and then, to finish off, I should lift the heel of my left foot, with the knee raised, and with my toe on the floor, shoot my right leg straight back at the same time that I look back, and toss my head in one gesture, and then arrive back to face my partner again. I should press my hand flat to my hip when I turn instead of allowing my arm to swing loosely and bent like a chicken wing. I should do this with my fingers slightly raised so the leader can easily find the hand he lets go of at the beginning of the rotation. Except for her advice on spinning closer to my partner, I was uncomfortable with all of her suggestions, all of which I associated with the flashiness of L.A. salsa.

Although in Costa Rica I had learned and incorporated some details about how women were supposed to move (for example, an overrotation of the woman's hip to punctuate the end of a turn marks salsa as Costa Rican, I was told), my Los Angeles instructor had some remedial lessons in mind for me. She observed that I focused too much on my hips and not enough on my arms. "It's easier for a woman to turn quickly and cleanly when she keeps her hips still. Otherwise, her hips pull her weight to one side and she loses her balance," she said. "With her hips centered, she can be ready to step in any direction her partner wants her to go after the turn."

José Piedra (1997) illuminates how dancing Latina bodies have historically been fetishized in terms of a mindless, excessively sexual swivel, sway, and swing of their hips. But he also theorizes how rumba-dancing Latinas, marginalized through colonialism, slavery, and gender, mobilized the eroticized, feminized hip, "defensively hiding their cultural participation behind a likely offensive show of skin and a pretended love of moving hips" (97). Piedra writes that rumba, an Afro-Cuban ancestor of salsa,[5] "suppl[ies] a poetics of the hip . . . that turn a meaningless body part into a signifying bodily attitude, compliance into defiance" (96). According to Piedra, *rumberas* were able to conceal their thoughtful mobilizations precisely because the sway of the hip was presumed mindless and associated with sex. It follows that Latina salseras in Los Angeles might also use their hips to move up salsa hierarchies in nightclubs.

But when I gazed out at the dancers in Los Angeles salsa clubs, the hips turned inconspicuous under the flourishes of the female arms that shot up to the ceiling, wrists bent, fingers spread as if reaching for something, and then caressing the hair. The arms demanded attention, and often eclipsed the hips as a site of focus, invention, and intervention. Rather than a Bakhtinian exaggeration of the lower body (the hips) to make class hierarchies visible through carnivalesque inversions of high and low, the exaggerated upper body (the inflation of arms) is part of a battle to reinforce class distinctions.[6] If culturally and economically marginalized rumberas defensively hid their incorporations into social spaces with the offensive maneuvers of the hip, might Latina salseras have found more success with the desirable maneuvers of the arms?

Latinas in Los Angeles salsa clubs rely more on their arms than their hips to move up club hierarchies. This shift of bodily emphasis from hips to arms resonates with Jane Desmond's (1997: 39) observation that as dance styles travel across borders and cultures, "dance forms originating in lower-class or nondominant populations present a trajectory of 'upward mobility' in which the dances are 'refined,' 'polished,' and often desexualized." While this shift from hips to arms may be a move toward upward mobility via sequined latinidad, this call to arms is not a move to desexualize salsa. It still references sexuality, but the shift of focus from the hips to the arms marks it as a more "refined" sexuality.

Latinas resexualize salsa in terms of their arms, contesting the limitations of the stereotype that equates Latinaness with a "hippy" sexuality that Piedra describes as socially offensive. If the hips offend because of their association with poor or working class, nonwhite, immigrant, and socioeconomically marginalized Latinas, the arms distance themselves from, yet still insinuate, that sexuality safely above the shoulders.

Given that many Latina salseras draw attention away from their hips, insisting on analyzing Latinas only in terms of their hips risks further confining Latina choreographies to their pelvic girdles. An analysis of arm gestures allows for an examination of alternative bodily techniques Latinas use to make themselves more desirable dance partners within salsa economies that value sequined latinidad. Many Latinas in such clubs reshape or resexualize their salsa practices to incorporate the upwardly mobile arms. As I apply Piedra's hip poetics to the arms I am not arguing that the hips and the arms are interchangeable parts; doing so suggests subtleties about gendered sequined latinidad that might otherwise be missed. A close look at the values associated with women's arm gestures sheds light on the parameters of Latina mobility in clubs and less hippy configurations of Latinaness.

Moving up in clubs such as The Legend and Copa Cabana West or at the salsa congresses depends on a salsera's ability to display techniques that reference a reconfigured Latina sexuality in league with U.S. standards of femininity. Women's arms, in conjunction with a tempered rock of the hips, can allow for this seemingly contradictory coupling. Latinas distinguish themselves from the less "refined" bodies of women, often from Latinas who perform techniques associated with working-class immigrants, by inserting arm gestures like the reach-up-wrist-pop-hair-smoothdown. Latinos distinguish themselves from the less "refined" bodies of men in part by selecting a "refined" dance partner: she shoots her arm to the ceiling, wrist bent, fingers spread—reaching to differentiate herself from the offensive sexuality of poor or working class, nonwhite, immigrant Latinas—then caresses her hair. In this way, she reconfigures herself as sexually desirable within the economy of the salsa club. She then lowers her hand into his, complying with the dominant heteronormative salsa rules of leading and following. As Latinas and Latinos differentiate themselves from each other through salsa practices socially coded as "high" or "low," they reinscribe class hierarchies.

I ask Maria Elena, a Latina who performs on a local dance team, about the value she attributes to the reach-up-wrist-pop-hair-smoothdown. "The guy leads everything else, but we get to use our arms any time he lets go. Besides, what else are we supposed to do with our arms? The only thing we can do is play with our hair!" she says with matter-of-fact sarcasm. She complies with the gendered rules of leading and following but values the gesture for something else: it allows her a moment in which to initiate her own movement and hence to participate more fully in the authorship of the dance.

But how often is coauthorship possible? To what extent are salseras able to author the dance with their arms, given that a salsa partnership with a man usually means that he most often directs which body parts go where and when? My own experience in the clubs suggested complicated answers to these questions. I noticed that I was experiencing difficulty at interpreting some of my different leaders' cues. One night at Copa Cabana West, my partner would try to lead me into a spin with the most ambiguous indication. While my hand was bobbing along close to my mid-torso, he would suddenly fling it upwards. But which way was I supposed to turn? His fling did not seem to prefer one direction or the other. A few times, I tried turning to the right, always met by a pair of bewildered eyes after the rotation. Since turning to the right seemed wrong, with the next partner I tried turning to the left, because didn't his bottom finger exert a slight pressure hinting at leftness? Apparently not: this partner also looked bewildered when I responded by turning. The next time, I experimented by forgoing the turn, reading the fling as an invitation to direct my own moves outside of his embrace. I sank, twisted, bounced, and slithered while my partner maintained the basic, looking surprised.

As the deejay spun fast Puerto Rican salsa at The Legend on another night, Maria Elena and I wallflowered, watching the dancing from the edge of the band-free stage. A young woman from the suburbs wearing a backless halter top and shimmery silver skirt danced very upright with her Latino partner. Sabrina, a phenotypically white Latina, had just begun taking salsa lessons. It was her second night out dancing at a club, and, she later told me, she had danced almost nonstop from the time she walked in to the time the club closed. She told me that before each dance, she informed the guys that she was a beginner because then they told her what they expected her to do. And in fact throughout the night, her partners engaged her in impromptu salsa lessons in the middle of the dance.

When one partner flung her hand upward, Sabrina missed her cue. Her steps became very small and she looked to her partner for the correction. He leaned in to say something in her ear, then took her hand again. Instead of releasing her hand after the fling, he directed her arm upward, over her head, smoothing her hair on the way down. Next to me, María Elena also watched the instruction. I shouted to her, "Did you see him correct her? I've just realized how women are supposed to respond to this hand-flinging lead. I thought women initiated the reach-up move themselves, but now I find out that men direct it."

María Elena said, "Sometimes the woman initiates it, but, yeah, when the guy goes like this, the woman does this." She shot her arm to the ceiling, popped her wrist, and brought it down around her head, caressing her hair.

Men had learned to direct the reach-up-wrist-pop-hair-smoothdown, one of the few gestures that women direct on their own. The male direction of the gesture that I witnessed attested to its worth within economies of sequined latinidad and the desire of men to be seen with women who reference this resexualized Latinaness. Although Sabrina was a beginner who did not perform the gesture on her own, her partner moved up the salsa hierarchy by stepping into the position of instructor, performing his valuing of the gesture and the women who execute it. Sabrina's performance of compliance with the patriarchal codes also allowed her to move up the salsa hierarchy. She allowed him to teach her to shoot her hand to the ceiling, wrist bent, fingers spread, reaching for a higher position in the hierarchy. Together they caressed her hair before he lowered her hand into his.

Los detalles de la mujer do not remain constant over time and across salsa economies. However, women will likely have to conform to the rules of sequined Latinaness if they want to move up salsa hierarchies. Even if women desire to commit themselves wholeheartedly to these rules, the transformation is not automatic or necessarily logical. Some women have the perfect silver dance heels, but their dresses are out of style. Some have the most expensive, exquisitely sequined halter tops, but they have not learned how to hear the salsa rhythm. Others have polished all the latest moves, but they don't think about mopping up their perspiration and runny eye makeup in between dances.

One cold and rainy Saturday at The Legend, I leaned against the wall, intent on observing women perform the reach-up-wrist-pop-hair-smoothdown. A winter wind blew through the door and I crossed my arms to my chest, shivering. A Latina in her forties wearing what looked like an oversized First Communion dress caught my eye. The dress was made of a white chiffon gauzy material with sheer long sleeves; the full skirt fluffed out above the knees over her sparkly silver heels. Her hair was styled in a blunt bob, parted in the middle, with thick bangs.

Earlier a waitress from Ecuador who now lived in Fontana had pointed the woman out to me, saying that she thought she was a good dancer. When *she* initiated the reach-up gesture, her arm moved as a whole unit: no finger articulations or bent wrists, and no hair swipe. On the one hand, it looked like a half-hearted afterthought, and yet it simultaneously looked like the cocking of a military rifle.

Did she consider this a variation of the reach-up-wrist-pop-hair-smoothdown? Were the Communion dress and the militaristic performance part of a deliberate mocking of sequined Latina femininity and the salsa wars, or an imitation gone awry?

"Wanna dance?" A male voice interrupted my research.

"No, thanks," I said.

He extended one arm to lean against the wall, trying to get my attention, but I was focused on how this woman in the Communion dress had made it to the dance floor in attire that was not just unsalsa but decidedly bizarre. Again she cocked the rifle: up-down. Could this move in any way parallel the sexually offensive maneuvers of the hip that Piedra would conclude defensively hides a break with dominant salsa practices? Or was it ludicrous of me to attempt to put into dialogue his analysis of the hip with arms that could hardly be considered offensive because they lacked an overt reference to sexuality?

The guy leaning against the wall persisted with the unsuccessful seduction. "Hey, did you know that standing with your arms crossed like that is an offensive gesture?"

The Traffic in Salseras: Choreographies of Display and Exchange

As in salsa clubs, the economies of the salsa congress dictated that a woman's desirability—and hence the frequency of her appearance on the dance floor, how well she is seen as following her partner's lead, and the club ranking of her partner—is mediated through men. Women also move up congress hierarchies by outdoing each other with their performances of sequined Latinaness. They cultivate commodities such as clothing, makeup, and dance technique, all of which, when put into play with sequined Latinaness, allows them to become more desirable dance partners. In particular, the West Coast Salsa Congress in Los Angeles is a hotbed of sequined latinidad, with the focus almost entirely on the latest innovations in salsa dancing that emerge from the exaggerated performances of salsero masculinity and salsera femininity.

In salsa clubs and congresses, where an exoticized Latinaness circulates as a commodity fetish, displays of both unsequined Latina femininity and white American femininity often hinder women's attempts to move up club hierarchies.

The salsa economy operates in tandem with desire. If you do not look and move like a sequined Latina in the dance economy, you will likely not generate enough desire, whether homosocial, homosexual, or heterosexual, to make it to the dance floor. In order to demonstrate sequined Latino masculinity, men choose to dance with a salsera who becomes more desirable through her exchange with other men, thus generating salsa capital, the capital most evident in the salsa club nighttime economy. Women in salsa clubs, as objects of salsero desire, become the bodies around which the economy revolves, although without the same kinds of gains as the men. Within this economy, women move up salsa hierarchies based on their desirability among salseros.

The year I attended the West Coast Salsa Congress, "SalsaLand" was enormous, with several white tents pitched in the parking lot of the Hollywood Park Casino. The tent where people danced socially to live music overwhelmed me with its six dance floors (an advertised twelve thousand square feet) arranged with asphalt walkways in between. As I scanned the layers in the crowd—the ones dancing, the ones watching, and the ones shifting positions along the asphalt grid—in search of my friend Luis, I noticed that most of the people I recognized were from El Reino de la Salsa in Hollywood. I was surprised that I didn't see many from the Chuck's Grill–Alexandre's–The Legend circuit, a trio of clubs where patrons cultivate sequined latinidad. It may have been that the forty-dollar-per-night entrance fee was exorbitant for the many working-class Latinas/os who frequented those clubs.

I finally ran into Luis dancing near the band with some of his other friends from El Reino: Rogelio, Juana, Memo, and two Anglo women he had recently met there, Stacy and Lynn. A Mexican who had learned to dance salsa in New York City, Luis had insisted that I would not be sorry if I went to the congress to hear his favorite New York band, the Spanish Harlem Orchestra. He led me out to the floor to dance his smooth East Coast style, but we had barely begun when we were drawn to a crowd that began to gather around a couple of dancers who were amazingly fast and animated.

She was wearing big silver hoop earrings, pleather purple pants, and a matching backless halter. She had pinned her hair back tightly into a bun, probably so as not to thwack her partner across the eyes with her hair when she turned. Her partner, in all black, wore a lacy long-sleeved blouse, velvet pants, and a fedora that he held onto with one hand, posing with his legs apart as she spun. She whirled faster than anyone I had ever seen, and as she came out of one spin, another guy emerged from the surrounding circle of onlookers, stepping in opposite the guy in velvet. A half rotation before the one who initiated the spin had planned to transition into the next step, the second guy stopped the spinning salsera by the shoulders and tugged her into a new partnership. The man in velvet retreated back to the circle to watch. This kind of exchange happened several times throughout the dance as, one at a time, men from the outer circle jumped in to steal the lead from the salsero already dancing.

I had seen this kind of exchange before at places like The Legend, but on a much smaller scale, usually between one woman and two men. One man would invite the woman to dance, his friend would break in, and the first man would stand aside, watching as if disinterested. Within the same dance, this first guy might reappear and take over. When it had happened to me once, all I could think about while dancing with the second guy was, "Hey, I only agreed to dance with the first guy." The second one had assumed that I would go along with the exchange. The primary contract for the exchange took place between the men, although the men required the cooperative participation of the woman in order for the game to take place.

Gayle Rubin (1975) analyzes how the exchange of women from one man to another underlies male status within a phallic economy. Placing Lacanian psychoanalysis within a Marxist framework, she explains the exchange of women for marriage within the *Kula* ring: "Women move in one direction, cattle, shells, or mats in the other. . . . It [the phallus] is where we aren't. In this sense, the phallus is more than a feature which distinguishes the sexes: it is the embodiment of the male status, to which men accede, and in which certain rights inhere—among them, the right to a woman. It is an expression of the transmission of male dominance. It passes through women and settles upon men" (131).

Within the male homosocial salsa dynamic, women become symbols of male status. Although this value exists in the abstract as salsa capital, it gets deposited upon female bodies. As men compete with one another in the salsa ring through the display of their dance partners, they join in the fraternal competition to show off the most cutting-edge, deterritorialized, sequined Latina phallus. Simultaneously, as in the exchange of cattle, shells, or money, the phallus as salsa capital is transported through salsera bodies in the act of exchange among men. The exchange also generates salsa capital.

At the salsa congress, the expanded scale of the exchange took on the quality of a game with several players. The competition among men relied upon the circulation of the salsera's body among them. Does he outdo the one who came before him? Does he surprise his partner, leading her in one direction when she thought she was supposed to go in another? Does he tangle her up in so many twists, only to suddenly drop his arms and let her loose? Does he turn her more, turn her faster, cause her to lose her equilibrium and then, in the most creative way, catch her up in a dip? How close to the ground can he throw her before she narrowly misses crashing into the floor?

Comparison of this exchange to a game may seem far-fetched, given that games are supposed to be fun. However, games can also be violent. Players often enter games with preconfigured alliances. Players also do not all have the same skill or necessarily agree on all the rules; some make up rules as they go along and have enough status so that others back them up against those who dispute the fairness of a decision. Some players cheat. So this exchange at the salsa congress, steeped in the practice of homosociality among men nestled within a framework of heterosexuality, can at least temporarily be classified as a game for the sake of this analysis.

The male objective of this game was less about holding on to the female partner than it was about the act of exchange. A guy who wants to break into the dance would do so by tapping the shoulder of the salsero already dancing, by walking around the inside edges of the circle, getting closer until the first guy backs away, or by more aggressively stealing the salsera away by cutting off the first guy. As I watched, one guy stole the salsera as she was being turned. When her partner launched her into a turn, the challenger stood on the other side of her, grabbed her by the hips, and halted her turn in front of him, with her back to the old partner.

Another time, the challenge was initiated by the salsero already dancing. He simply glanced at one of the guys who had not yet danced, challenging—or perhaps encouraging—him to take over. When Damián, the most alpha of male dancers, signaled to a younger guy in a satin plum blouse that he should attempt to take the salsera, the younger man met the dare reluctantly but accepted, as if preparing to go through an initiation.

Significantly, each time a salsero made his move to cut in, the salsera in transfer never seemed caught off-guard. In fact she facilitated the exchange. When the exchange occurred during a turn, she adjusted her speed almost imperceptibly, slowing down or speeding up to synchronize with her new partner. When he failed to correctly anticipate which leg she would step on as he stepped in, she seamlessly double-stepped into his frame. She thus allowed the exchange to happen gracefully, as if the "theft" were really a game after all.

In this way salseras were complicit in the exchange of sequined latinidad. At times, however, salseras would challenge their male partners, some more successfully than others. For example, a salsero might let go of his partner and start to do his fancy footwork or fast, multiple spins, and she would either copy him with a fast turn of her own or with fancier footwork, or else would whip out some other solo steps she had in her repertoire involving her arms and hips.

In a few instances, the women, possibly newer to the game, looked as if they were just trying to stay on their feet. Other women, like Sofía in the purple pleather, were very grounded, graceful, quick-witted, and innovative. In one improvisation, Sofía flung one arm straight out to the side while bending the other one, elbow lifted, beating her fist toward her chest twice percussively, and then alternating to the other side. I had never seen anyone incorporate arms like that in salsa, and she did so in synchronization with the music.

When Sofía and her partners finished their dance, I followed her and a white American girlfriend of hers, Dot, out of the tent as they slowly headed toward the rows and rows of Porta Potties. When I approached her to ask about the circle, she was wiping the sweat from her face. The song had lasted at least fifteen minutes. She had danced the entire time and needed a break. The guys, on the other hand, had completed much shorter segments and had plenty of energy to begin the game again with another woman.

From Honduras, Sofía had lived in Los Angeles for six years. I learned that she was a student at East Los Angeles College and wanted to be an elementary school teacher. In the meantime, she was a clerk at Lady Foot Locker. (She wrinkled her nose at this.) She had started dancing two years earlier, at first dancing every night of the week. At the time of the congress, she was going out only once a week because she had prioritized school and work. When I asked her how it was decided which women got to go into the circle, she explained that it was an honor to be chosen to go in. Since her boyfriend, Damián, was the unofficial ringleader of the group and often initiated the dance with a new woman, Sofía sometimes advised him on which women to select. "Not all the women can keep up with those guys!" she laughed, acknowledging not only her own ability to gain a high position in the hierarchy of women but that a woman's entrance into the circle depended on the recognition and desire of the men.

Back at the circle, Damián was scanning the onlookers, searching for the next woman to bring in as the last song drew to a close. He did this with subtlety, so that when the next song began, he and the woman he had invited to dance would appear in the center from the very first beat, as if by magic. Damián, and sometimes other high-status fellows, would choose partners from around the circle, giving the appearance that all the women would get their turn. However, an observant onlooker could distinguish which women would and would not be chosen, who were spectators, and who were hopeful practitioners busy with wall-flowering. The main dancers were primarily from Los Angeles and were previously acquainted with each other; occasionally they included dancers from other countries. The women who did not get asked to enter the circle were slightly older, over twenty-five, were dressed more casually, did not have their hair tied back, and did not project the same kind of serious salsera image as did Sofía.

The salseras who were asked into the circle all sparkled. They had paid attention to every detail of their makeup, earrings, and shoes. They covered up their partner's miscues with smiles. Their belly did not pop out from under their halter top. Their bodies were lean and muscular, as if they had undergone rigorous training. Exceptions to this presentation were not chosen by salseros. For example, no one ever seemed to glance at the tall Anglo woman standing around the circle. With her light brown unbrushed hair, lack of makeup, and heavy flat shoes, she looked more like a very large, unsophisticated schoolgirl than a salsera.

One of the guys who was less skilled than Damián chose to dance the next one with Sofía's friend Dot, recently back from the trip to the outdoor facilities. Dot looked like a professional ice skater or a ballroom dancer. Her blonde ponytail and a leotard bodice—with white, glittery strips of fabric that flowed from her hips down her legs—signified her commitment to perfect her dance abilities. Technically, however, she was not as strong as Sofía and some of the others. For example, Sofía initiated her arm movements from her shoulder blades, while Dot worked her limbs as if they were disconnected from the rest of her body. Her arms would stiffen instead of project out to the sides or up into the air. The guys who had danced with Sofía opted out of dancing with Dot. They relinquished the center so that the second tier of salseros, the intermediates who were trying out new moves and personas, could have a chance to position themselves among other intermediates with a woman who had not yet successfully crafted herself as a fashionable salsera.

Cristina, in a tall baseball-style cap, the kind that mechanics often wear, was brought into the circle. She wore a ripped T-shirt tied at the waist and a short jean skirt cut off at the hem. No glitter, no sparkle, no shine. Initially the more advanced dancers held back, as if letting the younger guys dance with her so that they could assess her abilities. Was she worth dancing with? Would she raise or lower the status of a more advanced dancer? Cristina stepped back into a solo, bending her knees and moving from her hips, taking advantage of a lower center of balance than most of the other women, who often shifted it to their chests. She continued to surprise the onlookers with sudden thrusts of the hips and her ability to spin quickly.

Her partner, who was wearing a brown bandana and matching T-shirt that said "Papi Chulo," was taken off-guard a couple of times. He kept repeating his routine—cross-body lead, spin, break open, dip, solos—unable to come up with new variations. Then Rico, in a long purple coat and white shoes with black tips, skidded into the circle and snapped Cristina away from Papi Chulo. He immediately increased the intensity of the dance by introducing more complex turns, neck drops, and lifts. Whether he had benevolently rescued Papi Chulo or had taken advantage of the lackluster performance by outdancing him, Rico moved up the hierarchy. Ready to meet his challenge, Cristina took off her cap and tossed it to a friend who was standing on the inside of the circle. Her gesture indicated that she was ready to get down to business, and the crowd cheered in the excitement of the competition. The primary competition, however, was not between Rico and Cristina, but between Rico and Papi Chulo, who put their masculinity on the line to try to increase their cultural capital by outperforming one another.

From across the circle, I observed Sofía indicate to her boyfriend that he should dance with a more mature-looking woman of about twenty-six, Eva. She had an especially sophisticated look in her all-white, strapless pantsuit that ended just below the knee. The pants clung to her legs and she had not an ounce of cellulite. Damián followed Sofía's cue, and Eva was a fantastic dancer; she never wasted a move. When Damián threw out some intricate footwork, she instantly duplicated his series of steps, catching up to him so that they performed in unison. But she performed them better, more gracefully and cleanly, and extended the sequences with steps he could not pick up. None of the guys seemed eager to interrupt this dance.

More than just enthralled by Eva and Damián's virtuosic dancing, the other guys seemed intimidated. Near the end of the song, a skinny salsero in a white straw fedora took Damián's place. Eva did not appear to be thrilled with the exchange. As soon as the song ended, she left the circle. Eva was not playing the game by the same rules as the men or the other women. All the other women who had danced, even though they had danced well and had challenged the men, never interrogated the rules of the game. But Eva did. She tended not to smile excessively, never stumbled, and never looked flustered. She also exposed the limits of the male homosocial bond in the game that threatened to unravel when no one stepped in right away to relieve Damián.

An analysis of the gender-based rules of the game provides insight into what it means to move in and move up within this setting. While women must be chosen to dance by a man of high salsero status, any man from around the circle with enough skill and confidence can participate simply by edging out the salsero already in the circle. The salseros who oversee the game appropriate the authority to select the women who will perform and, to a lesser extent, which men will dance with them. The men have more opportunities to perform at a greater frequency of short-lived, energized intervals, while the women compete with each other for fewer yet relatively long-term available positions. Even though the men and women perform together, male homosociality and social positioning take center stage.

In this way, men perform exaggerated sequined Latino masculinities as part of a strategy to gain a foothold in and move up the hierarchy of other male salseros. When a man of higher salsero status approves of or recognizes one of the neophyte salseros enough to challenge and coax him into the circle of exchange, both men move up the hierarchy. The younger salsero moves up because the salsero of higher status selected him to prove his masculinity—his willingness to hone his skills in the likeness of his mentor—from among the crowd. The mentor moves up the hierarchy of men through the act of selection, demonstrating not just his authority to do so but his ability to coerce or encourage the new salsero to join his ranks, much like the process of initiation, or hazing, in a college fraternity.

One way a salsero measures a salsera's desirability is by her performing L.A. salsa well enough to challenge him but not to surpass him. Cristina, fashionably dressed down, at first appeared not to subscribe to the aesthetic demands of L.A. salsa, even evoking images of working-class masculinity with her outfit rather than more exotic images of sequined Latinaness. When her dancing belied her outfit and she pushed her partners to keep up with her, however, she increased her desirability by taking off her hat, signaling that she was actually the one who had to exert the effort to endure her partner's electrified performance.

Eva's ability, however, surpassed that of the highest-ranking salsero, and she did not apologize for, accommodate, or cover up his impotence. Her performance reminded spectators and practitioners that the rules of the game were constructed to uphold salseros' naturalized authority to regulate dance hierarchies and belonging. Through her performance, Eva fleetingly gained the ultimate status of the evening, but she also relinquished belongingness. Recall that simply moving around the club and moving up the hierarchy are related, but not equivalent. Salseras who challenge the limits of the game's rules by earning more salsa capital than salseros do not get to stay in the game, and may not want to anyway.

Unlike Eva, Sofía cooperated so well with the rules that she generated enough salsa capital to suggest that Damián choose Eva as his next salsera. Intentionally or not, and without implicating herself, Sofía managed to disrupt the game via Eva's performance. She thus demonstrated the possibility that a high-status salsera can hijack the trafficking in salseras from men, thereby challenging their dominance without the threat of losing her own place within the system.

Men and women both perform heightened renditions of their gender in order to gain approval and acceptance from men who are higher up on the salsa hierarchy. Although men need to attract a desirable salsera to accomplish this, they ultimately desire the salsa capital that they can flaunt among men when dancing more skillfully with a salsera than had the last man who danced with her. Women who wish to move up salsa hierarchies do not usually care whether they gain approval or acceptance from other women, since women are not the ones who dominate the social scene at the club. Because of this, homosociality among men flourishes and is supported by men, women, and the choreography of the salsa economy itself.[7] Among women, homosociality—the desire for same-sex approval and inclusion—does not.

Los Muertos de Hambre

The circulation of women underpins homosociality among men, allowing men the opportunity to gain, or sometimes demand, the approval and admiration of their gender peers. This gendered dynamic is flexible enough to occur in more than one way in more than one economy. In places like the salsa congress, practitioners determine value by how well one dances out a masculinity that has been shaped by sequined latinidad. How well do they detach themselves from their media images as undocumented, exploitable labor? How successfully do they disguise their desperate, frustrated attempts to attain social and economic stability in the United States? Can they repress their memories of the violence of the war in the place they came from or the everydayness of the war against Latinos in (or trying to enter) the United States?

A *San Francisco Chronicle* article titled "Governor Signals He'd Welcome Minutemen on the California Border" elucidates former California governor Arnold Schwarzenegger's role in this war. The *Terminator* (1984) star praised an armed group of Arizona volunteers who have been patrolling the U.S.-Mexican border to prevent undocumented crossings into the United States through Arizona.[8] Thus at this site of violence, another group of men, this time volunteers for the vigilante group in California, enacted *their* masculinity by enforcing anti-Mexican, anti-immigrant sentiment as patriotic through images of the Revolutionary War. And they did so with gubernatorial encouragement.

This performance of a racialized, nationalized, historicized white masculinity matters to latinidad. Such homosociality, in play among primarily white men and outside salsa economies, affects male homosociality among Latinos in clubs. Through their enactments of sequined Latino masculinity, salseros sublimate the socially unacceptable references to this particular violence, channeling it into libidinal stylizations of violence in salsa performances. Salseros play out themes of violence intertwined with sexuality upon the bodies of salseras, as in the exchange game at the salsa congress.

The violence can emerge between salseros in other ways as well. In clubs like Valentino's on "Colombian Night," men do not configure homosociality by comparing themselves to each other in electrifying performances of L.A. salsa and sequined Latino masculinity. Rather the men at Valentino's gain status homosocially when they prove their masculinity by comparing their economic worth, their heterosexual potencies, and occasional unstylized acts, threats, and fights. They do this in more overt, gritty performances of violence and sex, as well as through references to their economic status in daily life that would shatter the sequined Latino veneer of the salsa congress.

Valentino's economy attracts mostly migrants and working-class Latinas/os and parallels the Las Feliz Edades crowd, the members of which primarily come from Mexico and Central America. While patrons at these clubs do not value dancing as a way to move up hierarchies, homosociality among men is still measured through social exchanges between them as well as through the display and exchange of women.

On one Friday night at Valentino's, the club was packed, standing room only. When I first arrived, I had a clear view of the dance floor from my spot standing along the wall, but as the night wore on, people filled in the spaces between me and the dancers. The space between bodies along the wall also diminished. "Friday night's a meat market at Valentino's," Sarita, a Chicana I knew from other salsa clubs, had warned me. "If I were you, I would not go alone, because it will look like you are after something besides ethnography. You know?" I did know. Women who went to clubs alone had bad reputations. I planned to speak to the women, however, and not the men, so I did not think I would have too much trouble.

As I was surveying the crowd, a voice behind me asked, "What do you think of this Colombian salsa?" His pickup line recategorized the club that I had only been to on Wednesdays as more pan-Latino than I had experienced. Alfredo, I learned, went to Valentino's only on Fridays, when the club switched deejays and changed the music to include Colombian genres of *vallenato* and cumbia, along with the usual salsa and merengue. On Wednesdays the club opened its doors to an entirely different crowd, mostly made up of Colombian immigrants, according to Alfredo. He told me that practically the same people went every Friday, so he knew just about everyone there. He identified himself as a Colombian, although he made sure to tell me that he was not an immigrant. Born in south Texas to a Mexican father and a Colombian mother, he moved to Los Angeles with his mother when he was just a baby. I learned all this in the first two minutes of knowing him.

When I told him I was researching salsa, he told me that in Colombia, salsa people hardly ever do turns or move quickly. "It's not like the flashy L.A. salsa. It's more about enjoying each other's company than trying to show off." He did not like to dance much but came to the club every week after work to see his friends and "enjoy *mis copas*." He tipped his plastic cup and polished off his beverage of choice: Cristal, the Colombian aguardiente. Then he invited me to dance. Most of the time, couples turned together at a leisurely pace without breaking from the embrace. Stepping away from each other to perform turns singly seemed to require too much space for this crowd. Elbow to elbow and butt to butt with other couples out dancing, no one tried to execute more than just a couple of tiny, slow rotations.

Our space along the wall had been swallowed up during the dance, but we managed to reclaim it when others moved away to dance the next set. Once Alfredo had distinguished himself and the crowd at Valentino's from the L.A. salseros at clubs like The Legend and events like the salsa congress, he also began to distinguish himself from the other men at Valentino's with stories of his ambition, ingenuity, and business acumen. "Did you know I own my own business? I repair fax machines in office buildings," he said. I found out that, before opening his own business, he had previously worked for another repair company and had kept records of all the clients' names and phone numbers. When he went solo, he called up each one, offering cheaper rates, gaining his first regular customers in the process. "Even though my rates are less, I overcharge them or charge them for parts that aren't broken, so financially the business has been very successful. I'm thinking of renting an office space and getting someone to help me. Are you looking for a job? I could use a good secretary, because the business is really starting to expand."

Alfredo owned and operated the repair business, but his big dream was to eventually buy into a fast-food burger chain and manage his own site. He would need about fifty thousand dollars to get that going and was saving up. He was also saving up to buy a house.

After sketching out his ambitions, he gestured with his chin toward the dance floor. "Most of these guys out there, my friends at this club, are *muertos de hambre* [the ones dying of hunger]," he said.[9] "They have no jobs, no ambition. Some of them get by selling phone codes or drugs, but most of them have nothing. No real places to live, no families here. These guys aren't in control of anything. Even their girlfriends make more money than they do. *Son muertos de hambre—sin donde para caerse muerto*," [without anyplace to drop dead] he finished, putting together two sayings that commented on the extreme poverty and hopelessness of his peers. *Muertos de hambre*, without even a place for their dead bodies to fall. Alfredo portrayed los muertos as failures, displaced not only in life but also in death.

Even though Alfredo, with his one-man van-based repair business, did not seem so distant from those he classified as muertos de hambre, he did everything he could to convince me that he was not like his friends. He had established himself within the capitalist system, but the others were still searching for a way to survive, clinging to the lives they still but apparently barely had. I glimpsed los muertos on the dance floor, cradling their girlfriends and moving in time to the music.

Within the club these men do not have to negotiate the same social and economic hierarchy as they do outside the club, a hierarchy in which they get placed near the bottom in relation to Anglo men. Yet even in relation to one another, they do not have equal access to resources outside the club. Alfredo made it known that he was more established financially and had many more resources and contacts upon which to draw in order to start up a business. Although he attributed his success to his own cleverness and determination, he was also likely benefiting from the stability of having lived in Los Angeles most of his life.

Of course, this claim of stability and success is relative. Inside the club Alfredo appeared stable and successful in comparison to his portrayal of *los muertos de hambre*. Outside the club even his lucrative job as a fax machine repairman and business owner does not have the same prestige as those held by accountants, lawyers, or doctors. If los muertos de hambre barely survived by working at the kinds of job they needed to keep secret, as in selling phone codes illegally, outside the club they would scarcely register at the lower end of socioeconomic hierarchies in their attempt to maintain invisibility. The ability to survive would correlate with the ability to disappear, to occupy as little space as possible.[10] As I reflected on Alfredo's classification of his friends, the salsa ended. The couples on the floor melted off to occupy the places opened up by the next group of dancers.

While I had been listening to Alfredo's story, he had reduced the space between our bodies considerably, somehow managing to put his arm around my waist without my noticing. "I'm going to the bathroom," I said.

After making my way across the club, I opened the door to the crowded women's room carefully; several women had congregated around the mirror to fix their hair and makeup. Two other women were looking at one another intently. One, who was in tears, said, "No sé que voy a hacer. No me puedo creer que está aquí con otra."

"Es un cabrón, ese hombre," said the other. "No puedo creer que apenas acabo de pagar su educcaión como plomero."[11]

This brief exchange reminded me of other stories and scraps of stories that women at Valentino's had told me, or I had overheard, regarding their relationships with men at the club; the stories provide a glimpse into these Latinas' assessments of masculinity, homosociality, and the circulation of women.

> **SEDUCTION**
>
> And then he started telling me all about how he is the protector of his cousin who owed money to a drug dealer. The dealer had been harassing his cousin. That night in the club, he went over and sat down at the table where the drug dealer sat. It was where the dealer always sat. Everybody knew him, what he sold, and where he sat. He was like the king of the club, Hector said. But the waitresses also knew Hector, who sat down at the king's table. Hector snapped his fingers and the waitress came running. I'm serious. This is how he told it!
>
> "Beers for me and him," Hector says he said. When the waitress set the bottles in front of them, Hector took his bottle by the neck and busted it apart on the edge of the table. He held the jagged end up against the dealer's neck and said, "Don't mess with my cousin again." The drug dealer got scared and left, so Hector claimed the table after that. He said, "I owned that club that night."
>
> **HOW SEDUCTION CRUMBLES OUTSIDE THE CLUB**
>
> When I first met my man, he said he had four cars, but when I started going out with him, I found out that two didn't even have wheels or engines, and the third he had crashed, because he drives too fast. The only one working was his delivery truck.
>
> **MALE HOMOSOCIALITY AT A WOMAN'S EXPENSE**
>
> I slept with him before I found out he had a girlfriend and two kids. He just wanted to parade me around the club in front of his friends.
>
> **WHAT HAPPENS WHEN A WOMAN DOESN'T COOPERATE WITH THE RULES OF MALE HOMOSOCIALITY**
>
> When I told him he was full of crap in front of all his friends, he stopped calling me.

Although on different terms than those of the exchange game at the salsa congress, women at Valentino's also move up when they cooperate with the homosocial desires of men who wish to gain club status among other men. The discussion in the bathroom and the other stories women have told me suggest that women are variously aware of how they fit into the economy of the club and the consequences of belonging on the men's terms. However, as in the last story, if women openly confront the men about the exaggerated stories they tell in order to bolster their masculinity, they work against such bolstering. They risk becoming alienated through men's acts of display and exchange.

Salseros at Valentino's invent or exaggerate their out-of-club economic positionings in competition with other men present.[12] At salsa clubs like The Legend or at the salsa congress, men rarely discuss in detail their positioning outside the club in the interest of reproducing the exotic imaginations of latinidad. Discussions within salsa economies most often revolve around someone's status according to locally developed standards of dancing "right." They create themselves within the sequined Latino economy of dance, as if disconnected from the political economy.

Unlike dancers at The Legend or the congress, those at Valentino's do not become sophisticated consumers of salsa in order to belong at the club. Patrons at Valentino's reject the L.A. salsero dance moves and instead perform salsa "Colombian style," dancing in opposition to what they regard as the Americanized sequined latinidad. At Valentino's, many of the practitioners have immigrated to the United States from the shared homeland of Colombia and identify as Colombian, forming a much more homogeneous group than is possible among patrons at The Legend. Cultural conceptions of how to socialize in a nightclub remain to some degree shared at the advertised Colombian night.

One of the things that keeps the dancers at this club from being "united" as Colombianos, however, is the competition for upward mobility outside the club. Men's success in moving up club hierarchies depends on how well they perform their success within the economy of daily life. But because they maintain club connections to an extent outside of the club, it is harder to reinvent their identity at night, since enough people know who they are by day. Hence men like Alfredo waste no time in making connections with female outsiders like me who do not already know the details of their lives outside the club.

The men at Valentino's generate club capital and possibly economic capital when they successfully integrate values from the political economy at work outside the club within the nightclub valuation system. And capital relating to both circulate through the bodies of the women. Men move up in the club hierarchy when they perform their desirability to women for each other. Appearing desirable to women depends upon a combination of their sexual clout and economic prowess. The men brandish female bodies to claim their space in the club and use them to potentially gain economic opportunities or simply the chance to survive outside the club. Los muertos de hambre, the men in this working-class club, the men who are dying of hunger without even a place to lay their dead body, build themselves up and tear each other down at the expense of women's bodies.

This does not mean that women in clubs like Valentino's are passive victims of latinidad. It is critical to note, however, that the heterosexist choreographies within the nightclubs are produced in dialogue with and in opposition to the dynamics of white male hegemony outside the clubs. In both spaces, even when women seem to break with the choreography, they often first learn how to succeed within them in order to do so.

At Chuck's Grill, dancers crowd onto a long rectangular dance floor filled with sparkly, blurred bodies. One particular night, in the middle of that floor and surrounded by a crowd of men, danced Amber, a Latina salsera who had won third place in a recent salsa contest with her kung-fu salsa choreography. She wasn't performing kung-fu moves that night, but instead comically cited hip-hop by popping and locking at top speed (with her arms), then punctuating her move with the reach-up-wrist-pop-hair-smoothdown. I overheard a woman say, "She is the only one who dances with a sense of humor!" She flawlessly followed the lead of her partner, who tried to keep up with her. Then, in the middle of the song, she swiftly replaced her partner with another man.

In contrast to the exchange game at the salsa congress, in which men oversaw the process of exchange, Amber initiated the replacement of partners she selected. I had never seen a woman occupy this position. She defied many rules of the gendered leader-follower relationship. She initiated many of her own movements, creatively incorporated arm techniques not commonly associated with Latinas, decided with whom she would dance, and then tired them out. Still, many men desired to dance with her. Had she managed to increase her "discursive participation," as Piedra (1997: 96) would call it, through her arm gestures? Had she used the arm gestures to increase her nocturnal value, ultimately liberating her arms to pop, lock, and swing in kung-fu punches?

The lights brightened after the dance ended, indicating that it was the last dance of the night. A cadre of men gathered around Amber, recklessly throwing out compliments and fighting for her attention. The scenario appeared to reverse the postdance dynamic I had witnessed another time at Copa Cabana West, when the salsero gained access to the actors from *Days of Our Lives*. Amber was a breathtaking exception to the positioning of most salseras, even high-status salseras, in L.A. salsa clubs. Yet, despite her example, in order to win a salsa competition in Los Angeles, to become a salsa celebrity who can create a few of her own rules, a salsera first had to become complicit with the spectacularization of the heterosexist choreography.

CHAPTER 5

"Don't Leave Me, Celia!"

SALSERA HOMOSOCIALITY AND LATINA CORPOREALITIES

When you walk into the women's bathroom at The Legend, you enter a small lounge with two red-velvet couches and a large, chipped mirror. Bright fluorescent lights illuminate the curling edges of the wallpaper, revealing the building's cosmetic flaws. Nothing is fancy in here. Even the velvet on the couches has worn thin; you can't help noticing this as you sink into the springs.

"This place is dingy," my friend Mónica said one night. Sniffing, she added, "And these couches could use a good dose of Febreze."

In the hypergendered spaces of the salsa club, the women's bathroom is a space of refuge away from men's constant assessments of how successfully women perform sequined Latinaness. The word *Mujeres* carved into the wooden bathroom door at The Legend restricts all but women's bodies from passing through and checking themselves out in the mirror. The only space in clubs to which men do not have access, the women's bathroom becomes a small zone in which women have the opportunity to engage with one another without interruption or aggressive pokes in the arm by men. The women's bathroom is an ideal site in which to begin to theorize the relationships among women in salsa clubs.

Mónica pointed out a woman primping in the mirror, possibly preparing to compete in the contest scheduled to start in a few minutes. "She's covered in hot-pink sequins!" I didn't assess the contestant's costume, since a group of four young Latinas had caught my attention. Three of the women were sitting next to Mónica and me on the second couch, sipping margaritas. The fourth had headed off to the bathroom stall around the corner, imploring, "Don't leave me, Celia!" The plea underscored that for women, moving around the club's economy of pleasure is no leisurely walk in the park. The woman had either been warned about or knew firsthand what can happen to women who separate from the group. A woman who travels alone often finds herself being herded into the meat market of one-night stands and alienated from the economy of salsa dancing. If she wishes to hone her desirability as a salsa dancer, she will stay with the group until she attains the presumed respectability of the heterosexual dyad.

Latinas risk being associated with those relegated to the fringes of the crowd if they do not cooperate with the codes of sequined Latinaness. If they do not camouflage their unsequined citizenship and class status of daily life and do not take lessons in L.A. salsa to learn the desired codes of femininity, they may be met with antimigrant, anti-Mexican hostilities. The woman's cry for Celia's companionship articulates that homosociality among women must be consciously fashioned in a harsh environment that exoticizes abstract Caribbean Latinas and criminalizes Mexican migrants. Furthermore women must negotiate the club codes of sequined Latina femininity that produce black Caribbean Latinaness as sexy and pleasurable and Mexican migrant Latinaness as repulsive and subhuman. They must do so even while the entertainment and media representations often displace, consume, target, or dismiss Latina bodies associated with both of these configurations of femininity. The violence of these representations circulates in newspaper articles, in online video games, on salsa website advice columns, and in the movies. Such violence directed at Latina bodies contributes to the tensions among women as they activate themselves as salseras inside nightclub bathrooms and other spaces in the clubs.

Unity through women's homosociality might appear to have a chance in the women's bathroom, but a salsera's removing herself temporarily from the heteronormative club economy does not necessarily grant her a reprieve. In the absence of men, the bathroom does not blossom as a welcoming, comfortable, amicable space of sisterhood, in part because the antimigrant politics that affect salsa hierarchies in the club do not dissolve in the bathroom. In the protected space of the bathroom, women negotiate these antimigrant politics as they forge relationships with each other and compose salsera femininities designed for circulation in the hierarchical salsa economy. Though I have suggested that the cry for Celia is a commentary on the antimigrant heteronormative choreography in the dance space of the club, "Don't leave me, Celia!" may have been expressed so that Celia would not leave her friend alone to face the antimigrant, heteronormative choreography in the bathroom, a choreography activated and enacted by the other women.

Breeders, Borders, and Bathrooms: Criminalizing Migrant Latinas at The Legend

In a global economy that relies on the transnationalization of labor, U.S. representations of Latinas/os as "wetbacks" who toil in sweatshops, fields, and other people's kitchens compose the flip side of the hypersexualized stereotype of sequined latinidad.

In an article in the *New York Times* in 2005, James C. McKinley Jr. reported, "In the heavily polluted New River near the California border, Mexican migrants plunge through filth, knowing the Border Patrol will not wade in to arrest them."[1] McKinley located undocumented migrant bodies as Mexican laborers willing to swim through feces and chemicals for low-paying jobs that confine them to the bottom of the social and economic hierarchy in the United States:

> At night, migrants strip to their underclothes and slip into the fetid water of New River, a polluted waterway that smells of feces, chemicals and all other manner of putridity. They float by silently in clusters amid odd patches of white foam caused by detergents, while Border Patrol agents watch from the shore, waiting to see where they will try to get out and run. "They know we won't go into that water after them," said one agent, who did not give his name. "It's not worth the risk."

The act of crossing the border through polluted water only to be chased by the Border Patrol dehumanizes migrants and even nonimmigrant Latinas/os.

The performance of sequined latinidad helps some salseras/os create alternate identities. But it is not easy. Pop-cultural representations of women migrants in the act of crossing the border are particularly difficult images to displace. In the crudely designed Internet video game *Border Patrol*,[2] the Mexican woman who crosses the border is depicted as pregnant, with hairy armpits, sweating, and towing two children as she dashes barefoot into the United States. She is "The Breeder." This and other representations of Mexican women feed stereotypes that depict women as crossing the border in order to exploit U.S. social services and to give birth to what the media have called "anchor babies," children whose birth in the United States entitles them to U.S. citizenship.

The object of the game is to protect the United States by gunning down migrants who run for their lives into the country. While the shooter earns one point for every migrant man executed,[3] a single strategic bullet kills The Breeder, her children, and the fetus, earning the shooter four points. Patriotic exterminations are quantitatively worth four times as much when directed toward female rather than male migrants.

The stereotype of the migrant Mexican woman as a breeder circulates widely in the United States. In 2006 at the University of Illinois, Urbana-Champaign, the Zeta Beta Tau fraternity and the Tri-Delta sorority hosted a Mexican-themed costume party in which the men dressed up as farm workers and the women as pregnant. This is just one example of a fear of the Latina breeder that can be linked to a history of surgical sterilization of Puerto Ricans, Latinas, and other minorities, as well as poor women more generally. This is both old news and new news: Project Prevention was founded in 1997, offering to sterilize women who are drug addicts.[4] The organization's billboards in predominantly black and Latina/o California neighborhoods offered women addicted to drugs two hundred dollars to be sterilized. The ideological and physical violence of stereotyping video games, Greek system parties, and eugenics movements are the ones that Latinas attempt to leave behind upon entering a salsa club in the borderlands.

Yet the clubs are not utopian spaces in which these kinds of violence dissipate. As noted earlier, in order to be considered desirable dance partners in the embattled salsa economy, salseras must dislocate their dance techniques from Mexico. They should not dance too slowly, repeat moves, bounce, or perform a basic step that crosses behind or they may be accused of "dancing like a Mexican." Salseras instead infuse their forward-and-back basics with a standardized arsenal of speedy spins and stylized arm gestures. Indeed many salseras attempt to disguise bodily features that could locate them as unskilled, Mexican migrant labor. They dress in short skirts, sequined tops, and glittery silver shoes with leather soles. They take bathroom breaks to prepare to reenter the fantasy space of latinidad: there they tuck away unruly strands of soggy hair, reapply lipstick, and paper-towel the dampness of their smoothly shaven armpits in order to distance themselves from the tousled and terrifying body of The Breeder. Given the antipathy directed toward pregnant Latinas, it is not surprising that during my research I encountered only one visibly pregnant Latina in the salsa economies.

In the corner of The Legend's women's bathroom, across from the couches, in a chair that looked like it was taken from somebody's kitchen, sat a bathroom attendant selling little bottles of lotion, tissues, bandages, and breath fresheners. She expertly avoided eye contact with anyone, even when someone purchased one of her wares. Her own efforts to make herself as invisible as possible were evenly matched by the efforts of the other women in the bathroom who looked past, through, and away from her. Her gray-uniformed body, the kind of body that many of the women disguised, was an unwelcome reminder of the kind of Latinaness the club patrons were associated with in everyday life. While many of the women recalibrated their femininity to stand out as desirable, the bathroom attendant did not blot out her working body with makeup or disguise it with sequins.

Although the attendant did not draw attention to herself, her very presence pointed to the patrons' frustrated attempts at social mobility in daily life. The attendant earns twenty-five dollars a night in cash, approximately the same amount it takes for one patron to pay for an evening's parking and admission. To acknowledge her presence would threaten the myth that there is no class difference among the women at The Legend and that club hierarchies of belonging and desirability do not interlace with the politics of migration outside the club. In the nightclub setting, her body disrupts a choreography in which patrons disavow the capitalist economy of daily life by activating the libidinal features of the salsa economy.

Homosociality, Alliances, and (Undoing) the Mystique of El Papi Chulo

Celia's friend emerged from the stall and rejoined the friends waiting for her in the bathroom lounge at The Legend, assured she would not have to make her way through the club on her own. In nightclubs, homosociality among women includes friendships such as Celia's, romantic relationships, dance teacher–student relationships, and familial relationships. Even as the politics of migration and class threaten to dismantle homosociality among the women, the strictly enforced gender divisions in nightclub bathrooms facilitate homosociality.[5] Latina salseras configure femininity and homosociality in competition with the Latinas and non-Latinas who have become increasingly skilled at performing sequined salsa techniques and personas.

Although some of the women at The Legend are connected through long-term relationships outside the club, homosocial interactions among women in the bathroom are usually brief, and for a number of reasons. Other than providing a respite from the traffic in salseras on the other side of the door,[6] the bathroom is not an especially pleasant locale. Along with spritzes of perfume and deft smearings of scented lip gloss, it stinks of musty wallpaper, mildewed crevices, perspiration, unflushed toilets, and occasional puddles of regurgitated alcohol. It is also not entirely socially acceptable to spend long periods of time in the bathroom, causing people on the outside to wonder what exactly you are up to and thus diffusing the bathroom's aura of secrecy. At The Legend, the bathroom feels almost like a lounge because of the couches and the spaciousness. Even so, when women enter alone, the interactions among them are few and fleeting:

> Are you in line?
> *Con permiso.*
> There's no toilet paper in this one.
> *¡Ay!* I didn't know anyone was in there.

In other words, the bathroom is not the place to make new friends. Unknown women are often regarded with suspicion, mistrust, and belligerence, just as baseball players of opposing teams might look upon each other if they had to share the same dugout.

The homosocial relationships between club-goers like Celia and her friends comprise not only homosocial friendships but also alliances. The Latinas in the bathroom form their alliances amid a heterogeneous salsa club society stratified by differences in class, race, and nation. Celia's alliance is situated within a space of leisure that largely produces social and racial hierarchies in dance terms.

Evaluations based on sophistication, complexity, line, and style tend to disconnect dance practices from associations with race, class, and nation. And alliances are difficult to forge among women whose conceptualizations of salsa club femininity do not correlate. Celia and her friends' connections before their bathroom break, as well as their apparent cultural and class similarities, facilitate their nightclub alliances. Their conformity with codes of femininity, in which women, specifically Latinas, should not move around singly in the club, holds their homosocial alliance in place. From what I witnessed, the alliance between members of Celia's group is about effectively navigating the patriarchal nightclub economy, not necessarily about undoing it.

Outside of the bathroom, women homosocially demystify (rather than attempt to undo) the gendered practices and antimigrant codes within the club economy in order to participate more fully on their own terms. Some have learned that romanticized Hollywood versions of the salsa-dancing nightlife can play out with unwanted complications off-screen. They renegotiate the terms of their club participation, passing their knowledge on to other women.

One night at The Legend I was sitting at a table next to a woman in her thirties who had driven all the way from a town past Riverside, almost two hours away. Flor had come to the club to meet up with her niece Silvita, her niece's friend Doris, and two male friends. Until recently she had worked in la limpieza. Many Latinas speak of la limpieza as one of the main industries available to them in Los Angeles, along with the more high-profile and glamorous entertainment and media industry. Recently Flor had to stop working to have carpal tunnel surgery in both wrists and was supporting herself temporarily on worker's compensation while she recovered.

When the guys got up to get a drink, Flor told me that she had come to the club as a way to move on with her life after her recent divorce. The previous December, she had gone home to El Salvador for a month; when she returned she found another woman living in her house with her husband, sleeping in her bed, washing her dishes, and listening to her music. She was devastated and wondered if her husband had replaced her because la limpieza had taken a toll on her body.

Silvita and Doris, who had been dancing, returned to the table when the merengue ended and the deejay switched to salsa. Silvita pointed past me to a guy in a fedora, a gold chain, and a long coat who was strutting by the tables. "Es un papi chulo," Flor shouted through the music. She laughed, and the three of us joined in. A term of endearment employed by a spouse, a lover, or even a mother, *papi chulo* literally means "beautiful man." A papi chulo also connotes a man whom women desire, can't help but fall in love with, or fight over for his affections. More than simply beautiful or desirable, a papi chulo is so irresistibly sexy that he seduces women with very little effort, is probably involved with more than one woman at a time, and is capable of breaking someone's heart when he finds a more desirable, probably younger lover with a body undamaged by la limpieza.[7]

If any of us at the table had been susceptible to Papi Chulo's seductive aura, Flor broke the spell with her revelation. She called our attention to how carefully he had cultivated and performed a masculinity that most likely withered outside of the salsa club economy. Her laughter demystified the performance as she passed on her insight to the younger women and me. Perhaps she saw in him a younger version of her husband, so that her story illuminated the class-based consequences of getting involved with a papi chulo. Unlike many of the middle- and upper-class Latinas and non-Latinas in the club, a working-class Latina like Flor might find that she has no choice but to return to la limpieza to support herself when her papi chulo moves on to a woman he finds more desirable.

We laughed in the midst of a thick crowd, and the music that blasted from the speakers both confined and protected our homosocial interaction. Flor's decoding of salsero masculinity occurred unnoticed by all but the women at our table, as she passed on the wisdom of her experiences.

Nalgas, Freakish Advice, and "the Old Country": Competing Codes of Salsera Femininity

As they negotiate antimigrant demands to perform sequined Latinaness, salseras often simultaneously find themselves pressured to identify with sequined Latinaness at the expense of other practices of Latinaness. At issue are their identifications with and rejections of classed and racialized femininities that overlap with antimigrant politics.[8] If many of the Latinas at The Legend identify with a sequined Latinaness in Los Angeles, they also may identify with practices of femininity from other localities.

In various Los Angeles nightclubs, Latinas navigate the tensions between the femininities of daily life and nightly life in the United States and Latin America.

They thread together practices associated with more than one locality, not with the aim of fully resisting and overturning antimigrant, patriarchal club economies but often to smooth their way through them, perhaps creating moments of disruption as they go. In salsa clubs like The Legend, when women compete with each other for dance partners, they also compete with women who have cultivated their skills at performing sequined Latinaness.

María Elena, a Mexican salsera, incriminates white non-Latina women for breaking with what she considers the respectable codes of Latina femininity by flaunting excessive mobility and hypersexuality in the clubs. At The Legend she often visually tracked the traffic patterns of white women and voiced her observations to me:

> White women do not know the culture of the club. They just walk in alone, walk around the club by themselves like they own the place, and ask Latinos to dance. And it works. Men dance with them all night. They come dressed in all these freaky outfits pretending to be "Latina." Look at those two over there in their poodle skirts! What do they think this is? The sock hop? That one in the mini skirt is wearing a thong and you can see her *nalgas* [butt cheeks] every time she spins. She looks like Barbie. But white women can get away with that because no one expects them to know any better. My boyfriend would be horrified if I did what they did.

María Elena is among the Latinas who perceive that the men in the club treat Latinas differently than they do the white women who attempt to perform sequined Latinaness. I have noticed that she is careful to go to the bathroom in the company of other women and dances only with her boyfriend, Aldo, who leaves her at the table to dance with whomever he pleases, including white women. He taught María Elena how to dance and is the only man with whom she has ever danced and with whom she ever wants to dance.

"I know it's not exactly fair," she said to me, calling attention to the gendered disparity in their dance club relationship. But she seemed to locate the injustice at least in part in the behavior of the white women; she refused to endorse a set of practices she associates with the ignorance, disrespect, entitlement, and promiscuity of white women.[9] She spoke lovingly of Aldo, who she said treats her respectfully, does not cheat on her, and supports her and their children. "He's no papi chulo," she said.

María Elena's response suggests a critique of white women for their interpretations of abstract Caribbean Latinas as hypersexual. This particular interpretation of sequined Latinaness not only reinforces the Hollywood industry's depictions of fictive black Caribbean Latinas as sources of eroticism and passion, but it also ignores and displaces the codes of femininity that the actual Latinas at the club navigate. Even though I have walked around by myself and defied my male partners' "protective" instructions ("Wait right here, I'll be back for you later"), I am very conscious of the codes of femininity that María Elena observes. Though I sometimes break with those practices, I am very aware when I do, so that a walk across the club to go to the bathroom on my own also involves a silent battle of rationalizations that mark my own (red-haired) Chicana feminist ethnographer positionality.

> *I'm passing as white and walking right into the meat market.*
> *Not all Latinas enact the same practices of femininity as does María Elena.*
> *But as a fair-skinned Chicana roaming around the club unattended, I feel like I'm reinforcing the perceived binary between women (including elite Latinas) who identify with middle-class Americanized ideologies of femininity and Latinas who identify with ideologies from other localities. In other words, I feel like I'm being disrespectful.*
> *If I don't walk around like this, I'll never get any work done. It's part of my research.*

As María Elena spoke, I found myself identifying to some degree with her critique of white salseras. What white women were able to "get away with," as she put it, was the displacement of the unsequined Latinas who come to dance as part of socializing.

My conversation with María Elena suggests that some Latinas interpret white women's performance of sequined Latinaness and excessive mobility as entitled, misguided, and vulgar and that these particular white women are unaware of or do not care how their actions affect Latinas. When I spoke with Valerie, a white salsera, about María Elena's perception that white women break with club codes of femininity by moving around the club by themselves, she was shocked. "But I do that all the time!" she told me. From María Elena's standpoint, Latinas must be more conscious of their actions in the clubs because the setting is an extension of their daily lives. When she leaves the club, she continues to interact with other Latinas/os with whom she socializes at night. She and Aldo have children together and extended family in common and are part of a larger sociocultural network that shares similar ideologies of gender.

María Elena also accuses white women of enacting erotic fantasies while poorly performing a temporary Latinaness. She conflates whiteness with a privileged disconnection from the everyday and nightly challenges and violence that she sees Latinas negotiating inside and outside the clubs. This does not mean that all Latinas identify with each other or do not identify with white women. It also does not mean that María Elena and other Latinas do not come to the club with fantasies of their own, including desires to dissociate themselves from stereotypes of Latinas as undocumented migrants, laborers, and breeders. María Elena's trip to the salsa club, however, is less of a fantasy and more of an outing not drastically detached from the Latina corporealities of daily life.

Edie "the Salsa Freak" would likely accuse migrant women like María Elena of being oppressed by traditions of what she would label "the Old Country." Edie "the Salsa Freak," via her popular salsa website and dance classes in the global salsa network, has become a primary ideologue for the practices of salsa, especially for her advice on gendered club etiquette. Several of the Latina salseras I have spoken with openly admire Edie and seek her approval, advice, and encouragement.

Edie Lewis of Colorado became more commonly known among salsa dancers as Edie "the Salsa Freak" after she visited a salsa club for the first time in Long Beach. She found herself enraptured by the passion of the "sexy bombshell Latina gal" who "was living what I was missing."[10] Thus she exclaims on her website what Savigliano (1995) theorizes as the First World's desire for the passion of the exotic Third World Other. She also complicates the theory precisely because many of the salsa practitioners with whom I have spoken, although they locate her as American, are unsure whether to identify her as Latina or white.

On her website's "Dear Edie" advice page, a male ballroom dancer expressed his frustration that women in salsa clubs will not accept his invitations to dance. He had no such problem in ballrooms, spaces that many Latinas/os like María Elena racialize as white. He wrote, "I wonder if a bit of ballroom-style socialization might make salsa clubs friendlier places in which to dance." In response to his suggestion that salseras need to be resocialized, Edie explained that salsa clubs are

> highly influenced by the conservative Latin culture—"the old country"—which is still very much alive today, and yes, right here in the United States. Let me define a typical standard "The Old Country" way of life for a young woman: This is where she doesn't leave mom and dad until she gets married, must be accompanied by a big brother on dates until she's 18 or 21, never looks a man in the eye, wears a shawl over her head, is an avid Catholic, is super shy, is expected to get married, have many children, stay home, take care of the house, never question . . . all that. Many Latin women simply will not dance with people they don't know. Period.[11]

Edie could have attributed the unfriendliness to the competitiveness of salsa clubs in which both men and women strive to reach the top of the social hierarchy by dancing only with highly skilled sequined partners. She could have suggested that the troubled dancer sign up for one of her salsa boot-camp weekends to make himself a more attractive partner. Instead she blamed his problem on the Latinas in the club, wielding racism under the guise of postfeminism. She did not refer to the conceptualizations of Latinas as sexy and exotic but described specifically Mexican and Central American women who bring their "conservative Latin culture" with them when they migrate to the United States. She portrays these "conservative" Latinas as childlike and unable to challenge their families who raise them to be Catholic breeders. Edie effectively reduced the complexities of María Elena's decision to dance only with Aldo to a stereotypical narrative that defines Latinas as conservative, Catholic migrants. Her description of the Latinas that plague ballroom dancers in salsa clubs contrasts with her portrayal of Latinas as sexy and passionate, embodying the Latinaness she desires to cultivate.

In conversation with me, Olivia, a Mexican woman from Orange County, reflected on the way the desires of white women to dance with sexy, papi chulo types influence Latino expectations of women in a heterosexist economy. The Latinas I have spoken with who could pass for white because of their skin color have expressed resentment toward white women who "fuck with our guys."

"Word is getting out among the Anglo women that this is where to come to pick up Latinos," Olivia, who is fair-skinned, said to me one summer night at The Legend.[12] "They make it harder for us, because the guys start to think all women with lighter skin want sex, will treat them like kings, or let them grope us when we dance." For emphasis, she points out a white woman who thrusts her hips back and forth then shakes them side to side with her back to her Latino dance partner, butt to pelvis. The implication is that the white women use "our guys" for nighttime pleasures (i.e., sex and dancing with "your nalgas hanging out"), rarely incorporate them into their daily lives, and leave Latinos dissatisfied with the Latinas of daily life who do not accommodate the exaggerated gender roles of the sequined Latino–sequined Latina club dynamic.

Now that she has cut her hair short, Olivia said, Latinos don't recognize her as Latina anymore. They treat her like a white woman who is looking for a brief sexual encounter with a Latino. She resents being drawn into the dominant dynamic between white women and Latinos, having to negotiate her identification with Latinaness while being assigned the identity of whiteness in the salsa club. As Olivia explained her frustration, I found myself able to relate, recognizing the limitations of the primary ways we have learned to read the body in the United States, privileging skin color. The whiteness of a woman's body often overshadows her culture, class, ethnicity, and history.

I have noticed that when someone who classifies me as white invites me to dance, my moving, speaking body complicates his perceptions. These men often ask me how I learned to dance "like a Latina," meaning someone who did not take classes to learn how to dance, and why I speak Spanish. My moving body does not signify either whiteness or Latinaness, but rather like-Latinaness—the kind of Latinaness that necessitates parenthetic qualifiers such as "(red-haired)."

I discussed this with Olivia, who said that once she explains to potential dance partners that she was born in Mexico, they seem to feel that they can't get away with the same kinds of behavior they might with someone they would consider an outsider. She thus corroborates the conjecture that within the club economy, women abide by, and are expected to abide by, different practices of femininity. Even if a white woman performs virtuosic sequined Latinaness while dancing, she may not identify with the codes that María Elena and Olivia associate with the Latinaness of their everyday lives.

Although María Elena, Olivia, and I have discussed differences between Latinas and white women in terms of a binary racial relationship, the observations can be reinterpreted within a framework that accounts for differences in class and nation. Another woman, Bianca, said she is fed up with the gender games at salsa clubs and hardly ever goes out dancing anymore. Bianca identifies as Chicana, comes from a solidly upper-middle-class family, and is a graduate student in English at the University of Southern California, while María Elena identifies as

Mexican and an immigrant, comes from a working-class family whose mother is a seamstress in a downtown factory, and is an undergraduate at UCLA.

The night I met up with Bianca at The Legend marked her return to the club after about a year's hiatus. On my way back to our table after observing the negotiations of women in the bathroom, I noted a Latino with dark curly hair and green contact lenses slowly easing out of the chair and slinking away. It turns out that Mateo had bought Bianca a margarita and, not unexpectedly, tried to get her phone number. "I have a boyfriend," she told him, which was actually the truth.

"Where is he?" Mateo had asked, looking over his shoulder nervously. Bianca explained that her boyfriend did not like to go out dancing and stayed at home. Finishing the story, she said, "That's when he said, 'If you were my girlfriend, I would never let you go out to a salsa club by yourself.' And *I* said, 'That's why he's my boyfriend and not you.'"

Bianca thus confronted Mateo, insisting that his projection of what constitutes a good boyfriend did not correspond with her own desires. To me she acknowledged that Mateo perceived her boyfriend as callous for not accompanying her to the club. Yet intertwined with what Mateo may have intended as a compliment was his notion of the power differential between genders. Bianca told me that she was not interested in being in a relationship with someone who acted like her supervisor. As soon as Mateo indicated that he would never let her go out alone, Bianca lost interest in the conversation.

A salsera like Bianca might suggest that women like María Elena restrict their own mobility and passively uphold a salsa patriarchy that oppresses them. When lamenting the difficulties of making it to the dance floor or the discomfort of walking around by myself for the sake of ethnography, I too have been scolded by women, mostly at the university, for the same thing, challenged with claims like these:

> *Why didn't you ask him to dance if you were tired of being a wallflower?*
> *You should dance with other people besides your boyfriend!*
> *You shouldn't be ashamed to dance with another woman!*
> *Don't be afraid to turn him down if you don't want to dance with him.*

Admonitions such as these came from both Latinas and non-Latinas who identify with the values of American liberal feminism or have established themselves socially and economically outside the club. They tend to reduce a woman's perceived lack of mobility to her level of individual confidence and assertiveness. But similar claims might be based on a different, albeit equally stereotypical critique.

Jennifer, a white salsa dancer I met in L.A., criticized not the individual woman but what she called "conservative Latin American culture." She rationalized that Latinas in salsa clubs have less mobility than white women because "in traditional Latin American culture, women are not used to having so much freedom." In other words, Latinas are accustomed to victimization within a culture of "backwardness." Both kinds of critique are unsatisfying and reinforce the need to reflect upon the differences among women and their identifications with conflicting and multiple practices of femininity in relation to class.

As a woman's social and economic status outside the club increases, there is less at stake in breaking with the codes of Latina femininity in nightly practices. In many cases, the Latinas and non-Latinas who break with these codes have established themselves in the economy outside the clubs. They are often middle- and upper-class women with a university education, like Bianca, or Hollywood celebrities. Those who move around on their own move with the same or even an increased kind of entitlement to which they are accustomed outside the club, whether they do so consciously, like Bianca, or not, like Valerie. A temporary brush with the exotic or marginalized classes will not likely negatively affect their social class and respectability outside the club. On the contrary, they may gain cultural capital because of their knowledge of "other" cultures. And they may gain cultural capital within postfeminist circles that celebrate women for choosing to awaken their presumed repressed sexualities through "forbidden" activities, such as salsa dancing.[13]

Sex and Revolutions

"Ladies, Let's Start a Revolution!" proclaims Edie "the Salsa Freak's" website. The dance-floor revolution is meant to allow women to bring back their supposedly lost sex appeal, and the dance floor is an acceptable place in which to "get away with" being sexy. Unless you are a "woman from the islands," that is, "if you don't have, nor were born with, natural sex appeal, the 'natural' island hip movement, the look, the attitude, and the flaring of the hands, ballet and Latin ballroom dance training is the next best thing."[14] Edie's description of the sexually repressed, "super shy" migrant Latinas contrasts with her invocation of the uninhibited, passionate

Latina of the islands, the one whom women without "natural" sex appeal can learn to emulate in order to incite or take part in a dance-floor revolution.

Her representations inscribe Latinas as either a conservative migrant who will dance only with men she knows or a hypererotic woman of the islands. The website thus manipulates two dominant Latina stereotypes, both of which come up lacking in global North standards of civilization measured in modernist terms of progress. It is the modern women of the global North who presumably can benefit from a salsa sex revolution. Unlike Marxist ideologies of revolution in which working-class laborers contest their exploitation within a capitalist system, the proposed salsa sex revolution appropriates revolutionary terminology in support of the continued exploitation of the exoticized dance practices of women of the global South.

The revolution page of Edie's website exoticizes not the practices of the Latinas observed on a nightly basis in Los Angeles nightclubs but the fictive, singular Latina who exudes her sex appeal effortlessly on the island. As in salsa clubs, circulations of salsa dancing in the Hollywood industry often reproduce the scenarios in which nameless Latinas who are featured extras or supporting actresses are displaced by white leading ladies who learn to connect with their sexuality by becoming "Latina" on the dance floor. Such is the case in *Dirty Dancing: Havana Nights*, as the protagonist Katey Miller, an American (played by Romola Garai), discovers her sexuality while learning to dance with Javier Suarez (played by Diego Luna), a young Cuban waiter at her hotel. Katey's intercultural coming-of-age happens at the expense of—and through—the displacing and dispensing of the black Cuban women in the film.

Katey reconstructs the memory of her unexpected and undesired relocation to Cuba in November 1958. Interrupting the trajectory of her senior year of high school and college plans, her father follows his career with Ford Motor Company and moves his white, upper-middle-class family to Havana. In her introductory narrative, Katey identifies herself as more intellectual and less frivolous than the other girls at her American high school—they want to talk about prom, while she wants to read Jane Austen—and implies that her intellectual goals will not be achieved while living in a place like Cuba. Cityscapes of Havana flash into postcards with captions that read "Land of Romance" and "Holiday Isle of the Tropics" and back into live-action shots. The images freeze the U.S. imagination of prerevolutionary Cuba as a playground for (U.S.) Americans.

Popping in and out of this colorful opening collage, snapshots of Katey and other girls from her U.S. high school yearbook black-and-whitely fuel the binary opposition between a modest upper-middle-class female sexuality of a rational, stable United States and an uncontained female sexuality of a volatile Cuba. The postcard image of a smiling Cuban woman dancing beneath a palm tree, swirling the white ruffles of her skirt, contrasts severely with Katey in a somber black sweater, withdrawn in the backseat as she rolls into Havana. The visual dissimilarities between Katey's austere ballroom-trained body and the bodies of dancing Cuban women in the first minute of the movie not only distinguish the women from each other in terms of race, class, and nation but also foreshadow Katey's thirst to learn mambo in the "land of fiestas and siestas."

Fifty-seven seconds into the opening sequence, the film continues to represent Katey's ballroom femininity as associated with the intellect, in sharp contrast to Cuban femininity as associated with a hypersexualized body.[15] Katey and a Cuban woman briefly partner each other, though not in the same frame. Katey stands stiff and uncertain before a lifesize postcard of Havana. The scene cuts to a blurred image that gains focus as the camera pulls away and the music from the background gains volume. The blur where Katey once stood takes the shape of a Cubana filmed from behind, wearing tight pants that accentuate the rhythmic wiggle of her hips as she dances with a crowd of happy Cuban men and women in the street. Cinematically Katey's body becomes a Cuban body.

This leads into a series of shots of black Cuban bodies writhing against each other and glistening with sweat in a Havana nightclub we come to know as La Rosa Negra (The Black Rose).[16] The words "*Dirty Dancing: Havana Nights*, Based on True Events" emerge over the bodies, situating their moves as dancing, as dirty, as black, as Cuban, and as in the realm of the factual. Back in the car, Katey continues in voiceover, "I was really scared." Although she refers to her transition to Cuba in general, her statement of fear also frames the visual representation of the black dancing bodies—bodies that perform an exotic sexuality that both frightens and fascinates.[17]

By the end of the movie, the day after the Cuban Revolution and the day before the Americans return to the United States, Katey and Javier successfully attain the status of King and Queen of the Night at La Rosa Negra, displacing the Cuban woman who previously held the title. While Katey may be queen for one night, she does not occupy the political position of Cubans by day. The Revolution curtails her reign at La Rosa Negra. With her U.S. passport, she returns to the

United States, as Javier and the Cuban women at La Rosa Negra stay put to deal with the everyday realities of the Revolution. Katey's displacement of the Cuban woman at the club may be temporary, but it establishes the triumph of a white liberal bourgeois American ballroom femininity over a static, hypersexualized Cuban femininity, unchanged by revolutions on or off the dance floor.

Edie's salsa sex revolution dovetails with this kind of dance-floor displacement of Caribbean Latinas, and it also involves a further disavowal of the predominant Mexican and Central American Latinas in Los Angeles. Her representation of these Latinas as passive, naïve, static, and obedient, always willing to sacrifice their own desires in order to please their boyfriends, husbands, brothers, fathers, and sons, interlaces with the politics of migration and gender. Her portrayal of migrant femininity, however, contradicts the Latinaness enacted by Flor, Olivia, and María Elena. The migrant women with whom I interacted at The Legend are active, not passive and obedient, participants in salsa clubs with their own critiques and desires. They are incredibly astute about the contentious gendered nightclub choreographies and violence directed toward their migrant Latina bodies.

How to Take a Break from the Dance Floor, Con Respeto

I returned to Las Feliz Edades, the club that the sequined classify as the place where undocumented migrants from Mexico and Central America go to socialize and pick up sex partners, to further understand the codes of migrant Latina femininity and homosociality.[18] This time I planned to go with my friends Ilana and Beto, salsa dancers who had never been to the club. Beto couldn't make it at the last minute, so Ilana and I went together, or *solitas*, without the company of a man. When we arrived, the manager offered to find us a place to sit but said we might have to wait a little while by the bar before a table opened up.

This time I would make it a point to talk with the women at the club, although I knew that being new and standing in the bar area meant we would be thrust into constant interactions with men, something that Beto's presence might have thwarted or at least reduced. So Ilana and I danced with a couple of guys from El Salvador before we had time to find a place to stash our jackets. Back by the bar, a very young, skinny guy popped up in front of us, still wearing his jacket, and offered to buy us beers. From Guatemala, Enrique was twenty years old and had recently moved to Van Nuys after the death of his mother. He told us that she had died of a broken heart when his father left with another woman.

Los Angeles was a beautiful place, he beamed, full of opportunities. He wanted to practice his English with us, even though Ilana and I had both been speaking Spanish with him. Please, could he buy us a beer? We refused multiple insistent variations on the invitation, knowing that "just one beer" could mean one beer plus one man's claim on a woman for the entire night. But we were two women intent on sticking together in this scene, and he was just one earnest young man who seemed desperate to join us. Ilana and I had both been to plenty of clubs before and had some experience navigating the gendered pitfalls, but against our better judgment we finally gave in to his pleas. Not quite persuaded that the opportunities in Los Angeles had provided him with enough extra cash to pay for three beers on top of a thirteen-dollar entrance fee, we said that we would have a beer with him but would buy our own. He was thrilled. "Don't worry," he said, "mi hermano mayor pagará [my older brother will pay]!" And suddenly he was dragging his big brother, Saulo, away from his dance partner to buy us drinks.

The next thing I knew, I was holding Ilana's jacket, purse, and barely sipped beer, along with my own, and drinking with Enrique, while Saulo and Ilana danced. Despite our intention of learning more about codes of femininity and homosociality among the women in the club, Ilana and I had been there for less than ten minutes before we had been split up into heterosexual couples. Enrique had scouted out the scene and recruited us for him and his brother. On my previous trip to the club, I had been seated with a table of men but had been placed there by the manager, who had entrusted my care to his good friend Lorenzo. Without the explicit pact between men to treat a woman *con respeto*, a woman often has a lot of convincing to do before a man will discontinue unwanted advances. I could not tell how things would unfold with Saulo.

Even when women at clubs like Las Feliz Edades don't want the company of men who have approached them, just saying no can exacerbate situations. As I stood at the bar with Enrique, I recalled Sarita's story about the night she went to Valentino's when a burly bodyguard type who hung out at the drug dealer's table kept approaching her table to ask her to dance. Not wanting to get mixed up with the drug ring, she declined him each time he asked throughout the night. Finally, she said she had to get very firm. "I just roared 'No!' and gave him a dirty look. Then he got irritated, looked me in the eyes, and muttered something like, 'No te creas que seas tanto' before he left me alone.[19] Now I don't really want to go back to that club for a while." Sarita said that she had learned the skill of respectfully turning down an invitation to dance, so that the guy would understand that she meant to decline the dance, not reject him. "Guys face a lot of rejection every night. They need pretty big egos just to walk into the club." Unfortunately, she said, this guy took the rejection personally. "He got really aggressive," she said, "which is an exception to how most of the guys take getting turned down."

Sarita is also somewhat of an exception. At clubs in which patrons desire sequined latinidad, many middle- and upper-class women decline a man's invitation to dance based on his inability to distance himself from practices and outfits associated with the working class or with Mexicanness. Unlike many of these women, Sarita was very conscious that by declining to dance with someone, she might appear to be "snobby" and to reinforce club hierarchies. In order to avoid disrespectful breaches of club etiquette or angry insults, it is especially useful for women to learn some of the club-specific refusal techniques that correspond to the heterosexist economy predominant at each site.

Ilana and I were working on it at Las Feliz Edades. When she returned to collect her beer and personal effects, Saulo trailing right behind her, she quickly hollered in my ear (so that no one else could hear), "When he started getting into the groping dance, I told him I wanted to take a break!" Saulo then turned to talk to me, asking why I came to the club. I told him about my work, and then I said, "Hay como cinco hombres por cada mujer en este club. ¿A qué vienen los hombres aquí? ¿Por qué vienes tú aquí?"

"Los hombres vienen aquí en busca de sexo."

"¿Por qué vienen las mujeres?" I asked.

"Vienen a lo mismo," he responded.

"Bueno, nada mas para que sepas, mi amiga y yo no venimos a eso. Trabajamos en un proyecto."

"Sí, ya sé. Yo les trataría con el mayor respeto."[20]

Later that night, after Ilana had had a few more dances with Saulo, she grabbed me by the arm and said, "We've got to go to the bathroom!" The security guard outside the women's room would not let me enter with my beer, so I had to leave it on the deejay's counter. "I think he finally got the message that I am not interested in taking him home with me," she said to me, after locking us together behind the stall door.

He was trying to get my phone number and kept touching my arm. I think he's getting desperate because it's after one o'clock and the club is going to close in an hour. I told him I had a boyfriend and he said we could just be friends, but that in the U.S., you could have sex without a committed relationship. I told him I was from a very Catholic family and didn't believe in sex without marriage. Then I said I had to go to the bathroom. By the way, I don't think they are really brothers, because Saulo calls Enrique his amigo.

Ilana's idea to hang out in the bathroom for a few minutes so that Saulo would move on proved effective. Or maybe she ruptured his sexual desire for her with the invocation of Catholicism. He had told Ilana that none of the people at the club would ever dare to be so publicly sexual with each other back in Guatemala, or Honduras, or wherever they had come from. Sexual promiscuity was an American behavior, he explained. When we emerged, he was wrapped in the embrace of the woman he had been dancing with earlier that night.

When Enrique saw that his "brother" had given up on Ilana, he decided to step in. Earlier he had abandoned his quest for my affections, disturbed by my focus on the women at the club. He quizzed Ilana about my queer behavior after I left to join a table with two women, both about forty-five, who had been laughing and dancing with each other and with several different men during the night. The way they seemed to enjoy every moment of the evening reminded me of my friend's aunts with whom I used to socialize at the afternoon dances in Costa Rica.

Unlike my interactions with some of the younger women at Las Feliz Edades who wanted little to do with me, the three of us clicked right away. I suspect they did not view me as competition or did not care even if I was. I spoke mostly with Angélica, who said that each week she and her best friend, Yesenia, came to Las Feliz Edades in between their work shifts. They both work in la limpieza, she said, and the only time they got to see each other was during a short window of time on Saturday nights after one got off work at 7 o'clock and before the other began work at 3 in the morning. They had each carefully done up their short hairdos, makeup, and outfits and were the most elegant of all the women present.

Angélica wore a white embroidered dress that fell past her ankles. Yesenia wore a black polyester evening gown with a shimmery rhinestone fringe that hung below the bustline, and a matching rhinestone necklace. In contrast to the short skirts, fishnets, and bare bellies of the younger women, and the cleaning uniforms they said they wore on their day jobs, their outfits made them look like queens—the queens of the night. Their table was right in the thick of the club, giving them the best possible vantage point from which to see and be seen. A cumbia came on, and the two, excited by hearing one of their favorite songs, pulled me up to join them in a trio. We danced for just a short moment together, and then three young guys joined us, steering us into three groups of two.

None of us experienced the groping problem that Ilana had mentioned. Angélica and Yesenia were obviously not interested in picking up anyone and must have already established that with numerous dance partners. I noticed that their protected positioning extended to me. Just as the aunts in Costa Rica liked to joke that they were my chaperones, my liaisons who taught me how to navigate a club culture unfamiliar to me, Angélica and Yesenia seemed to briefly step into chaperone mode. Or rather, since I had sat myself at their table, I had instigated the dynamic, one in which I was to benefit from their savvy.

Soon the three of us were back at the table, where I asked Angélica what she thought about Saulo's claim that both men and women came to the club seeking sex. She wrinkled her nose, forehead, eyes, and mouth and shook her head forcefully side to side. She held up her margarita in front of her and said slowly, "Nosotras pagamos nuestras propias bebidas. Ganamos suficiente para cubrir nuestros gastos. No dependemos de nadie."[21] As Angélica implied, a drink was not simply a polite or friendly social gesture but could double as a man's attempt to buy time with a woman. By financing her own drinks, she foreclosed the possibility of a man's haggling over the terms of her involvement with him. I wondered if the impetus for this particular information had resulted from her observation that Ilana and I had each accepted a beer from Saulo and Enrique.

"Quisiera bailar?" a guy asked me, breaking into our decodings of gendered relationships. He offered his hand, palm up, waiting for my acceptance. "Gracias, pero no," I said.

"Come on," he said, extending hand farther.

"No, gracias. Tengo una rodilla mala," I said. [I have a bad knee.] (That was at least part of the truth.)

"Just one dance," he stated, as if sealing the deal.

"Maybe later. We're having a conversation," I said, as he reached across me toward Angélica. All she had to do was drop her lids a little, peer straight at him, wrinkle her nose, and shake her head with a kind half-smile, as if she had a previous understanding with him and expected him to take her seriously.

Angélica's no was the kind that invited no negotiation. He immediately nodded and departed, disappointed but with the respect that she induced.

Without going to the bathroom, Angélica and Yesenia removed themselves intermittently from participating in the traffic in women. When they reentered, they almost imperceptibly challenged the patrons within the heterosexist economy to include them on their terms. They stand in contrast to Eva, the salsera who overtly challenged her dance partner's masculinity in front of an audience, and in doing so could not continue to participate with that particular clique at the salsa congress. Eva stunned the crowd with her unbelievable dance moves, while Angélica and Yesenia bopped around the floor with no evidence of formal dance training. However, Angélica and Yesenia, old enough to be the mothers of some of the women at Las Feliz Edades, were some of the most popular dance partners that night. They knew how attain their desires as they navigated the heterosexist choreographies of the club without displacing other women or rejecting the men. In a club where gaps between the richest and the poorest patrons are not as profound as in salsa clubs, the Las Feliz Edades patrons bring sometimes clashing fantasies with them to the club as they seek to stabilize themselves within, or escape from, the antimigrant violence of daily life in Los Angeles. Despite codes of sequined salsera femininity in which women try to hide their association with la limpieza or histories of migration, Angélica and Yesenia, in their rhinestones and evening gowns, defied stereotypes of Latinas as laboring bodies. On Saturday nights they regularly perform an alternate femininity than that allotted them in daily life, and yet they do not disavow that they are women of la limpieza.

Together Angélica and Yesenia dislodge stereotypes of migrant Latinas as victims of a conservative patriarchy. Like them, the men at Las Feliz Edades negotiate hegemonic white patriarchy in everyday life. As migrant women in transition to another locality, Angélica and Yesenia develop social tactics for participating in heteropatriarchies also in transition. Through their participation they exercise the power to craft gendered nightclub relationships as respectful alliances that can potentially transform their mobilities within the U.S. war on Latinas/os. What Angélica and Yesenia seem to know is that an empathetic, critical consciousness of the relationships among multiple Latina/o corporealities can give them an edge, a way out of the war.

Conclusion

Pause.

Salsa is danced latinidad. Over the last two decades salsa has surged across borders of nation, race, and class and has become the dance through which Latinas/os are identified on a global scale. Although cumbia, merengue, and tango have also crossed borders, none of these genres has achieved the same massive presence that salsa has in Los Angeles and around the world. No other popular dance associated with latinidad has been so relentlessly commodified and packaged as a "crossover" genre to the extent that salsa has. Salsa has "crossed over" to upper- and middle-class populations of Latinas/os and non-Latinas/os not because the form offers an essential appeal but because of the political, social, cultural, and economic value ascribed to the moves.

I have dwelt upon the movement practices in salsa clubs in order to understand latinidad as a social choreography that intertwines with power. Much of the material in this book has focused on the moods, judgments, alliances, perceptions, and hierarchy formation between bodies. Through choreographic ethnography, a methodological collaboration between choreographic and ethnographic analytical strategies, I have considered how moving bodies enact often clashing notions of latinidad.

Step-step-step.

My partner dips me, conking my head against the head of another woman during the next pause. A couple dancing salsa does not dance alone. Even an intimate partnership cannot evade becoming embedded within the continually changing social body of practitioners that often determines a person's identity by how and with whom that person moves. Who you desire to be and how you desire to move do not always coincide with how others interpellate you. For many Latinas and Latinos, dancing salsa becomes a way to claim a presence, both globally and in Los Angeles. Yet by elaborating on inter-Latina/o relations and Latina/o corporealities within salsa spaces, I have found that some salseras/os dance "wrong." Those who are labeled as dancing "wrong" are socially recognized as having failed to convert dance practices recognized as Mexican and Central American to dominant local standards of dance practices.

The pause marks a supple stillness that maintains mobility. Like the pause, latinidad as situated in Los Angeles is neither static nor homogeneously embodied. The pause in salsa spaces becomes a way to understand that enactments of latinidad are relational, contingent upon the social and political choreographic codes of time, space, and moving bodies. Latinidad may appear stable but is constantly in motion as dancers create and re-create it. This book pauses to challenge utopian frameworks that position salsa dancing as primarily resistive to the racial and economic violence of globalization.

Step-step-step. Pause.

My partner turns me away, holding my arms behind me so that I lean uninvited into the partnership of another couple. Across the time of six steps and two pauses, we dance as if a threesome. My elbow knocks a salsero in the jaw as I am whisked back around, duo restored. As couples, we share and compete for the same square footage but have to maneuver in such a way that we do not drop into the same spot simultaneously.

Given that Latinas/os are homogenized in U.S. migration policies and in hierarchies of racialization, this study has offered insights into interethnic gendered relationships in salsa clubs and a discussion of how salseras/os in Los Angeles reify and/or erase blackness. Rather than focusing on the kinesthetic dynamic between two dancing bodies in this partner dance, I have expanded salsa to the social realm, asking: Which bodies do not make it to the dance floor? How, where, and with whom do dancers move when they are not dancing? Broadened notions of movement in salsa spaces have decentered dominant areas of dance studies concern, such as the center stage, the dance floor, the dancing, and heteronormative couple dancing.

Pause.

Someone's sequined toes trail up my leg as her partner lowers her into a slow dip. Cologne lingers in the space that my partner swings us into. It reminds me of Benicio. The memory washes away with the aroma of stale, sweaty armpits. I think they belong to my partner. He turns my body into a weapon that harvests more of the tightening space around us. As more dancers fill up the floor, he still attempts the big, fast turns. A thick ponytail swats away my center of balance and I spin unsteadily without enough room between my partner and me to recover. He fakes a steady landing, converting my off-keel prestumble into a dip. A woman limps off to the bathroom to patch up a bloody foot. Salsa injuries can temporarily impede a dancer's participation but are rarely fatal. Salsa spaces are meant to be pleasurable, after all.

Crossing the salsa dance floors of this global city, we zoom forward, back, and down, in and out, up and around, overlapping spaces. Awareness of the other bodies dancing upon, between, and against us allows us to keep moving, even as the collisions threaten to land us in a collective, immobilized heap. When we forget about the other bodies moving around us in all directions at once, when we don't negotiate the shared space with enough precision, we step on each other.

Reflected upon in the abstract, the signature moves and moods of salsa accommodate a diversity of techniques and qualities and flow across borders of class, race, region, and nation. Dancers in couples mirror their partner's footwork and oppositional hip shifts. On the beat or on the offbeat, dancers cross behind, step forward and back, side to side, around one way and back another, or travel across the room. They embrace tightly, loosely, or with a frame, forging a song's-length attachment. Even when backing out of the embrace, dancers maintain the partnership through embodied calls and responses, through flirtatious glances met and averted, often during the pause. Because salsa was not standardized within a ballroom context early in its history, as was the waltz, for example, the multiplicity of interpretations and trajectories of development within each locality in which salsa has circulated offers flexibility in the way that practitioners perform the dance.

The L.A. couple dancing casino, or "Cuban salsa," moves in patterns that curl around one way and back the other. The two look as if they are about to dance off to opposite sides of the club, but during the pause his hold on her wrist snaps them back together. She has to pay attention to the cues from his grasp to note the sudden changes in direction. He playfully deludes her, intercepting her momentum with an unexpected turn. Pause. He returns her emergent grin. Without slowing or straightening the arc of their trajectory, they draw close together in an embrace, legs entwined, elbows reaching out and torsos rocking side to side.

They bend their knees deeply on one beat only to pop up and back down on the next beat. Still embraced, with a little more room between them, their torsos dip forward and butts push out, feet planted into the floor as they pivot around each other. The pause does not mean that they stop all the action. In casino, a pause arrests the flow of movement in one direction for just one flirtatious beat. In that beat, slight reverberations ripple up their bodies from the relaxed groundedness of the feet, to a sink in the knees, a rotation of the hips, followed by the ribs, an accent in the shoulders, a glimmer in the eyes. As the ripple moves out through the crowns of their heads, they savor the entire length of the pause before they shift their weight and drop into the rhythm on the other side. Through their posture, they acknowledge Cuban son, the popular dance that emerged in Cuba in the early 1900s. Through the reverberations of rhythm through their bodies, they evoke the image of Cuban rumba. Both references claim salsa as a legacy of Cuban music and dance.

With an air of superiority, the mambo dancer turns down offers of men she has seen dancing "on the one." At last someone she recognizes as a mambo dancer arrives and takes her by the hand. They have danced together before and belong to a small number of dancers in Los Angeles who "break on the two." That is, they pause on the first count, sometimes tapping in place, chins lifted slightly, holding their first step until count two. They not only follow the offbeat rhythm but embody the different layers of the recorded music, having memorized the irregular beats of the plentiful drum solos to which they synchronize the swift, percussive flicks, toe taps, and double heel digs of the footwork.

They embrace: out and near shoulder height, their elbows extended away from each other without raising or lowering in opposition to minute hip displacements. Torsos lifted, they swivel their hips around a vertical axis more than they allow their pelvises to pull their weight to the side. Brief shoulder shimmies and hip swivels rarely influence their unbending spines. The more skilled dancers, such as this couple, appear elegant rather than stiff. When he leads her into a string of spins, she centers her hips to maintain her balance and increase her speed. It is during the pause at the end of the turn sequence that she accents the hips, a gesture that reclaims their mobility. The contained energy of their upper bodies contrasts with the meticulous fervor of their feet, the dual vitalities a replication of practices associated with New York Palladium dancers in the 1950s.

While mambo dancers affix themselves to practices of a legendary time and place, L.A.-style salseras/os embody a contemporary, premeditated superstardom. His hand on her throat, she plunges into a neck drop, propelled back to standing by his foot. While the gendered interactions of the casino dancers allude to a playful attraction, the mood between leader and follower in L.A. salsa is overtly orgasmic tinged with violence, managing to exaggerate (possibly even parody) cinematic stereotypes of Latino dancing bodies. Before they hit the nightclub floor, they have carefully rehearsed routines, elements, and personas at home or in a studio. The partners selectively jump into the rhythm of only the faster-paced songs, considering the slower salsas more appropriate for beginners or *viejos* (old people).

L.A. salseras/os do not luxuriate in holding a beat for as long as possible, as casino dancers do, or arriving sharply on time, as mambo dancers do. Rather their steps tend to arrive with or slightly ahead of the beat. They perform the very first steps with an accelerated energy that only escalates, as their feet seem to rarely make contact with the floor. L.A. salseras/os embellish their moves with "tricks," like splits and back flips. They adapt moves from other genres such as hip-hop, tango, and swing. They incorporate personas from Hollywood blockbuster films. During the pauses, they mark the end of each series of intricate footwork, spectacular lifts, and stunning spins with triumphant poses: they extend their arms up and out, away from their bodies with clean lines, no rippling; they anchor themselves with the big toe of a knee-locked leg stretching behind them; they cock their heads to one side. Unlike the circuitous body rolls of the casino dancers, all of these gestures require their own momentum in order for dancers to initiate them as if each part were disconnected from the motions of the others.

When observing salsa as an embodied practice within a specific Los Angeles club, the practices of casino, mambo, and L.A.-style salsa are not ranked equally. Globalization's pressures to homogenize the practices of salsa in L.A. butt up against increasingly sophisticated processes of differentiation. Practitioners attempt to reinstate stylistic and identitarian boundaries when they blur and flow into one another without a moment of pause. Thus borders based on hierarchies of nation, race, and class are reinforced. Salsa practitioners dispute, concede, and proclaim L.A.-style salsa's growing dominance over all other local styles. With the rise of L.A. salsa, new techniques, such as keeping the hips centered so as to be ready to move in any direction rather than allowing them to pull one's weight to one side, call into question the legitimacy of other, hip-based practices.

Stipulations that the forward-and-back step is the one and only basic step do not recognize the crossing-behind step, associated with Mexico and Central America, as salsa. Such codifications that mark L.A.-style salsa challenge notions of salsa as a coherent, stable genre. The dance hierarchies that follow cut into visions of salsa as a uniting force.

Salseras/os in L.A. have always been seen as beneath New York salseras/os, my friend Maricruz told me, because L.A. salseras/os are associated with Mexicanness. In hierarchies of danced latinidad, practices associated with Nuyoricans and other Caribbean Latinos in New York rank higher than practices associated with Mexican and Central American Angelinos. Yet Los Angeles dancers are finally making a name for themselves. We have created our own style, Maricruz said, a style that people at congresses around the world are beginning to respect and emulate, even the dancers in New York.

The global salsa network expanded to include the first-ever Mexico World Salsa Congress at the Crowne Plaza in Acapulco in December 2005. What kinds of local dance politics will begin to accompany Mexico's membership in the global salsa network? With the intensifying global flow of L.A. salsa, what will happen during the pauses? As L.A.-style salsa takes a firmer hold on dance practices in Mexican nightclubs, old and new hierarchies of nation, class, and ethnicity have likely already begun to develop. Will Mexicans in Mexico value L.A.-style salsa over cumbia-inflected salsa practices? Will they straighten the crossing-behind step into a forward-and-back basic, smooth out the bounce, quicken the music, add tricks, and pose during pauses, as the Mexican dance teams have begun to perform at recent West Coast Salsa Congress exhibitions?

At Las Feliz Edades, Angélica and Yesenia, wearing the most elegant outfits in the club, sat at the most coveted, central table closest to the dance floor. From the third chair at the table, I glanced at the cumbia-inflected moves that accompanied the deejay's choice of salsa music. Most dancers stepped crossing behind, not forward and back. They sank into their hips, casually leaning back or eagerly tipping their weight forward. They tangled their fingers together loosely. Tentative frames arose and dissolved into close, cheek-to-cheek embraces. Dancers clung to each other in desperate romances that had nowhere else to go.

During the pauses, they accented a foot with a small ankle-height kick to the diagonal between the front and side. No poses, no slides into splits. No references to other localities for the purpose of out-authenticating other practices. No corrections, discussions of proper technique, or accusations that they were dancing salsa wrong. Dancers of casino, mambo, and L.A.-style salsa—salsa styles that circulate as part of world salsa congresses—do not register, exclude, or disavow the techniques practiced at Las Feliz Edades as salsa. Yet, week after week, the Las Feliz Edades patrons return to perform these "not-salsa" moves to salsa music, disrupting local efforts to spectacularize and deterritorialize latinidad through the production of global salsa.

The band follows the recorded salsa music by kicking off a lively set of cumbia. Angélica and Yesenia bounce up and beckon me to join them on the dance floor.

Notes

Preface

1. I have changed the names of most people and places. I use the real names of public and well-known figures (i.e., Carmen Nelson, Liliana Valle, Albert Torres, and Edie "the Salsa Freak").
2. A dance associated with the Garinagu culture on the Caribbean coast of Belize, Honduras, Nicaragua, and Honduras.
3. See Ana López (1997) for an analysis of the historical relationship between Hollywood films and latinidad.
4. I identify the people who made these comments only as "non-salseras/os" and not as individuals because several patrons across clubs made these same or similar statements. "No bailo salsa, bailo cumbia!" means "I don't dance salsa, I dance cumbia!"
5. See Deborah Root (1998: 30) for a discussion of violence as a trope of exoticism.
6. For works on women's employment of their own racialized eroticism, please see Parreñas Shimuzu (2007), Cooper (2005), and Kempadoo (2004).
7. For an analysis of the hypersexualization of Latinas, please see Aparicio and Chávez-Silverman (1997). For work on the circulation of Latinas in popular culture, please see Peña Ovalle (2011), Mendible (2007), and Molina Guzmán and Valdivia (2004).
8. For more on native ethnographers, please see Narayan (1997).
9. "All by yourself (as an unaccompanied woman).

Introduction

1. I realize that a surname does not necessarily indicate whether someone identifies as Latino or Latin American or not, but in this case I am interpreting surnames such as Torres, Moreno, and Cruz as signifiers of Latina/o-ness.
2. The website for Albert Torres Productions advertises its own West Coast Salsa Congress in Los Angeles and offers a link that lists "Congresses around the world." See https://alberttorresevents.com/congress/.
3. The global salsa network has since expanded to Latin America, as well as a few cities of the global South such as Lima, Quito, Acapulco, Medellín, and San José (Costa Rica).
4. The genres that preceded salsa, such as *danzón*, *guaracha*, bolero, son, cha cha chá, rumba, and mambo, have been circulating within Cuba, the Caribbean, the Americas, and beyond since colonization. For works that trace these genres, see Ortiz 1950, Linares 1974, and Rondón 1980.
5. Please see Roberts 1999, Quintero Rivera 1998, Ospina 1996, Rodríguez 1994, Ulloa 1992, Rondón 1980. See also Priscilla Renta (2004), who has noted the lack of scholarship on salsa dance.
6. I deliberately use *baile popular* rather than *Latin dance* to highlight the popular and creative practices of the dances such as salsa, cha cha chá, bolero *clásico*, and merengue, for example. I find that *Latin*, a term that drops the *American*, makes invisible the Latina/o and Latin American bodies that developed the practices. See also Waxer (2002: 5), who finds that the term *Latin* "tends to collapse difference in a way that can perpetuate oppressive stereotypes."
7. Aparicio (1999) highlights the ways that competing authenticities construct notions of latinidad.
8. See, for example, Mendible (2007: 7) who theorizes the Latina body as a transnational floating signifier.
9. This allusion to war references Limón's (1994) discussion of the war between the United States and Mexico and the contemporary class warfare experienced by Mexican Americans in Greater Mexico (the Mexican land lost to the United States). Limón analyzes how working Mexican Americans in south Texas battle the everyday conditions of postmodern socioeconomic domination through the nighttime practice of polka dancing, a residual tradition.
10. For a detailed account of this history, see Sánchez (1993), especially 87–107.
11. I would like to bring in Sánchez's analysis of the anthropologist Manuel Gamio, who, in the 1920s and 1930s, described Mexico's effort to forge a national unity by incorporating the indigenous populations into the vision of the nation. Gamio attributed U.S. economic success to what he considered a racially homogeneous population with a culturally harmonious set of beliefs and practices. In contrast, he ascribed the backwardness of Mexico and other Latin American countries to a racial heterogeneity (Sánchez 1993: 121).

12. Scott Gold, "Border Agents Warn of Influx," *Los Angeles Times*, May 16, 2004.
13. As I frame dance more broadly as movement practices, I echo Paul Scolieri's (2008: v) assertion that dance and migration studies both foreground movement as an analytic, each field poised to bring complex considerations to the other. In a 2008 special issue of *Dance Research Journal* with the theme "Dance and Migration," Scolieri traces the ways that migrants new to the United States forge identities through dance in the context of anti-immigration legislation and racism. In that volume Cruz-Manjarrez addresses the ways that Zapotec dance and identity change in their migration from Yalálag, Mexico, to Los Angeles. Like Cruz-Manjarrez, I am concerned with the ways that dancers conceptualize this migration.
14. My consideration is influenced by Lucy Burns (2008), who critiques the idea of Filipino men as "splendid dancers," an apparent affirmation that contributed to a historical amnesia, erasing the violence of U.S. colonization of the Philippines and the hostile climate to Filipinos in the United States outside of the dance halls.
15. The Treaty of Guadalupe-Hidalgo states that Mexicanos in the surrendered territory had one year to elect to become citizens of the United States or retain citizenship status as Mexicans. Those who did not respond were to automatically become incorporated as U.S. citizens at the end the year.

1. The Salsa Wars

1. Thompson (2005: 336) credits the Afro-Cuban composer and musician Orestes López with popularizing the mambo.
2. Cuban casino, commonly called Cuban salsa in Los Angeles, can be practiced either "on the one" or in contratiempo. Casino may also be practiced with several pairs dancing together in a circle; this is known as Rueda de Casino.
3. For more on the social and political practice of rumba in Cuba, see Daniel 1995.
4. See also Dixon Gottschild 1996: 8–9.
5. Recorded with RCA and released in 1951.
6. See Radanovich 2009, especially 35–57. In his biography of Benny Moré, Radanovich writes that a number of Cuban musicians went to Mexico City after the Cuban Revolution, creating what is referred to in Mexico today as *música tropical* (35).
7. Rondón (2008: 61) specifically acknowledges that Fania Records helped create salsa as a commercial success in urban centers from New York to the Caribbean: "Never before had salsa been distributed with such commercial success. Never before had this music been adopted so absolutely as the contemporary expression of the urban Caribbean. The old naïve and provincial guarachas that expressed life in those large urban centers euphemistically called 'great cities' were now a thing of the past. Although this contemporary music shared the same clave as before, it was as bitter and full of irony as the city that produced it."
8. Albert Torres promotes salsa music and dance events in Los Angeles and is the founder of the West Coast Salsa Congress.
9. The son and casino of Cuba complicate classifications of nation according to rhythmic

interpretations. Whereas in Cuba son is danced on clave (or "on two" in U.S. categories) and casino is danced either "on one" or "on two," in Los Angeles practitioners of casino tended to dance "on one."

10. Mexican dancers who live in Mexico City, Victor Burgos and Gaby Bernal from the salsa group Salsa con Clave, performed a routine that mixed salsa with *quebradita* at the 2002 West Coast Salsa Congress. In an online posting of an interview with the reporter Dena Burroughs, they suggest that L.A. Mexican salsa dancers cheered for their performance because they were Mexican rather than because they were innovative. For their discussion of the local politics of salsa in Mexico City and its relationship to L.A. salsa, see the interview at http://www.tosalsa.com/goto.asp?http://www.tosalsa.com/forum/interviews/interview020615dena_victor_gaby.html.
11. When I refer to "Mexicanness," I am applying the term used by practitioners to generalize techniques associated with Mexicans, Central Americans, and sometimes other non-Caribbean Latinas/os from South America.

2. Dancing Salsa Wrong

1. For example, the Vásquez brothers, Johnny, Luis, and Francisco, emigrated from Guadalajara and contributed to the early development of L.A. salsa.
2. I agree with Lisa Lowe (1996: 172–73), who writes that the realms of education, law, and popular culture become activated as "regulating sites" through which "'immigrants' are 'naturalized' into 'citizens' or through which 'immigrants' are disciplined as 'aliens' and 'foreigners.'"
3. Please see, for example, Isabel Wilkerson's *The Warmth of Other Suns: The Epic Story of America's Great Migration* (2010). Wilkerson also specifically addresses the history of African American migration to Los Angeles.
4. Lowe (1996) argues that the globalization of capital relies more heavily on the forces of differentiation than on homogenization in order to refine divisions of labor. She suggests that economic globalization requires an increased sophistication of the efforts to distinguish one kind of laborer from another, in order to more efficiently exploit the bodies that supply labor. Differentiation allows for increased knowledge of the characteristics of workers within various regions or nations to whom jobs may be outsourced. Hence, with greater efficiency, profit increases. The distinctions that Lowe writes about occur not only within corporations and workplaces but also within and through other structures of society, such as education, law, and popular culture.
5. Homogenization of techniques never completely occurs among those who practice L.A. salsa either. There is constant competition to introduce new moves. Only those with high status can initiate the incorporation of new moves or the refinement of old moves, increasing their status and making mundane the "older" moves still practiced by the majority of dancers.
6. In the documentary film *Mad Hot Ballroom* (Paramount Pictures, 2005), teachers

in New York adapt a ballroom methodology to teach children in the public schools, teaching "rhumba from Cuba" with the same "quick, quick, slow" technique.

3. Un/Sequined Corporealities

1. I refer here to the decline in the economy that began during the administration of George W. Bush, escalating after September 11, 2001.
2. Savigliano (1995) specifically addresses what she calls "the Exotic" in her work on tango. For other texts that apply more generally, see Lyotard (1993), who theorizes that the political economy is a libidinal economy in which desires and affects circulate together with capital, and Wilson (2004), who writes on the interconnections between the global economy and social identities formed in the everyday life of Bangkok.
3. The sitcom *Welcome Back, Kotter* aired from September 9, 1975, to August 10, 1979, on ABC.
4. I base the following description of Manny's procession from the street to the dance floor on my own observations of this sort of entrance pieced together from various points in the club over a period of several years, as I have never before been a member of such a party; I also include insights from other attendees and club employees.
5. Reggaetón is a genre of music influenced by hip-hop and reggae. One of the moves commonly associated with reggaetón is called *perreo*, as in the pelvis-to-butt "doggie-style" sex position. According to the article, "A Rowdy Sound Leaves Salsa Behind on the Dance Floor" by Agustin Garza in the *Los Angeles Times* on April 30, 2005, reggaetón's popularity is replacing that of salsa, as evidenced by record sales.
6. Translation: They go to other clubs. We dance salsa too, but without so many moves.
7. In chapter 5 I discuss gendered exceptions to this pattern of accommodating space and dance styles.
8. I translate *respeto* as the respect one enacts as part of a sociocultural responsibility among Latin Americans and Latinas/os. For more on *respeto* as a cultural marker of latinidad, see Limón (1994: 110, 113).
9. Translation: But look, we are two Mexicans, two Salvadorians, and one Nicaraguan, all at the same table, friends. We are all Latinos.
10. Translation: We are two Mexicans, two Salvadorians, and one Nicaraguan, all at the same table. We have the same Latino culture, the same language.
11. Translation: Each one of us, each place has different details, but it's always the same story.

4. Circulations of Gender and Power

1. Translation: "They're crazy!" he told me. "Why?" I asked, glancing their way. "They're lesbians," he said.
2. In *Epistemology of the Closet*, Eve Kosofsky Sedgwick (1990: 212) argues that men closet their attractions to each other through their joint attentions to women in compliance with "*compulsory* heterosexuality."
3. Susan Foster (1996: 12) writes that the homoerotics of two female dancers per-

forming both the male and female characters in ballet heterosexual partnerings "invited the erotic attachment of both male sexual orientations." Male audience members gazing upon the female ballerina and the travesty dancer could imagine the dance performed by a male couple, thus closeting male same-sex desires through the spectacle of dancing female bodies. For a detailed analysis of the ballerina as phallus, see "The Ballerina's Phallic Pointe" (1996).

4. The salsa performances of lesbianness in Latin America and at other nightclubs in Los Angeles deserve further investigation. For an analysis of the politics of sexuality among immigrants of color in the United States (primarily from Mexico, Cuba, El Salvador, and the Philippines), see *Queer Migrations: Sexuality, U.S. Citizenship, and Border Crossings*, edited by Eithne Luibhéid and Lionel Cantú Jr. (2005).
5. Piedra (1997: 115) specifies that salsa is one of the "symbolic survivors (or martyrs?) of the worldwide rumba heyday of half a century or so ago."
6. Stallybrass and White (1986: 6–19) inform my interpretation of Bakhtin (1968), as they explain that the lower-class participants of carnival recode and reinscribe categories of high and low even within the context of carnival in which participants transgress bodily codes of the upper-class dominant.
7. Male homosociality at the salsa congress constituted a Latino "boys' network," what middle- and upper-class white men have benefited from among themselves for generations, outside of the club. This Latino boys' network that succeeds within salsa economies rarely exists or gets defeated in the economy outside the club. A single Latino, or sometimes a Latina, may be admitted into the network of elite white men as a token but not as part of a network of other Latinos within the outside economy.
8. "Governor Signals He'd Welcome Minutemen on the California Border," *San Francisco Chronicle* James Sterngold, Mark Martin, and Chronicle Staff Writers, April 30, 2005. See http://www.sfgate.com/politics/article/Governor-signals-he-d-welcome-Minutemen-on-2637959.php
9. *Muertos* can include both men and women who are starving, but in this scenario, the club patron who uses this phrase does so in reference to men.
10. See also Arturo Arias's (2003) analysis of the invisibility of Central Americans in the United States.
11. Translation: "I don't know what I am going to do. I can't believe he is here with another woman. Did you see him making out with her against the deejay booth in front of everybody?" "He's a bastard, that man," said the other. "I can't believe I just finished paying his way through plumber school."
12. The men at Las Feliz Edades also discussed their working-class daytime positions with me. They are more recent arrivals in the United States than are the men at Valentino's. The five men I spoke with at Las Feliz Edades did not seem to have the time, the contacts, or the inclination to figure out how to survive economically in the United States by selling illegal phone numbers, as Alfredo had mentioned.

5. "Don't Leave Me, Celia!"

1. James C. McKinley Jr., "At Mexican Border, Tunnels, Vile River, Rusty Fence," *New York Times*, March 23, 2005.
2. See Sangent Games, "Border Patrol," http://nerdnirvana.org/g4m3s/borderpatrol.htm.
3. Male characters are "Mexican Nationalist" and "Drug Smuggler."
4. See "Should Drug Addicts Be Paid to Get Sterilised?," *BBC News Magazine*, February 8, 2010, http://news.bbc.co.uk/2/hi/uk_news/magazine/8500285.stm.
5. Carroll Smith-Rosenberg's analysis of homosociality among women in *Disorderly Conduct: Visions of Gender in Victorian America* (1985) addresses the cultural and social aspects of often life-long friendships among women. She includes in her scope of homosociality "relationships [that] ranged from the supportive love of sisters, through the enthusiasms of adolescent girls, to sensual avowals of love by mature women" (60). Unlike the women of the Victorian era in Smith-Rosenberg's research, however, many of the women in Los Angeles salsa clubs occupy marginalized positionings in the United States.
6. I refer to "The Traffic in Women: Notes on the 'Political Economy' of Sex," by Gayle Rubin (1975).
7. In some cases, *papi chulo* is code for "pimp."
8. Negotiations of femininities do not play out as binary oppositions. Latina salseras identify with conceptualizations of femininity from many different nations, social classes, and ethnicities, for example. Gloria Anzaldúa (1999) theorizes the awareness of the multiple, conflicting ideologies, cultures, and languages that crisscross a single body and a cultural body as mestiza consciousness. The awareness of contradictory ideologies correlates with Sarker and De's (2002: 20) concept of "placetime," the basis by which trans-status subjects "re-member (that is, bring back from memory and reassemble)" modes of belonging, survival, and resistance. Chela Sandoval's theory of differential consciousness in which the oppressed potentially transform spaces as they walk through them informs Sarker and De's analysis of placetime (26). Without sticking to one ideology, differential consciousness is effective due to the "tactical subjectivity" of the oppressed, "the ability to read the current situation of power and of self-consciously choosing and adopting the ideological form best suited to push against its configurations, a survival skill well known to oppressed peoples" (Sandoval 1991: 14, 15).
9. Gina M. Pérez's (2004) work on the relationships between Puerto Rican women and Mexican women in Chicago demonstrates that Puerto Rican women find Mexican women "too forgiving" of their men when they cheat on them or otherwise mistreat them. Summarizing the flaws that Puerto Rican women attribute to Mexican women, Pérez writes, "They don't stick up for themselves, and they either don't know—or choose not to know—their rights" (106). Mexican women in Chicago characterized Puerto Rican women as "unforgiving." In this section of my work, I analyze the

relationships between Chicana, Mexican, and Central American Latinas and white women. Further fieldwork might indicate that the relationships between Puerto Rican women and Chicana, Mexican, and Central American women in Chicago correlate with their relationships in Los Angeles.

10. "Edie, The Salsa FREAK . . . My Story," http://www.salsafreak.com/mystory.html.
11. "Dear Edie," http://66.102.7.104/search?q=cache:Y_M02qPBJRIJ:www.dancefreak.com-/edie/edie1.htm+edie+conservative+culture+salsa&hl=en&client=safari. Accessed on May 15, 2008.
12. I have depicted The Legend as a club in which men and women focus primarily on dance and look down on those who participate in the meat market, looking for romance, sex, love, or connections. When the contest season ends at the club in May, participants and their desires shift from dancing to the pickup scene; dancing becomes secondary. Many people who participate in the contest season go to The Legend only at that time, describing the off-season crowd as "rough" or "more urban."
13. This kind of interpretation tends to omit concerns of race, class, and nation and assumes that practices of sexual "repression" and "freedom" look the same across all cultures.
14. See Edie "the Salsa Freak," "Ladies, Let's Start a Revolution, http://www.dancerhangout.com/content.php?r=685-Sex-Appeal. Accessed on November 15, 2012.
15. The dance scholar Susan Leigh Foster (1998) challenges ideas of the mind-body split that have often historically been used to equate racialized (and classed and gendered) Others of the global South with the body and those of the global North with intellect, serving as a rationale for oppressive laws and racist practices. Foster brings together mind and body in her theory of choreography, an intellectual plan for movement done by thinking bodies. Her theory assists in the denaturalization of racialized, classed, and gendered hierarchies.
16. The name presents the club as a space of blackness. Javier, played by the Mexican actor Diego Luna, is not actually black but more of a light brown. Luna-as-Javier's performance of Cuban popular dance in the film associates him with a black Cubanness. Hence the film depicts him as legitimately occupying space as an accomplished and desirable dancer at La Rosa Negra. The film does not address the racial politics among Cubans.
17. See Ana López (1997) on Hollywood representations of Latinas as sexualized.
18. *Con respeto* means "with respect." I use this term here to signify respect within a Latino and Latin American cultural context.
19. Translation: "Don't think you are all that." This is an insult, meaning, "You aren't as hot as you may think."
20. Translation: I told him about my work, and then I said, "There are about five guys for every woman in this club. What do the men come here for? Why do you come here?" "The men come here looking for women to have sex with." "Why do the women come to the club?" I asked. "Same thing," he responded. "Well, just so you know, my friend

and I aren't here for that. We're working on a project." "Yes, I know. I would only treat you with the utmost respect."

21. Translation: "We buy our own drinks. We earn enough money to take care of our own expenses. No one can make a claim on us."

References

Published Works

Abu-Lughod, Lila. 1999. "The Interpretation of Culture(s) after Television." In *The Fate of "Culture,"* edited by S. Ortner, 110–35. Berkeley: University of California Press.

Acosta-Belén, Edna. 1999. "Hemispheric Remappings: Revisiting the Concept of Nuestra América." In *Identities on the Move: Transnational Processes in North America and the Caribbean Basin,* edited by Liliana R. Goldin, 81–106. Albany: Institute for Mesoamerican Studies, University at Albany.

Althusser, Louis. 1971. *Lenin and Philosophy, and Other Essays.* New York: Monthly Review Press.

Anzaldúa, Gloria. 1999. *Borderlands/La Frontera: The New Mestiza.* 1987. San Francisco: Lute Books.

Aparicio, Frances R. 1999. "Reading the 'Latino.'" *Latino Studies: Toward Re-Imagining Our Academic Location. Discourse* 21 (3): 3–18.

———. 1998. *Listening to Salsa: Gender, Latin Popular Music, and Puerto Rican Cultures.* Hanover, N.H.: Wesleyan University Press.

Aparicio, Frances R., and Susana Chávez-Silverman. 1997. *Tropicalizations: Transcultural Representations of Latinidad.* Hanover, N.H.: University Press of New England.

Aparicio, Frances R., and Cándida F. Jáquez. 2003. Introduction to *Musical Migrations:*

Transnationalism and Cultural Hybridity in Latin/o America, vol. 1, edited by Frances R. Aparicio and Cándida F. Jáquez, 1–12. New York: Palgrave Macmillan.

Appadurai, Arjun. 2000. "Grassroots Globalization and the Research Imagination." *Public Culture* 12 (1): 1–19.

———. 1996. *Modernity at Large: Cultural Dimensions of Globalization*. Minneapolis: University of Minnesota Press.

———. 1990. "Disjuncture and Difference in the Global Economy." In *Global Culture*, edited by Mike Featherstone, 295–310. London: Sage.

Arias, Arturo. 2003. "Central American–Americans: Invisibility, Power and Representation in the U.S. Latino World." *Latino Studies* 1: 168–87.

Arrizón, Alicia. 2000. "Conquest of Space: The Construction of Chicana Subjectivity in Performance Art." In *Latinas on Stage*, edited by Alicia Arrizón and Lillian Manzor, 352–69. Berkeley: Third Woman Press.

———. 1999. *Latina Performance: Traversing the Stage*. Bloomington: Indiana University Press.

Attali, Jacques. 1985. *Noise: The Political Economy of Music*. Minneapolis: University of Minnesota Press.

Bakhtin, M. M. 1981. *The Dialogic Imagination: Four Essays*. Edited by Michael Holquist. Translated by Caryl Emerson and Michael Holquist. Austin: University of Texas Press.

———. 1968. *Rabelais and His World*. Translated by H. Iswolsky. Cambridge, Mass.: MIT Press.

Balibar, Etienne. 1998. *Race, Nation, Class: Ambiguous Identities*. 1988. London: Verso.

Behar, Ruth. 1996. *The Vulnerable Observer: Anthropology That Breaks Your Heart*. Boston: Beacon Press.

Berríos-Miranda, Marisol. 2000. *The Significance of Salsa to National and Pan-Latino Identity*. Ph.D. diss. University of California, Berkeley.

Bharucha, Rustom. 1996. "Somebody's Other: Disorientations in the Cultural Politics of Our Time." In *The Intercultural Performance Reader*, edited by Patrice Pavis, 196–212. London: Routledge.

Blanco Borelli, Melissa. 2008. "Y Ahora Qué Vas a Hacer, Mulata? Hip Choreographies in the Mexican Cabaratera Film *Mulata* (1954)." *Women and Performance: A Journal of Feminist Theory* 18 (3): 215–33.

Boggs, Vernon W. 1992. *Salsiology: Afro-Cuban Music and the Evolution of Salsa in New York City*. New York: Excelsior Music Publishing Company.

Brunsdon, Charlotte, Julie D'Acci, and Lynn Spigel. 1997. *Feminist Television Criticism: A Reader*. Oxford: Clarendon Press.

Burns, Lucy Mae San Pablo. 2008. "'Splendid Dancing:' Filipino 'Exceptionalism' in Taxi Dance Halls." *Dance Research Journal* 40 (2): 23–40.

Butler, Judith. 1995. "Melancholy Gender/Refused Identification." In *Constructing Masculinity*, edited by M. Berger, B. Wallis, and S. Watson, 21–36. New York: Routledge.

Camacho, Alicia Schmidt. 2008. *Migrant Imaginaries: Latino Cultural Politics in the U.S.-Mexico Borderlands*. New York: New York University Press.

Chatterjea, Ananya. 2004. *Butting Out: Reading Resistive Choreographies through Works by Jawole Willa Jo Zollar and Chandralekha*. Middletown, Conn.: Wesleyan University Press.

Clifford, James. 1997. "Spatial Practices: Fieldwork, Travel, and the Disciplining of Anthropology." In *Anthropological Locations: Boundaries and Grounds of a Field Science*, edited by A. Gupta and J. Ferguson, 185–222. Berkeley: University of California Press.

———. 1988. *The Predicament of Culture*. Cambridge: Harvard University Press.

———. 1986. "Introduction: Partial Truths." In *Writing Culture: The Poetics and Politics of Ethnography*, edited by J. Clifford and G. Marcus, 1–26. Berkeley: University of California Press.

Colón, Hector Manuel. 1985. "La calle que los marxistas nunca entendieron." *Comunicación y Cultura*, July, 81–94.

Colón, Willie. 1999. Foreword to *¡Música! The Rhythm of Latin America: Salsa, Rumba, Merengue, and More*, by Sue Steward, 6–7. San Francisco: Chronicle Books.

Concepción, Alma. 2002. "Dance in Puerto Rico: Embodied Meanings." In *Caribbean Dance: From Abakuá to Zouk: How Movement Shapes Identity*, edited by Suzanna Sloat, 165–75. Gainesville: University of Florida Press.

Cooper, Carolyn. 2005. "Sweet and Sour Sauce: Sexual Politics in Jamaican Dance Hall Culture." Lecture, Centre for Research on Latin America and the Caribbean, York University, Toronto.

Cruz-Manjarrez, Adriana. 2008. "Danzas Chuscas: Performing Migration in a Zapotec Community." *Dance Research Journal*, 40 (2): 3–22.

Dallal, Alberto. 2000. *El "Dancing" Mexicano*. Mexico City: Universidad Nacional Autónoma de México Instituto de Investigaciones Estéticas.

Daniel, Yvonne. 2005a. "Cuban Dance: An Orchard of Caribbean Creativity." In *Caribbean Dance From Abakuá to Zouk: How Movement Shapes Identity*, edited by Susanna Sloat.

———. 2005b. *Dancing Wisdom: Embodied Knowledge in Haitian Vodou, Cuban Yoruba, and Bahian Candomblé*. Urbana: University of Illinois Press.

———. 1995. *Rumba: Dance and Social Change in Contemporary Cuba*. Bloomington: Indiana University Press.

Dávila, Arlene. 2001. *Latinos Inc.: The Marketing and Making of a People*. Berkeley: University of California Press.

de Certeau, Michel. 1988. *The Practice of Everyday Life*. Berkeley: University of California Press.

De Genova, Nicholas, and Ana Yolanda Ramos-Zayas. 2003. *Latino Crossings: Mexicans, Puerto Ricans and the Politics of Race and Citizenship*. New York: Routledge.

Desmond, Jane C. 1998. "Embodying Difference: Issues in Dance and Cultural Studies." In *The Routledge Dance Studies Reader*, edited by Alexandra Carter, 154–62. New York: Routledge.

Desmond, Jane. 1997. *Meaning in Motion: New Cultural Studies of Dance*. Durham: Duke University Press.

Dixon Gottshild, Brenda. 2003. *The Black Dancing Body: A Geography from Coon to Cool*. New York: Palgrave Macmillan.

———. 1996. *Digging the Africanist Presence in American Performance: Dance and Other Contexts*. Westport, Conn.: Greenwood Press.

Emerson, Robert M., Rachel I. Fretz, and Linda L. Shaw. 1995. *Writing Ethnographic Fieldnotes*. Chicago: University of Chicago Press.

Fabian, Johannes. 1991. *Time and the Work of Anthropology, 1971–1981*. Philadelphia: Harwood Academic Press.

Fanon, Frantz. 1967. *Black Skin, White Masks*. Translated by Charles Lam Markmann. New York: Grove Weidenfeld.

Featherstone, Mike. 1996. "Localism, Globalism and Cultural Identity." In *Global/Local: Cultural Production and the Transnational Imaginary*, edited by R. Wilson and W. Dissanayake, 46–77. Durham: Duke University Press.

Febres, Mayra Santos. 1997. "Salsa as Translocation." In *Everynight Life: Culture and Dance in Latin/o America*, edited by Celeste Fraser Delgado and José Esteban Muñoz, 175–88. Durham: Duke University Press.

Fernández Retamar, Roberto. 1989. "Caliban: Towards a Discussion of Culture in Our America. Caliban Revisited." In *Caliban and Other Essays*. Translated by E. Baker, 3–55. Minneapolis: University of Minnesota Press.

Flores, Juan, and George Yúdice. 1993. "Living Borders/Buscando America: Languages of Latino Self-Formation." In *Divided Borders: Essays on Puerto Rican Identity*. Houston: Arte Publico Press.

Foster, Susan Leigh. 2002. *Dances That Describe Themselves: The Improvised Choreography of Richard Bull*. Middletown, Conn.: Wesleyan University Press.

———. 1998. "Choreographies of Gender." *Signs* 24 (1): 1–33.

———. 1996. "The Ballerina's Phallic Pointe." In *Corporealities: Dancing Knowledge, Culture and Power*. New York: Routledge.

———. 1986. *Reading Dancing: Bodies and Subjects in Contemporary American Dance*. Berkeley: University of California Press.

Foucault, Michel. 1995. *Discipline and Punish: The Birth of the Prison*. 1975. Translated by Alan Sheridan. New York: Vintage Books.

———. 1980. "Two Lectures: Power/Knowledge." In *Selected Interview and Other Writings 1972–1977*. Edited by C. Gordon. Translated by C. Gordon, L. Marshall, J. Mephan, and K. Soper, 78–108. New York: Pantheon Books.

Frankenberg, Ruth, and Lata Mani. 1996. "Crosscurrents, Crosstalk: Race, 'Postcoloniality,' and the Politics of Location." In *Displacements, Diaspora, and Geographies of Identity*, edited by Smadar Lavie and Ted Swedenburg, 273–93. Durham: Duke University Press.

Fraser Delgado, Celeste, and José Esteban Muñoz. 1997. "Rebellions of Everynight Life." In *Everynight Life: Culture and Dance in Latin/o America*, edited by Celeste Fraser Delgado and José Esteban Muñoz, 9–32. Durham: Duke University Press.

Fregoso, Rosa Linda. 1993. *The Bronze Screen: Chicana and Chicano Film Culture.* Minneapolis: University of Minnesota Press.

García, David F. 2009. "Embodying Music/Disciplining Dance/The Mambo Body in Havana and New York City." In *Ballroom, Boogie, Shimmy Sham, Shake: A Social and Popular Dance Reader*, edited by Julie Malnig, 165–81. Urbana: University of Illinois Press.

Geertz, Clifford. 1973. *The Interpretation of Cultures: Selected Essays.* New York: Basic Books.

Glick Schiller, Nina. 1999. "Who Are These Guys? A Transnational Reading of the U.S. Immigrant Experience." In *Identities on the Move: Transnational Processes in North America and the Caribbean Basin,* edited by Liliana R. Goldin, 15–43. Albany: Institute for Mesoamerican Studies, University at Albany.

Goldin, Liliana R. 1999. "Transnational Identities: The Search for Analytic Tools." In *Identities on the Move: Transnational Processes in North America and the Caribbean Basin*, edited by Liliana R. Goldin, 1–11. Albany: Institute for Mesoamerican Studies, University at Albany.

Goldman, Danielle. 2010. *I Want to Be Ready: Improvised Dance as a Practice of Freedom.* Ann Arbor: The University of Michigan Press.

Gramsci, Antonio. 1992. *Selections from the Prison Notebooks.* Edited and translated by Q. Hoare and G. N. Smith. New York: International Publishers.

Grewal, Inderpal. 1998. "On the New Global Feminism and the Family of Nations: Dilemmas of Transnational Feminist Practice." In *Talking Visions: Multicultural Feminism in a Transnational Age*, edited by Ella Shohat, 501–32. Cambridge, Mass.: MIT Press.

Gupta, Akhil, and James Ferguson. 1997. "Discipline and Practice: 'The Field' as Site, Method, and Location in Anthropology." In *Anthropological Locations: Boundaries and Grounds of a Field Science*, edited by A. Gupta and J. Ferguson, 1–46. Berkeley: University of California Press.

Habell-Pallán, Michelle, and Mary Romero. 2002. Introduction to *Latino/a Popular Culture,* edited by M. Habell-Pallán and M. Romero, 1–21. New York: New York University Press.

Hall, Stuart. 1996. "Cultural Studies and Its Theoretical Legacies." In *Critical Dialogues in Cultural Studies*, edited by D. Morley and Kuan Hsing Chen, 262–75. London: Routledge.

———. 1994. "Cultural Identity and Diaspora." In *Colonial Discourse and Post-colonial Theory*, edited by Patrick Williams and Laura Chrisman, 392–403. New York: Columbia University Press.

Hamilton, Nora, and Norma Stoltz Chinchilla. 2001. *Seeking Community in a Global City: Guatemalans and Salvadorans in Los Angeles.* Philadelphia: Temple University Press.

Hondagneu-Sotelo, Pierrette. 2001. *Doméstica: Immigrant Workers Cleaning and Caring in the Shadows of Affluence.* Berkeley: University of California Press.

hooks, bell. 1991. "Narratives of Struggle." In *Critical Fictions: The Politics of Imaginative Writing*, edited by Philomena Mariani, 53–61. Seattle: Bay Press.

Jeyifo, Biodun. 1996. "The Reinvention of Theatrical Tradition: Critical Discourses on Interculturalism in African Theatre." In *The Intercultural Performance Reader*, edited by Patrice Pavis, 149–61. London: Routledge.

Joseph, May. 1999. *Nomadic Subjectivities: The Performance of Citizenship*. Minneapolis: University of Minnesota Press.

Kempadoo, Kamala. 2004. *Sexing the Caribbean: Gender, Race, and Sexual Labor*. London: Routledge.

Kipnis, Laura. 1993. *Ecstasy Unlimited*. Minneapolis: University of Minnesota Press.

Kondo, D. 1997. *About Face: Performing Race in Fashion and Theater*. New York: Routledge.

Laó-Montes, Agustín, and Arlene Dávila. 2001. *Mambo Montage: The Latinization of New York*. New York: Columbia University Press.

Limón, José. 1998. *American Encounters: Greater Mexico, the United States, and the Erotics of Culture*. Boston: Beacon Press.

———. 1994. *Dancing with the Devil: Society and Cultural Poetics in Mexican-American South Texas*. Madison: University of Wisconsin Press.

———. 1991. "Representation, Ethnicity, and the Precursory Ethnography: Notes of a Native Anthropologist." In *Recapturing Anthropology: Working in the Present*, edited by R. G. Fox, 115–35. New York: Oxford University Press.

Linares, María Teresa. 1974. *La música y el pueblo*. Havana: Editorial Pueblo y Educación.

López, Ana M. 1997. "Of Rhythms and Borders." In *Everynight Life: Culture and Dance in Latin/o America*, edited by Celeste Fraser Delgado and José Esteban Muñoz, 310–43. Durham: Duke University Press.

Lowe, Lisa. 1996. *Immigrant Acts: On Asian American Cultural Politics*. Durham: Duke University Press.

Luibhéid, Eithne, and Lionel Cantú Jr. 2005. "Introduction: Queering Migrations and Citizenship." In *Queer Migrations: Sexuality, U.S. Citizenship, and Border Crossings*, edited by E. Luibhéid and L. Cantú Jr., ix–xlvi. Minneapolis: University of Minnesota Press.

Lyotard, Jean-François. 1993. *Libidinal Economy*. 1974. Translated by Iain Hamilton Grant. Bloomington: Indiana University Press.

Marcus, George E., and Fred R. Myers. 1995. *The Traffic in Culture: Refiguring Art and Anthropology*. Berkeley: University of California Press.

Marx, Karl, and Friedrich Engels. 1998. *The Communist Manifesto*. 1848. New York: New American Library.

———. 1976. *Capital, Volume 1*. Translated by Ben Fowkes. London: Penguin Books, New Left Review.

Mendible, Myra, ed. 2007. *From Bananas to Buttocks: The Latina Body in Popular Film and Culture*. Austin: University of Texas Press.

Miyoshi, Masao. 1996. "A Borderless World? From Colonialism to Transnationalism and the Decline of the Nation-State." In *Global/Local*, edited by Rob Wilson and Wimal Dissanayake, 78–106. Durham: Duke University Press.

Mohanty, Chandra Talpade. 1998. "Crafting Feminist Genealogies: On the Geography and

Politics of Home, Nation, and Community." In *Talking Visions: Multicultural Feminism in a Transnational Age*, edited by Ella Shohat, 485–500. Cambridge, Mass.: MIT Press.

———. 1991. "Under Western Eyes: Feminist Scholarship and Colonial Discourses."/ In *Third World Women and the Politics of Feminism*, edited by Chandra Talpade Mohanty, Ann Russo, and Lourdes Torres, 51–80. Bloomington: Indiana University Press.

Molina Guzmán, Isabel, and Angharad N. Valdivia. 2004. "Brain, Brow, and Booty: Latina Iconicity in U.S. Popular Culture." *Communication Review* 7: 205–21.

Moraga, Cherríe. 2000. *Loving in the War Years: Lo Que Nunca Pasó Por Sus Labios*. Cambridge, Mass.: South End Press.

Moraga, Cherríe, and Gloria Anzaldúa, eds. 1983. *This Bridge Called My Back: Writings by Radical Women of Color*. New York: Kitchen Table, Women of Color Press.

Mulvey, Laura. 1989. *Visual and Other Pleasures*. Houndmills, U.K.: Macmillan.

———. 1988. "Visual Pleasure in Narrative Cinema." In *Feminism and Film Theory*, edited by C. Penley, 69–79. New York: Routledge, Chapman and Hall.

Narayan, Kirin. 1997. "How Native Is a 'Native' Anthropologist?" In *Situated Lives: Gender and Culture in Everyday Life*, edited by Louise Lamphere, Helena Ragoné, and Patricia Zavella, 23–41. New York: Routledge.

Noriega, Chon A. 2000. *Shot in America: Television, the State, and the Rise of Chicano Cinema*. Minneapolis: University of Minnesota Press.

———, ed. 1992. *Chicanos and Film: Representation and Resistance*. Minneapolis: University of Minnesota Press.

Oboler, Suzanne. 1999. "Racializing Latinos in the United States: Toward a New Research Paradigm." In *Identities on the Move: Transnational Processes in North America and the Caribbean Basin*, edited by Liliana R. Goldin, 45–68. Albany: Institute for Mesoamerican Studies, University at Albany.

Ortiz, Fernando. 1950. *La Africanía de la música folklórica de Cuba*. Havana: Ministerio de Educación, Dirreción de Cultura.

Ospina, Hernando Calvo. 1996. *Salsa: Esa Irreverente Alegría*. Nafarroa, Euskal Herria, Spain: Editorial Txalaparta.

Paranaguá, Paulo Antonia. 1995. *Mexican Cinema*. Consejo Nacional para la Cultura y Los Artes (Mexico); British Film Institute; Instituto Mexicano de Cinematografía. London: British Film Institute.

Paredez, Deborah. 2009. *Selenidad: Selena, Latinos, and the Performance of Memory*. Durham: Duke University Press.

Parreñas Shimuzu, Celine. 2007. *The Hypersexuality of Race: Performing Asian/American Women on Screen and Scene*. Durham: Duke University Press.

Peña, Manuel. 1999. *Música Tejana: The Cultural Economy of Artistic Transformation*. College Station: Texas A&M University Press.

Peña Ovalle, Priscilla. 2011. *Dance and the Hollywood Latina: Race, Sex, and Stardom*. Piscataway, N.J.: Rutgers University Press.

Pérez, Gina. 2004. *Migration, Displacement, and Puerto Rican Families*. Berkeley: University of California Press.

Piedra, José. 1997. "Hip Poetics." In *Everynight Life: Culture and Dance in Latin/o America*, edited by Celeste Fraser Delgado and José Esteban Muñoz, 93–140. Durham: Duke University Press.

Pietrobruno, Sheenagh. 2006. *Salsa and Its Transnational Moves*. Lanham, Md.: Lexington Books.

Pollock, Della. 1998. "Performing Writing." In *The Ends of Performance*, edited by P. Phelan and J. Lane, 73–103. New York: New York University Press.

Quintero Rivera, Ángel G. 1998. *¡Salsa, Sabor y Control! Sociología de la musica "tropical."* Mexico City: Premio Casa de las Américas.

Radanovich, John. 2009. *Wildman of Rhythm: The Life and Music of Benny Moré*. Tallahassee: University Press of Florida.

Radhakrishnan, Rajagopalan. 1996. *Diasporic Mediations: Between Home and Locations*. Minneapolis: University of Minnesota.

Renta, Priscilla. 2004. Salsa Dance: Latino/o History in Motion. *Centro Journal* 16 (2): 139–57.

Rincón, Bernice. 1997. "La Chicana: Her Role in the Past and Her Search for a New Role in the Future." 1971. In *Chicana Feminist Thought: The Basic Historical Writings*, edited by Alma M. García, 24–28. New York: Routledge.

Rivera-Servera, Ramón H. 2011. "Dancing Reggaetón with Cowboy Boots: Social Dance Clubs and the Politics of Dance in the Latino Southwest." In *Transnational Encounters: Music and Performance at the U.S.-Mexico Border*, edited by Alejandro Madrid, 373–92. London: Oxford University Press.

———. 2004. "Choreographies of Resistance: Latina/o Queer Dance and the Utopian Performative." *Modern Drama* 47 (2): 269–89.

Roach, Joseph. 1996. *Cities of the Dead: Circum-Atlantic Performances*. New York: Columbia University Press.

Roberts, John Storm. 1999. *The Latin "Tinge": The Impact of Latin American Music on the United States*. 1979. Oxford: Oxford University Press.

Rodríguez, Olavo Alén. 1994. *De lo Afrocubano a la Salsa: Géneros Musicales de Cuba*. Havana: Ediciones ARTEX.

Román, David, and Alberto Sandoval. 1995. "Caught in the Web: Latinidad, AIDS, and Allegory in *Kiss of the Spider Woman, the Musical*." *American Literature* 67 (3, September).

Rondón, César Miguel. 2008. *The Book of Salsa*. Translated by Frances R. Aparicio with Jackie White. Chapel Hill: University of North Carolina Press.

———. 1985. "Cero Salsa (o salsa cero)." *Comunicación y Cultura*, July, 94–105.

———. 1980. *El libro de la Salsa: Crónica de la músical del Caribe, Urbano*. Caracas: Editorial Arte.

Root, Deborah. 1998. *Cannibal Culture: Art Appropriation and the Commodification of Difference*. Boulder, Colo.: Westview Press.

Rose, Tricia. 1994. *Black Noise: Rap Music and Black Culture in Contemporary America.* Hanover, N.H.: Wesleyan University Press.

Rouse, Roger. 1991. "Mexican Migration and the Social Space of Postmodernism." *Diaspora* 1 (1): 8–23.

Rúa, Mérida, and Lorena García. 2007. "Processing Latinidad: Mapping Latino Urban Landscapes through Chicago Ethnic Festivals." *Latino Studies* 5: 317–39.

Rubin, Gayle. 1975. "The Traffic in Women: Notes on the 'Political Economy' of Sex." In *Toward an Anthropology of Women*, edited by R. Reiter, 157–210. New York: Monthly Review Press.

Said, Edward. 1978. *Orientalism.* New York: Vintage Books.

Sánchez, George. 1993. *Becoming Mexican American: Ethnicity, Culture and Identity in Chicano Los Angeles, 1900–1945.* New York: Oxford University Press.

Sanchez Gonzalez, Lisa. 1999. "Reclaiming Salsa." *Cultural Studies* 13 (2): 237–50.

Sandoval, Chela. 2000. *Methodology of the Oppressed.* Minneapolis: University of Minnesota Press.

———. 1991. "U.S. Third World Feminism: The Theory and Method of Oppositional Consciousness in the Postmodern World." *Genders* 10 (Spring): 1–24.

Sarker, Sonita, and Esha Niyogi De. 2002. "Introduction: Marking Times and Territories." In *Trans-Status Subjects: Gender in the Globalization of South and Southeast Asia*, edited by Sonita Sarker and Esha Niyogi De, 1–27. Durham: Duke University Press.

Sassen, Saskia. 2002. "Introduction: Locating Cities on Global Circuits." In *Global Networks, Linked Cities*, edited by Saskia Sassen, 1–36. New York: Routledge.

———. 2001. *The Global City: New York, London, Tokyo.* Princeton: Princeton University Press.

———. 2000. "Spatialities and Temporalities of the Global: Elements for a Theorization." *Public Culture* 12 (1): 215–32.

———. 1999. *Guests and Aliens.* New York: New Press.

———. 1998. *Globalization and Its Discontents: Essays on the New Mobility of People and Money.* New York: New York University Press.

———. 1996. "Analytic Borderlands: Race, Gender and Representation in the New City." In *Re-Presenting the City: Ethnicity, Capital and the Culture in the 21st-Century Metropolis*, edited by Anthony D. King, 183–202. New York: New York University Press.

Savigliano, Marta E. 2003. *Angora Matta, a Tango Opera: Fatal Acts of North-South Translation.* Middletown, Conn.: Wesleyan University Press.

———. 2001. "Translingual Choreocritics: Edgy Meditations on a North-South Flight." Paper presented at Congress on Research in Dance conference, October 27, 2001, Judson Church, New York, New York.

———. 1997. "Nocturnal Ethnographies: Following Cortázar in the Milongas of Buenos Aires." *Etnofoor* 10 (1–2): 28–52.

———. 1996. "Fragments for a Story of Tango Bodies (on Choreocritics and the Memory of Power)." In *Corporealities*, edited by Susan Foster, 199–232. New York: Routledge.
———. 1995. *Tango and the Political Economy of Passion*. Boulder, Colo.: Westview Press.
Sawhney, Deepak Narang. 2002. "Journey beyond the Stars: Los Angeles and Third Worlds." In *Unmasking L.A.: Third Worlds and the City*, edited by D. N. Sawhney, 1–20. New York: Palgrave.
Schechner, Richard. 1996. "Interculturalism and the Culture of Choice." In *The Intercultural Performance Reader*, edited by Patrice Pavis, 41–50. London: Routledge.
Scolieri, Paul, ed. 2008. "Introduction. Global/Mobile: Re-orienting Dance and Migration Studies." *Dance Research Journal* 40 (2): v–xx.
Sedgwick, Eve Kosofsky. 1990. *Epistemology of the Closet*. Berkeley: University of California Press.
Shohat, Ella. 2002. "Area Studies, Gender Studies, and the Cartographies of Knowledge." *Social Text* 72 (20/2): 67–78.
———. 2000. "Coming to America: Reflections on Hair and Memory Loss." In *Going Global: The Transnational Reception of Third World Women Writers*, edited by Lisa Suhair Majaj and Amal Amireh, 284–300. New York: Garland.
———. 1998. Introduction to *Talking Visions: Multicultural Feminism in a Transnational Age*, edited by Ella Shohat, 1–62. Cambridge, Mass.: MIT Press.
Smith-Rosenberg, Carroll. 1985. *Disorderly Conduct: Visions of Gender in Victorian America*. New York: Knopf.
Spivak, Gayatri Chakravorty. 1993. *Outside in the Teaching Machine*. New York: Routledge.
———. 1992. "Acting Bits/Identity Talk." *Critical Inquiry* 18 (4): 770–803.
Stallybrass, Peter, and Allon White. 1986. *The Politics and Poetics of Transgression*. Ithaca, N.Y.: Cornell University Press.
Surin, Kenneth. 1997. "On Producing the Concept of a Global Culture." In *Nations, Identities, Cultures*, edited by V. Y. Mudimbe, 199–219. Durham: Duke University Press.
Thompson, Robert Farris. 2005. *Flash of the Spirit: African and Afro-American Art and Philosophy*. New York: Random House.
———. 2002. "Teaching the People to Triumph over Time: Notes from the World of Mambo." In *Caribbean Dance from Abakuá to Zouk: How Movement Shapes Identity*, edited by Susanna Sloat, 336–44. Gainesville: University Press of Florida.
Thornton, Sarah. 1996. *Club Cultures: Music, Media, and Subcultural Capital*. Middletown, Conn.: Wesleyan University Press.
Tobin, Jeffrey. 1998. "Tango and the Scandal of Homosocial Desire." In *The Passion of Music and Dance: Body, Gender, and Sexuality*, edited by W. Washabaugh, 79–102. Oxford: Berg.
Trinh T. Minh-Ha. 1992. *Framer Framed*. New York: Routledge.
———. 1991. *When the Moon Waxes Red: Representation, Gender, and Cultural Politics*. New York: Routledge.

———. 1989. *Woman, Native, Other: Writing Postcoloniality and Feminism*. Bloomington: Indiana University Press.

———. 1988. "Not You/Like You: Post-Colonial Women and the Interlocking Questions of Identity and Difference." *Inscriptions* 3/4: Available at http://culturalstudies.ucsc.edu/pubs/inscriptions/vol-3-4/minh_ha.html./

Tsing, Anna Lowenhaupt. 1993. *In the Realm of the Diamond Queen: Marginality in an Out-of-the-Way Place*. Princeton: Princeton University Press.

Ulloa, Alejandro. 1992. *La Salsa en Cali*. Cali, Colombia: Centro Editorial Universidad del Valle.

Valle, Victor M., and Rodolfo D. Torres. 2000. *Latino Metropolis*. Minneapolis: University of Minnesota Press.

Valverde, Umberto. 1982. *Reina Rumba, Celia Cruz*. Universo Mexico.

Visweswaran, Kamala. 1995. *Fictions of Feminist Ethnography*. Minneapolis: University of Minnesota Press.

Wallerstein, Immanuel. 1990. "Culture as the Ideological Battleground of the Modern World-System." In *Global Culture*, edited by Mike Featherstone, 32–55. London: Sage.

———. 1989. *The Capitalist World-Economy*. New York: Cambridge University Press.

Waxer, Lise. 2002. *Situating Salsa: Global Markets and Local Meaning in Latin Popular Music*. New York: Routledge.

Wilkerson, Isabel. 2010. *The Warmth of Other Suns: The Epic Story of America's Great Migration*. New York: Vintage Books.

Williams, Raymond. 1980. *Problems in Materialism and Culture: Selected Essays*. London: Verso.

Wilson, Ara. 2004. *The Intimate Economies of Bangkok: Tomboys, Tycoons, and Avon Ladies in the Global City*. Berkeley: University of California Press.

Yarbro-Bejarano, Yvonne. 1994. "Gloria Anzaldúa's *Borderlands/La frontera*: Cultural Studies, 'Difference,' and the Non-Unitary Subject." *Cultural Critique*, Fall, 5–28.

Ziff, Bruce, and Pratima V. Rao. 1997. "Introduction to Cultural Appropriation: A Framework for Analysis." In *Borrowed Power: Essays on Cultural Appropriation*, edited by Bruce Ziff and Pratima V. Rao, 1–27. New Brunswick, N.J.: Rutgers University Press.

Films

Along Came Polly. Directed by John Hamburg. DVD. 2004.

Dirty Dancing: Havana Nights. Directed by Guy Ferland. DVD. 2004.

Shall We Dance? Directed by Peter Chelsom. DVD. 2004.

Index